BREAKING OUT

We had broken through the German inner ring, but there was still the outer ring, and a machine gun constantly barking from a bunker blocked our way. It had to be stopped.

Yuriy Mikheev stepped forward. "Comrade Petty Officer, let's prepare a bundle of grenades." There was no other way out. Everyone had to give up his last grenade for Mikheev's attempt.

Crawling forward, meter by meter, Mikheev approached the bunker. Then a flare burst into the sky—the Germans saw him and opened fire! Mikheev was our last chance. If they killed him or a bullet found its way into the grenades . . .

Suddenly Mikheev jumped up and hurled the grenades. They were still in the air when he was cut down by a machine-gun burst. The explosion in the bunker echoed in the mountains.

Thus, the last of the scouts who perished on Mogilnyy saluted us, the living.

BLOOD ON THE SHORES

Soviet SEALs in World War II

Viktor Leonov
Translated With an Introduction and Notes by
James F. Gebhardt

IVY BOOKS • NEW YORK

Ivy Books
Published by Ballantine Books
Translation Copyright © 1993 by James F. Gebhardt

This translation was previously published by Naval Institute Press in 1993.

Library of Congress Catalog Card Number: 94-96133

ISBN 0-8041-0732-7

Manufactured in the United States of America

First Ballantine Books Edition: November 1994

10 9 8 7 6 5 4 3 2 1

Dedicated to the Soviet *morskiye razvedchiki* [naval scouts], living and deceased, who fought against German and Japanese imperialism in World War II

Contents

Foreword

    A LONG TIME AGO I harbored the idea of publishing my book in America. There were good reasons for this. There was no detachment like mine in the Northern Fleet before the war. It was created at the beginning of the war from ships' sailors and fleet shore units. We studied and mastered this difficult and dangerous work during the war, in combat with the enemy.

From the beginning we fought *on a small bit of land*, seized from us by the *enemy in this region*, then later in Finland, and finally in Norway. Here a great part of our effort was directed at supporting convoys which Americans were escorting to Murmansk and Arkhangelsk with needed aid that we used for the common victory over German fascism. Many groups of scouts sat for months in the *snows of northern Norway*, conducting *careful observation* over the *activities of the enemy's combat forces*. These same *groups guided* our *strike forces against the enemy formations*, interfering with their attacks on the convoys. In addition, the detachment *conducted night raids on enemy roads and bases*. In these operations the detachment learned, matured, and won *respect and distinction among* the fleet's sailors. It was not by coincidence that our detachment was the only one of several analogous units to be designated *"guards"* status.

We also had personal contacts with American sailors in Murmansk and Polyarnoye. These were friendly, comradely encounters. We understood that we were working for a common end, the liberation of the world from fascism, and we rejoiced in our common victory. One thing hurt our feelings a bit—sometimes it slipped into the conversations of our American friends that our detachment was made up of *desperadoes and cutthroats*. Our own friends in the Soviet fleet also called us these names, and we tolerated it. But in truth, the detachment had the strictest discipline and *quite ordinary personnel*.

But later, racing through the ruins of burned-out Murmansk, extinguishing the incendiaries that had smothered the city, I very much liked the daring courage of the American sailors. After that I firmly resolved to write a book about the wartime comradeship of Soviet and American sailors.

This book was written in the early 1950s and accepted for publication by the Soviet Navy's official press. But shortly thereafter, that entity was dissolved and the manuscript was turned over to the Ministry of Defense's official press, which made additional changes to the manuscript. The release of the book was delayed. Finally realizing that the book was not only good but needed, the ministry decided to publish it without further delay. I was not in Moscow at the time, and the Cold War was under way by then. Who was fighting this war, our peoples or our governments, to this day I have not been able to understand. But as a result of the Cold War, the book was reduced almost by half. What I had written about the comradely friendship between Soviet and American sailors during the wartime period had been excised.

Now our wartime friendship is being renewed. We have begun better to understand each other, and we have begun more frequently to associate with each other. We now understand that we two great powers bear responsibility for peace and for the fortunes of the peoples of countries large and small. Therefore, I would like my book to be published in America.

Let our wartime friendship, bonded with the blood shed in the battles with fascism, remain an eternal guarantee of peace for all peoples.

V. N. Leonov
Moscow, USSR
21 November 1990

Acknowledgments

I WISH TO ACKNOWLEDGE the contribution and support of several people to the completion of this book. Major William H. Burgess III, U.S. Army, by his initial prodding and subsequent encouragement, caused me to investigate this subject thoroughly and write about it. Major Burgess and Robert Suggs read and provided insightful comments that improved the manuscript. Owen A. Lock, Editor in Chief at Del Rey Books, recognized the potential of this material and supported its publication. Harold S. Orenstein helped me over some rough spots in translating both the Russian and German. Robin Inojos prepared the maps and chart. My wife, Deborah, and my children, Kevin and Karla, gave me time and continuous moral support to stay on schedule. By his prolific writings, Hero of the Soviet Union Makar Babikov opened my eyes to the historiography of the Northern Fleet reconnaissance detachment. I especially want to acknowledge the assistance of Twice Hero of the Soviet Union Viktor Nikolayevich Leonov, who gave me a two-hour interview in Moscow in September 1990, and on 21 November 1990 invited me to celebrate his seventy-fourth birthday with him and his family.

James. F. Gebhardt
Leavenworth, Kansas

Translator's Note

BECAUSE THIS BOOK IS MUCH MORE than a simple translation of a Soviet-published memoir from Russian to English, a few words of explanation are in order. It begins with an introduction that places Viktor Leonov and his memoir in historical perspective. The introduction also contains relevant material that Leonov omitted from his first book but which appears in his second book and other sources.

The introduction is followed by the translation of Leonov's memoir, *Face to Face*. At several places in the translation I have inserted material in square brackets, occasionally to provide clarification, in other cases to supply material that was too lengthy to be placed in a note but relevant enough to warrant inclusion in the text. Notes explain terms, concepts, and geographical place names and offer other perspectives on the subject at hand.

Five appendixes supplement the material in the text. The first is a survey of the *reconnaissance detachments* of the Soviet Navy's other fleets and flotillas in World War II. The next two are translations of captured German documents that support material in the Introduction. The fourth is also a German document, mentioned by Leonov in the text. The last contains a table of rank equivalents of the U.S. and Soviet World War II navies. Soviet ranks were retained throughout the text, primarily because there was not a direct correlation between the rank structures of the U.S. and Soviet navies during that period. For readers who may not be familiar with naval ranks in general, U.S. Army World War II rank equivalents are provided. The bibliography lists books and articles that would be most useful to anyone conducting additional research on Soviet naval special purpose forces and reference works and other sources used to assemble this book.

The translation of one term in this book may lead to some confusion and therefore merits explanation. Throughout the text, Leonov frequently used the Russian *voin*, literally "warrior," or "fighting man," but most often translated as "soldier" in the contemporary context. It comes from the Russian word for "war" *(voyna)*. When the word *"soldier"* appears in the text, then, it does not refer to a combatant of the Red Army but rather *to a "warrior"* or *"fighting man" of the Red Navy*. A sailor in the Red Navy was always a "sailor" *(moryak)*, whether he be in the engine room of a submarine, on the deck of a torpedo boat, or in a *ground reconnaissance unit*. But in the latter case, he was also often called a *voin*, hence "soldier" in this text.

Introduction

VIKTOR NIKOLAYEVICH LEONOV. This name does not easily roll off the tongue of an American reader. It does not have the simplicity of "Sergeant York" or the glamour of "Audie Murphy." But the name of Viktor Leonov is acclaimed in the Soviet Union just as those names are among Americans of several generations. He is one of almost 12,000 men and women who received the award and title Hero of the Soviet Union for their courage or leadership in battle in World War II.[1] But Leonov is one of *only 115* Soviet World War II heroes to have received this highest award twice.

This is his story, but not his alone. He is representative of a small group of *Soviet naval scouts, morskiye razvedchiki in Russian*, perhaps fewer than six *hundred total*, who were the *Soviet Navy's World War II version of the modern U.S. Navy's SEALs (Sea, Air, Land commandos—a* special operations force). The memoir of Viktor Leonov was chosen to tell this story, both because it was the first of several personal accounts to be written in the post-Stalin period about this unique group of men and because among all these *daring raiders*, including nearly two-dozen Heroes of the Soviet Union, he *ultimately commanded in combat the detachments of two different* fleets, the *Northern and Pacific*. Today, Viktor Leonov remains *perhaps the best known of all the Soviet World War II naval* scouts.

Leonov was born 21 November *1916* in Zaraysk, a small city located about 135 kilometers southeast of Moscow.[2]

1

His father was a gardener, who apparently joined the Communist Party during the first decade of Soviet rule. When young Viktor finished seventh grade in 1931, encouraged by his father, he traveled to Moscow. There he took an apprenticeship at a factory that specialized in metal fabrication. Leonov finished training in 1933 and went on to become not only an outstanding worker and team leader but also an active participant in Komsomol (Young Communist League) activities.[3] While he was a factory worker, Leonov earned several sports rankings for his participation in his spare time in parachute jumping, boxing, precision rifle marksmanship, and cross-country skiing.[4]

Upon his induction into the Red Navy in 1937, Leonov was assigned to a submarine training detachment and then to the Northern Fleet. He served as a mechanic in the submarine's engine room for perhaps three years and then was transferred to a repair facility in the Northern Fleet base at Polyarnyy. In 1940 he was recommended for and accepted into membership in the Communist Party. Leonov was working in the Polyarnyy repair facility when the Soviet-German war began on 22 June 1941.

The organization that Leonov joined just days later was called *the reconnaissance detachment of headquarters, Northern Fleet (in Russian, razvedyvatel'nyy otryad shtaba, severnogo flota)*. The Soviet Military Encyclopedia describes the *generic reconnaissance detachment* as ranging in size from *platoon (25 to 40 men)* to reinforced *company (70 to 140* men) and subordinated to the *intelligence organs of headquarters of fleets, defensive regions, naval bases, and other commands.*[5] Its mission was to penetrate into the *enemy's rear area by surface or subsurface vessels or by* walking through the front *line to gather intelligence data or conduct diversionary-demolition activities.*[6]

The theoretical concept for such actions was first advanced in the Soviet Union in 1934 by a young naval officer, I. S. Isakov. At the time a staff officer in the operations section of the general staff, Isakov wrote a six-page essay on amphibious operations that was published in a naval professional journal.[7] He viewed *amphibious landings* as being of three scales: *strategic, tactical, and assault parties.* His definition of the latter is instructive.

> The landing of *assault parties* is characterized most of all by the following: (1) a quite small scale of operation; (2) the possibility of the conduct of a broad variety of missions, most often of a demonstrative nature (the sowing of panic in the rear, demolition of a bridge or tunnel, destruction of a shore battery put out of action by the fleet, cutting of pipelines, etc.); (3) a *rapidly moving operation of only several hours' duration;* and (4) normal return of the assault force to the ships and to base upon fulfillment of the mission on shore, if the goal was not the organization of partisan activities.[8]

From January 1937 to January 1938, Isakov was chief of staff and then commander of the Baltic Fleet, and from June 1938 to August 1939 he was commandant of the Naval Academy in Leningrad. Although when the Soviet-Finnish War broke out in November 1939 Isakov was serving on a higher naval staff in Moscow, he may have left his mark on the Baltic Fleet. There is a clear reference in Soviet sources to a detachment of sailors, based on Kronshtadt Island near Leningrad, who attacked Finnish rear areas on skis.[9] This may have been an early version of what later became known as the *fleet reconnaissance detachment.* In any case, the generic reconnaissance detachment of headquarters, fleet/flotilla, ultimately appeared in all four Soviet fleets and four flotillas before World War II was over.[10]

When Germany attacked the Soviet Union on 22 June 1941, the Northern *Fleet was quickly placed in a precarious position.* Beginning on 29 June, German ground forces crossed the Finnish *border some ninety kilometers northwest of Murmansk and began an offensive to capture* both Murmansk and *the railroad that* connected it with the Soviet heartland.[11] Murmansk is an important *strategic port,* the Soviet Union's only *year-round ice-free harbor with un-restricted access to the ocean*. Admiral A. G. Golovko, commander of the Northern Fleet, was concerned lest an element split off from the German offensive to attack his main naval base *at Polyarnyy* from its rear, landward side. He could not be sure that the Soviet 14th Army defending Murmansk would be able to halt the German offensive, nor could he depend on 14th Army intelligence sources for his daily estimates of enemy locations, capabilities, and intentions.

The Northern Fleet also had a forward base on the northern side of Sredniy Peninsula, only thirty kilometers by sea from the German-controlled port of *Petsamo*. Although Soviet Army and naval ground forces blocked the landward approaches to this base at the narrow Sredniy Isthmus, there was always the possibility that the Germans would launch amphibious operations against Sredniy or Rybachiy peninsulas or against Soviet territory farther to the east. Such operations could be launched from *Vardo and Vadso* on the *nearby Varanger Peninsula*, as well as from Kirkenes or Petsamo. German air force units based at Kirkenes and two forward airfields also were within easy striking range of Polyarnyy and Murmansk. For all these reasons, Admiral Golovko needed his own ground reconnaissance force.

With these problems in mind, Golovko met with his intelligence staff in the first days of the German offensive and assigned tasks, which they worked into a collection plan.[12] The area of immediate concern was the coastline on the left flank of the German offensive. The second area of interest was the German corps' rear area, particularly the location of headquarters and lines of communication. The third area of interest was Finnish and Norwegian ports, where the Germans could be gathering the forces necessary for amphibious operations.

The chief of the intelligence section of the Northern Fleet was Captain Third Rank P. A. Vizgin, who had served in the same capacity under Golovko when the latter com-

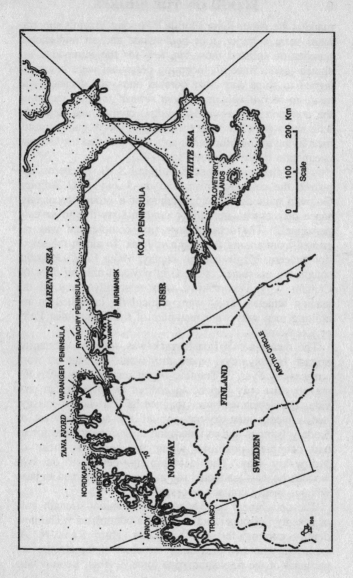

manded the Amur River Flotilla.[13] Among Vizgin's subordinates were a major, four lieutenants, and an undisclosed number of enlisted men, too few for the immediate assigned tasks. Since all incoming personnel were being assigned to ships and other combat units, the decision was *made to recruit volunteers from several sources*, including the commercial *fleet in Murmansk*, civilian and fleet athletic and sport clubs, and the group of Norwegian communists living in the Murmansk area who had fled the German occupation of their country in 1940.

The fleet chief of staff, Admiral S. G. Kucherov, approved the collection plan, and on *5 July 1941* Admiral Golovko authorized the formation of a ground reconnaissance detachment, initially to contain sixty-five to seventy personnel.[14] The detachment's first complement was recruited from among the *fleet's athletes*. To aid in the selection process, Vizgin and his deputy, Major L. V. Dobrotin, sought the assistance of the fleet physical training director, Captain V. V. Domozhirov, who personally knew all the leading athletes. They were particularly interested in recruiting men who were members of the Communist Party or Komsomol.

The detachment's first barrack was with the submarine brigade in Polyarnyy, where they would be "cut off from unnecessary eyes."[15] Training began immediately, with the urgency that only impending *combat deployment* can provide. The detachment was assigned its first combat mission just a week later, to reconnoiter the coastline east of Sredniy Isthmus and to determine if German ground forces had occupied positions along the southern shore of Motovskiy Bay. The detachment—deployed on two wooden boats—conducted the mission and returned to base without enemy contact or casualties.

The detachment quickly reached its initial strength goal of seventy personnel and acquired a commissar.[16] The new deputy commander was Intendant Third Rank N. A. Inzartsev, who was previously the chief of the athletic department of the fleet submarine force.[17] Viktor Leonov was among those recruited to the detachment during this early period.

Leonov's 1957 memoir picks up the story in mid-July 1941 and carries it through to the end of the war, but it ignores a major aspect of the fleet intelligence staff's activities: *covert intelligence operations* throughout northern *Norway from September 1941* to October 1944. Captain Third Rank Vizgin sent a small group of men to Varanger Peninsula in late September 1941 with two missions: determine the location, strength, and activities of German garrisons between Vardo and Vadso and establish contact with the Norwegian resistance as part of a plan of regional intelligence activities.[18] Although led by a Soviet lieutenant, half of this group of thirteen men were Norwegian communists who had fled the German occupation. They boarded a submarine in Polyarnyy and proceeded toward their landing site at Langbunes, twenty kilometers south of Vardo. On 26 September the group went ashore by rubber boat without incident and remained in the German rear area until mid-November, continuously moving about the eastern portion of Varanger Peninsula to gain information and avoid capture. They reported their positions and activities by radio, made numerous contacts with Norwegian civilians, and on

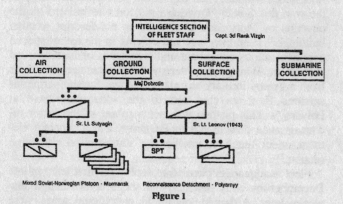

Figure 1

more than one occasion had to shoot their way clear of danger. Tight German population-control measures prevented them from establishing contacts with the resistance, but they did learn much about the several small local German garrisons. Part of the group returned to Soviet control by fishing boat on 22 October, and the remainder were picked up by a submarine on 15 November.

One of the conclusions drawn from this operation was that a protracted, *Soviet-sponsored partisan struggle* was not feasible on Varanger Peninsula. There was little cover and concealment; all the populated areas were concentrated along the coast, where the Germans could maintain tight observation and control; and the population base was too small to absorb strangers. The alternative to a Soviet-supported partisan effort was reconnaissance by small coast-watching teams of two or three men, inserted into the Varanger Peninsula to *monitor and report on German naval* traffic. Targeting data thus obtained *would be used to guide naval air and submarine* forces.[19]

Late in 1941 Vizgin reported the preparation of five teams, each consisting of two Norwegians and one Soviet radio operator (Figure 1). The commander of this group was Senior Lieutenant P. G. Sutyagin, and the political officer was a woman, Nina Krymova.[20] From the first days of the war, this Soviet-Norwegian platoon was billeted on the outskirts of Murmansk in a group of nondescript wooden buildings.[21] Here they received training in the use of special communications equipment and techniques of insertion and extraction. At night they deployed for parachute insertions from a nearby military airfield at Vaenga; for submarine insertions they traveled out to the submarine base at Polyarnyy. This platoon was not a subset of the larger reconnaissance detachment in Polyarnyy but a separate element under the fleet intelligence staff ground collection section.[22]

Fleet headquarters planned to deploy the first team in late December or early January and the second team a few weeks later. Although the initial operational areas were along the north coast of the Varanger Peninsula, Vizgin hoped to place teams near Nordkapp (North Cape) and Tromsø in February. In this manner the fleet intelligence staff could monitor German shipping along its entire route from the west coast of Norway into and out of Kirkenes, the main supply base for German ground forces on the Murmansk axis. To assure reliable radio communications, Vizgin requested and received from the fleet chief of staff the establishment of a separate signal communications center, manned for around-the-clock monitoring of these groups' operations. The chief of staff also assured Vizgin of close air support, and the placing of reconnaissance specialists on ships.[23] Thus submarine crews included personnel specially trained for inserting and extracting reconnaissance teams by rubber boat to act as boat handlers. If not Sutyagin himself, then some other officer from the fleet intelligence staff always went on the submarine to supervise the insertion or extraction.

In early *January 1942* the first team was inserted into the northern coast of Varanger Peninsula by submarine S-101, near Cape Nalneset (between Tana Fjord and Kongsfjord).[24] This group operated in the area between Berlevag and Cape Nalneset for two-and-a-half months, reporting not only on German naval traffic but also the activities of the local garrison. They maintained limited contacts with sympathetic local Norwegians, from whom they obtained information about German population-control measures, local military construction, and the results of Soviet air operations against Kirkenes. They communicated regularly with their base, sometimes three times in a twenty-four-hour period, and listened to reports given by other coast-watching teams. By the end of March, however, their provisions were exhausted, and they were in danger of exposure because of extending daylight hours.[25] On 29 March they were alerted that a submarine was en route to pick them up, and a few days later they were delivered to their base.

Not all attempts *to land reconnaissance teams in Norway* were successful. On 14 February a submarine approached

Mageroy (an island ten kilometers southwest of Nordkapp) and, after careful periscope reconnaissance of the landing area, surfaced to commence the landing operation.[26] While the small boats were taking the reconnaissance team to shore, strong winds and current pushed the submarine inshore, endangering it. The commander made another attempt to approach the shore to put off the teams' supplies, but without success. For three nights the submarine remained in the area while a storm raged. On the night of 18 February it returned to the landing area on the surface, only to discover German patrol vessels. During the ensuing crash dive, the submarine commander was left on the conning tower, believed to be mortally wounded. The Germans, however, quickly captured him alive.[27] On shore, meanwhile, three men of the reconnaissance team and two sailors were left without food, special winter clothing, and other items of equipment necessary for their missions.[28]

Three days later, another team was lost in a similar incident.[29] A submarine was inserting them on Arnoy (an island northeast of Tromsø) on 21 February 1942. Encountering problems, it managed to land the two Norwegians but not the Soviet radio operator. Although some weeks later these two Norwegians linked up with another team on the Varanger Peninsula, the two incidents together clearly indicated the need for better training of *submarine crews and reconnaissance* teams in handling small boats.

The next reported insertion of a team into Norway was on 4 April 1942, just a day after the extraction of the team from Nalneset. Submarine M-173 landed three men on the southeast shore of Sylte Fjord.[30] This team ranged east and west along the coast between Kiberg and Hamningberg, maintaining limited contacts with Norwegian sympathizers. In early May the two Norwegians who had been stranded on Arnoy in February joined them, and passed all the information they had gathered about German activities in the Tromsø area to their base by radio. The group remained in this area until sometime in the early autumn of 1942, resupplied periodically by air. Soviet sources credit them with providing information that led to the sinking of nine German transports.[31]

The insertions of these small reconnaissance teams by submarine continued through the remainder of 1942 and until September 1943.[32] It was not until September 1942 that German counterintelligence, through a prisoner-of-war interrogation, was able to determine the existence of the group and how it operated. Using this information, along with reports from Norwegian collaborators, by the summer of 1943 the Germans were able to kill or capture several agents, and even had minor successes in convincing agents to come over to their side, entering the radio net, and, in late October 1943, luring a Soviet submarine into ambush.[33]

During the summer of 1943 the Soviets also attempted to deploy two captured German personnel as a reconnaissance team. One had been snatched from a coastal artillery battery position in August 1942 and the other from a Stuka shot down over Murmansk on 26 December 1942. Both men were from Austria and were subjected to political reindoctrination by the Soviets. One of them had a brother in Dachau concentration camp, jailed there for communist sympathies. The men were given a radio and the mission to observe vehicular traffic on the Arctic Ocean Highway and air traffic at Salmijarvi and Nautsi airfields. As soon as they were inserted by parachute, on 31 May 1943, they turned themselves in to the nearest German unit. German counterintelligence was unsuccessful in using their damaged radio to enter the intelligence net of the Northern Fleet intelligence department.[34]

Having lost several teams to German counterintelligence, the mixed Soviet-Norwegian platoon no longer had sufficient manpower for mission requirements. Personnel from the reconnaissance detachment in Polyarnyy were detailed to assist them with their strategic reconnaissance mission.[35] Initially, Leonov's detachment provided boat handlers who went out on the submarines and assisted in the insertions and extractions. This first occurred on 30 September 1943, when four of Leonov's scouts departed on a submarine with an insertion mission to Nordkin Peninsula.[36] At about the same time, some of Leonov's men began to slip away to the safe house in Murmansk to prepare for other missions.

Although the submarine insertions continued, more frequently the men *were parachuted in*, despite the weather and terrain. A three-man team jumped into Varanger Peninsula on 10 February 1944, where they remained for nearly nine months. During this mission, Leonov's scouts reported on German ship traffic, searched for a downed Soviet pilot, and escaped and evaded German dog-equipped patrols. This group was extracted by a patrol torpedo boat on 26 October 1944.[37] Other parachute insertions included two Norwegians to the area west of Neiden on 24 March 1944, two Soviets to the Batsfjord area on 18 April, and two more Soviets to the area of Banak airfield, near Lakselvn in Norway, on 26 June. Two Norwegians jumped into Varanger Peninsula on 23 October, and even as the Germans were in retreat in late October, two Norwegians were parachuted into the Hammerfest area on the twenty-eighth.[38] The last team known to return to Soviet control was two Soviets and a Norwegian inserted near Hammerfest by submarine on 6 October 1943, who returned to Murmansk in January 1945.[39]

Although there is no tally of total airborne insertions, a recently declassified Soviet postwar report indicates that, in all, *thirty-nine* submarine insertions were attempted, of which *twenty-five* were successful.[40] By the Germans' own admissions, these *Soviet and Norwegian* teams were responsible *for the sinking of many* German ships.

What makes these generic fleet and flotilla reconnaissance detachments so unique? Why should they be called special purpose forces? How can these Soviet units be in any way compared to U.S. Navy SEALs? Several indicators, when taken together, point to these conclusions.

All the detachments bore the same generic name *in Russian: reconnaissance detachment of* a particular fleet or flotilla. Three carried the additional description as detachments of *osobogo naznacheniya*, or *special purpose*.[41] But, as the experience of the Dnepr River Flotilla detachment shows, the units sometimes had formal designations that did not indicate their actual organization or mission.

The linguistic evidence is more weighty. A 1972 Soviet journal used the Russian *razvedyvatel'no-diversionnyye gruppy* (reconnaissance-diversionary groups) to describe Viktor Leonov's Northern Fleet detachment,[42] and a 1985 article about naval support of partisan operations used the same term to describe the Baltic Fleet detachment.[43] Viktor Leonov used the term *razvedyvatel'no-diversionnyy otryad (reconnaissance-diversionary detachment)* in his 1985 book to describe the Northern Fleet group at its creation in 1941 and the Pacific Fleet detachment when he arrived there in June 1945.[44]

In a 1984 article about U.S. Navy SEALs, they were referred to nineteen times, eleven of which using the Russian phrase *razvedyvatel'no-diversionnyye (reconnaissance-diversionary)* and eight using *spetsial'nogo naznacheniya (special operations forces).*[45] A 1987 Soviet article used the term *razvedyvatel'no-diversionnyye gruppy* twice on the same page, first to describe U.S. Navy submarine-landed forces in the Gilbert Islands in August 1942 and then to characterize Soviet submarine-landed forces in German-occupied Norway in 1941–42.[46] In a September 1989 article about U.S. Navy SEALs in the Soviet Navy's journal *Morskoy Sbornik* (Naval Digest), the Russian *razvedyvatel'no-diversionnyye* was used twice and the term *spetsial'nogo naznacheniya* six times.[47] In an October 1989 article about U.S. special operations forces, both of these terms were used numerous times.[48] In the linguistic sense, then, the Soviets themselves see equivalency between U.S. special operations units, in general, and U.S. Navy SEALs, in particular, and Soviet fleet and flotilla reconnaissance detachments.

Historically, the detachments all possessed a common organizational structure: platoon-size units in flotillas, company-size units in fleets; subordination to the intelligence staff of the fleet or flotilla headquarters; direct action reconnaissance/raid elements in all fleets and flotillas; *covert action/espionage cells in all of the fleets and the Azov Flotilla.*

Like the special operations forces of many nations, the Soviet naval reconnaissance detachments were able to transfer as individuals and even entire units from one major command to another, even between theaters of war. Their capabilities were known and appreciated throughout the Soviet Navy, and their role was similarly understood by the upper command echelons of all fleets. This organization was clearly institutionalized throughout the Soviet naval forces.

Typical for special operations units, all the detachments were subordinated to the highest operational level of naval command, the commander of a fleet or flotilla. The example of the Northern Fleet suggests that fleet and flotilla commanders frequently were personally involved in the briefing and debriefing of detachment personnel. This allowed for the most rapid transmission of commanders' guidance and quick turnaround of information gained from reconnaissance. Although command and control of fleet reconnaissance detachments clearly rested with the local fleet commander, the Main Naval Staff in Moscow could assign fleet intelligence staffs specific collection tasks.[49] In the case of the Northern Fleet, it is likely that intelligence information of strategic interest and importance to the Royal Navy was being passed to Admiral D. B. Fisher at the British mission in Polyarnyy.[50]

As befits any *special operations organization, personnel* were selected very carefully. High *standards of physical fitness were prerequisite for assignment* to these detachments and were maintained in training. Many naval scouts *were fleet champions*, Masters of Sport, and even a few Meritorious Masters of Sport.[51] An equally important criterion for recruitment was political reliability. The need for linguistic skills led to the employment of non-Slavic Soviet citizens, as well as foreign nationals. Women appeared in the Northern Fleet, Baltic Fleet, Black Sea Fleet, and Azov Flotilla detachments as medics, language specialists, and intelligence agents.

Elite troops are frequently segregated from conventional units. Sources on the four fleet detachments emphasize physical separation of scouts from other fleet units, with explanations that suggest *security* and compartmentalization. Barracks were always near fleet headquarters, even if that was distant from the battlefield. *Detachments were self-contained*, with their own medics, clerks, cooks, supply personnel, armorers, political officers, and light vehicles for administrative support. It is also interesting that in the Danube Flotilla, the detachment did not operate from a Soviet military vessel, but rather from a trophy yacht that formerly belonged to a German admiral.[52] In the Pacific Fleet, Leonov's detachment sailed from Wonsan back to its base at Vladivostok, not on a Soviet naval vessel but on a trophy Japanese naval vessel, of which they were the crew.[53] This demonstrates the independent spirit that so many special operations units develop over time.

Naval scouts trained in all the fundamental *skills associated with special* operations, such as *parachuting, driving* (there were few motor vehicles in *the USSR before World War II*, and it was useful to be able to drive captured German vehicles), *communications, skiing, languages, demolitions, enemy weapons, land navigation, sniper marksmanship, unarmed combat, surveillance photography, and special methods of insertion and extraction.*

The missions performed by these *detachments were tactical by most criteria but operational-strategic in impact:* raiding, reconnoitering, organizing partisan activities, covert gathering of intelligence, low-level political assassination, abducting enemy personnel, vectoring air strikes, frequently wearing *enemy uniforms, and carrying enemy weapons*—all activities that are the *standard repertoire of special operations forces.*

These detachments had habitual relationships with their means of delivery. In the Northern Fleet in particular, there are references to the same boat captains and liaison personnel with submarine crews to help with *insertions* and *ex-tractions* and the repeated use of the *same air crews to conduct* parachute delivery of personnel and supplies.

Thus far only a single connection has been made between the Soviet Navy's emergency rescue service, called EPRON in 1941, and a reconnaissance detachment, that case being in the Baltic Fleet. But the history of the emergency rescue service clearly indicates that its units participated in amphibious landings of the other fleets as well. The currently postulated employment of small submersibles by Soviet naval special-purpose forces may be the result of this World War II liaison. This is an area that merits additional historical research.

Some detachments share a common historiography. Memoirs of fleet reconnaissance detachment veterans began to appear at around the same time, 1957–62, when many analysts believe the Soviets were re-creating their special operations forces.[54] This suggests a renewal of interest in their wartime experiences. Other recent writings, however, provide more direct linkages between naval special purpose forces past and present. In October 1988 an article appeared in *Morskoy Sbornik* that celebrated the seventieth anniversary of Soviet naval intelligence.[55] The article names the World War II Heroes of the Soviet Union of the Northern, Baltic, Black Sea, Amur Flotilla, and Pacific Fleet reconnaissance detachments in a single sentence. Just two paragraphs later in another single sentence are named the World War II chiefs of the intelligence sections of the staffs of Northern, Baltic, and Black Sea fleets, among others.

On the second page of this article one finds another list of eight names, men who are called the "leading officer-communists of intelligence/reconnaissance [*razvedka*]." In other words, these eight men were the current batch of intelligence officers of fleet staffs or occupied some leadership position in naval reconnaissance units. These eight men are important pieces of the current naval special-purpose force puzzle and should be tracked closely in the pages of Soviet military periodicals.

Viktor Leonov, *former submarine sailor and repairman, veteran, commander of both the Northern and Pacific Fleet reconnaissance detachments, and twice Hero of the Soviet Union,* retired from active duty in 1957 at the age of forty. He reappeared in the early 1960s, however, in the uniform of an army colonel and was involved in the personnel selection and training of ground force special-purpose troops. (This fact was established in an interview with a former Soviet soldier in 1987.)[56] This single association—and there may be many others—of a World War II veteran with development of contemporary special purpose forces clearly demonstrates the use by the Soviet special-operations community of past war experience as an organizational and doctrinal base for current force development.

When taken together, all these factors provide strong evidence that naval reconnaissance detachments of Soviet fleets and flotillas during World War II were *the forebears of the current Soviet naval special-purpose force.* A thorough study of the history of these groups is essential to an understanding of the organization and mission of Soviet naval special-purpose forces today. With this translation of the 1957 memoir of Viktor Nikolayevich Leonov, the *most famous naval scout of them all, this thorough* study may now begin.

JAMES F. GEBHARDT

1

Early Experiences

WE GREETED THE WAR beyond the sixty-ninth parallel, at one of the naval bases of the Northern Fleet.[1]

On the first day of the war [22 June 1941], the white hats and sailors' caps, which the inhabitants of this port city had become so accustomed to seeing, almost immediately disappeared. Summer was in full swing, the much-loved sun shone around the clock—normal for those latitudes—and a light southern wind promised steady weather. Now, though, such weather did not make us happy. The weather summaries said, "clear visibility," and German air reconnaissance was flying over the base, to Murmansk and back. Against the dark background of the granite of the piers and roadways, the white saucers of our sailors' headgear were easily seen; therefore, we were ordered to remove them.

After a short time we became used to the tiresome wail of the sirens and the endless pounding of hammers in the repair shop where we worked. They had sent Sasha Senchuk and me there from the submarine, saying, "You know sheet metal and lathe operations, so we are sending you to a combat assignment." We exchanged our sailors' dungarees for dark blue coveralls and went to the ship repair facility.

An order was an order. We had to obey it, though in no way did our work coincide with what we believed to be a "combat assignment," especially now that the war had begun. I didn't say anything, but Sasha Senchuk couldn't keep silent. He didn't have anyone to express his resentment to besides me. One night, after a long and tiring day, we were getting ready to sleep right there in the workshop, but Sasha could not sleep. He shook me by the shoulder. "Okay, you have something to say about everything! Tell me, Viktor, why is the working class taking up arms, but you and I are here in the workshop? Special assignment, you say? Orders? Is that so?"

I kept silent, but he shouted right into my ear, "Say something, damn it!"

Sasha paced from corner to corner. I knew that he would give me no peace and would come up with various plans to return to the submarine fleet, or, even worse, go to the naval infantry [the Soviet equivalent of the U.S. Marine Corps].

I was thinking about this very thing when Sasha ran up to me and, with a quick jerk, pulled me down off the workbench. "I have an idea!"

In Sasha's eyes there was the joyful brilliance and adamant decisiveness of a man who had challenged fate. In those minutes Senchuk seemed handsome and strong, though in fact he was homely. He was thin, narrow, and bony at the shoulders, and his dark oblong face under a shock of tar-black hair was thickly covered with blackheads.

"I have an idea!" Sasha exclaimed, and then laid out his plan, which I, still half asleep, understood included flight from his "combat post" to the front, to the *naval infantry brigade*.

"We will say that we are volunteers! They will sign us up."

I agreed to all of it only so he would leave me alone and give me an hour of sleep.

Morning came, and Sasha, eager to get on with it, pounded his hammer furiously on the half-polished head of a chisel and sawed and drilled, working with all his energy. Perhaps he had forgotten yesterday's idea because he urged me to finish the repair on the submarine quickly, and then we would immediately return to its crew. It was impossible to argue with Sasha, and I wanted to believe him, though the work load in the repair shop was increasing with each passing day.

The chief of the repair shop coldly promised: "We will replace you in good time." We would, undoubtedly, have suffered and waited if disturbing news had not reached us. Some of our friends from the submarine, the Three Nikolays and Aleksey, ran into the repair shop and told us that a special detachment of naval scouts was being created for action in the enemy rear area. As outstanding athletes, they had already been selected for the reconnaissance detachment.

"We missed it!" Sasha angrily reproached me, as if I were guilty of something. "You are a ranked skier and noted sailboat-racing champion." But suddenly he turned and showered our friends with questions. "Where is this detachment? Who do I ask about joining? Where do I get a transfer?" Sasha grimaced with annoyance as he stood before electrician's mate Nikolay "Kolya" Damanov—Kolya number one, we called him.

Kolya stuttered but was talkative just the same. "S-s-sasha! Don't get excited! At the headquarters they know that you and Viktor are good a-a-athletes. And we will tell S-s-senior Lieutenant Lebedev from the intelligence s-s-section about you. It is too bad that you will have to exchange your sa-s-sailor's uniform for infantry. Lebedev s-said that under the infantry fatigue shirt should be a s-sailor's soul. And the soul of a s-scout. Here it is!" stammered Kolya number one.

I didn't know anything about the soul of a scout, but to be honest, I was surprised that the Three Nikolays—Damanov, Losev, and Ryabov—whom I had taught to ski and throw grenades, had been selected into the reconnaissance detachment, but I had been overlooked.[2] I looked questioningly at Petty Officer First Class Aleksey Radyshevtsev, with whom I often contended for first place in competition.[3] Aleksey smiled encouragingly, "The detachment is just being formed. Everything will work out."

It turned out that a Major Dobrotin, a representative of the fleet staff, had gone to Murmansk to select some members of the Young Communist League for the detachment, and the Lesgaft Institute of Physical Training in Leningrad supplied another group.[4] But the main complement of scouts would consist of sailors.

"The people will be selected one by one, as n-ne-needed," Kolya Damanov said. "Hitler's crack units are operating against us here. Mountain infantry. We will gi-give those jaegers a hot time."[5]

They once again promised to try to find us a position and then left. We waited nervously for the evening, when we could submit a request to the Military Council of the Northern Fleet.[6]

If only it were possible to put on a scrap of paper one's true feelings! To write it down in such a way that a rear admiral, when he read this paper, would say: "Assign Senior Sailor Viktor Leonov, in his third year of service, to the detachment of naval scouts!" But I couldn't write that well.

"I request that I be assigned to the reconnaissance detachment of Headquarters, Fleet." Is that all? And sign it? How could the rear admiral understand my desire and calling to serve in reconnaissance? I wrote about it, but then crossed out the last lines, threw away the paper, and began again. It was not mine to judge about a calling, and it even sounded immodest. Sasha and I had a burning desire to become naval scouts. But a desire is not a calling.

Then I recalled how when I was a schoolboy, it struck me that I was called to become a poet. I'd read in the school newspaper the verse of a seventh grader about a snipe hunt. I decided that I could write better. I went home, sat at the table, and composed for such a long time that my father, not used to seeing me so deeply occupied in studies, asked, "Vitya, what are you so interested in?"

I showed my father the beginning of my poem. Father

smiled condescendingly, but then, having examined the text, began to frown. Finally, he read the first lines aloud, slowly and totally without expression:

> Once I was a pilgrim,
>   I believed in God and the tsar.
> Now I have become a Pioneer,[7]
>   A fighter for the society of labor!

"You wrote this?" my father asked sternly. "When were you, the son of a communist, ever a pilgrim? And to you the tsar is only something from a book. What kind of verse is this, if there is no truth in it? You read much, but you write clumsily."

Such a blow to a confident young poet did not pass without consequences.[8] When Sasha Senchuk helped me compose a verse about the northern sea, about service in the navy, I restrained his constant poetic outpourings as much as I could.

Sasha recited the first two lines of the latest stanza:

> We joyfully greet the frosty dawns
>   And with the song of bells want to say. . . .

"To say what? And how to say it?" Sasha looked plaintively at me: he waited for my prompting. We thought a long time.

"I've got it!" Sasha slapped me on the back. "A Northern Fleet sailor needs,

> And with the song of bells wants to say:
> Gray sea! Snow-covered hills!
> And I am prepared to tie my life with you forever. . . ."

I recalled a nimble pilgrim from the fifth grade, who immediately became a "fighter for the society of labor," and told Sasha about it.

"Nonsense!" he said resentfully. Sasha would not agree

that the soul could be transformed. "Viktor, you act like our verse is for the whole fleet."

Before the war, we dreamed together how we would return home after naval service, I to Zaraysk, near Moscow, and Sasha to Kiev. We would talk about faraway cruises in the Arctic Ocean, which we had not sailed yet, about the frozen sea[9] and the granite walls in the deep fjords, about the kingdom of the eternal night, illuminated by faded northern lights, and about many other things, which sounded attractive but to which we never intended to commit ourselves.

To commit one's life. Now here I was, writing a request to a rear admiral, and this request could change my life. I had to think and deliberate. Again and again I had to ask myself, Was I prepared for the difficult life of a naval scout? Did I have sufficient determination and courage to keep a promise that I was eager to make on paper? I would earn the title of naval scout!

I had dreamed about the navy. When I was a young factory worker at the Calibr plant in Moscow, I loved to read Stanyukovich's books.[10] I even wrote down from memory the old admiral's words that accompanied his young nephew to the fleet. "You will love the sea and love naval service. It is noble and good, and sailors are a straight and honest lot." It is from *Around the World on a Kite*. In the evenings I studied in the Osoaviakhim naval club.[11] In order to pass the very difficult examination of the draft commission, I took up sports. The doctors noted somewhat indifferently that for a height of five feet nine inches, I weighed 165 pounds. I held the second-class Ready for Labor and Defense badge[12] and a certificate of active membership in the Osoaviakhim naval club. Nevertheless, they painstakingly tapped on my chest and listened to my heart and lungs, spun me around on some kind of rotating stool, checked my vision and hearing, and then, finally, pronounced their decision. I was suitable for service in the navy.

The Komsomolists of Calibr, who had accompanied me

to Leningrad's Kirov Training Detachment, instructed me to be a deserving representative of the chief of the navy and, joking of course, predicted a head-spinning career as a captain of long voyages. The young girls sang a song about the captain, whose smile was the ship's flag. My father said a brief good-bye: "Serve honorably, my son!"

I served the entire three years in the north as prescribed. When they accepted me into the party, my father sent me a long congratulatory letter. "The entire Leonov family is proud of you," he wrote. "You understand today's international situation. I believe that in the dark hour of trials you will justify our party's faith in you."

Now that dark hour of trials had arrived. Above my workbench a poster beckoned. The artists had portrayed a woman—a mother. She was turning to me, as to her son: "The Motherland is calling you!"

"Viktor!" Sasha Sanchuk interrupted my thoughts. "Why aren't you writing?"

"I'm finishing!" I resolutely picked up the pen and dictated aloud to myself the last words of the request: "I will earn the rank of naval scout!"

"I will do the same!" Sasha said.

We put away our requests; we'd hand them over to the supervisor in the morning.

Two weeks later Sasha and I turned in our naval uniforms to the clothing warehouse and received the green khaki uniforms of infantrymen in exchange. After the baggy sailor's bell-bottoms and light sailor's boots, we felt clumsy in trousers that fit tightly at our knees and in heavy boots with inordinately broad canvas tops. A metal helmet either slipped to one side or weighed heavily on our heads, which were growing accustomed to it. We received semiautomatic rifles with bayonet-knives, grenades, and rucksacks designed for heavy loads.

Embarrassed by our unusual appearance, we stood before Senior Lieutenant Georgiy Lebedev. He scrutinized us suspiciously, as if wondering whether he should accept us into the detachment.

"From submarines? That's good! Petty Officer Motovilin!"

A tall sailor with light brown hair appeared in the doorway. He was the remarkable scout Stepan Motovilin, about whom the newspaper *Krasnoflotets* [Red sailor] had already written.

"Rookies," Lebedev pointed at us. "Get going."

After breakfast, Motovilin led us into the hills and showed us how to move and stay hidden in the rocks, how to throw a grenade, and how to thrust with a bayonet. We made a good effort, and after just two days Motovilin, satisfied with our initial successes, said, "Men, you're good, but don't tell anyone! Of course, you'll have to learn a lot more, but there is no time. We'll assemble tonight for more training."

Sasha Senchuk perished in our first operation.

He was the first dead man that I saw with my own eyes in the war. Sasha's death really shook me, though I tried not to display any emotion in front of my comrades.

Scouts who had returned from the operation were sleeping in the barracks. The bunk next to me, Sasha Senchuk's, was empty. Kolya Damanov, who almost died there in the mountains because of my stupidity, snored blissfully to the right.

I thought about Sasha, looked at Kolya Damanov, and was overwhelmed by unhappy thoughts.

My weary body demanded rest. I closed my eyes, tried to fall asleep, but wasn't able to put a single disturbing question out of my mind: Was I suited for service in naval reconnaissance? In front of Lebedev, Stepan Motovilin had boasted of my courage. Even the senior lieutenant himself had said: "You fought well, Leonov! You're not afraid of the jaegers—that's the main thing. Your knowledge will increase." No one mentioned—and, I hoped, no one suspected—what had happened to me when we crossed the low ground in the mountains. This was already after the death of Senchuk. Pursued by the Germans, we were withdrawing toward the sea, toward our boat. Behind me crept scout Grigoriy Kharabrin, a former driver for the Sailors' Home. Cursing mercilessly, he shouted at me: "Move it! Get down! You'll be killed!" But I did not get down. I went on, crouching, completely indifferent to the whistle of bullets. I did not have the strength to run but was afraid to lie on the ground. Yes, I was afraid to fall to the ground! It seemed to me that then my legs would cramp up again, and I would not be able to stand up, just as Sasha Senchuk could not get up.

Grisha Kharabrin then lashed out at me for bravado and for childishness: "You're giving the jaegers fodder! But they are missing it."

Kolya Damanov didn't tell anyone about the confusion with the grenade. I consoled myself that such things could happen to anyone in his first battle. They should not judge me for this. I would judge myself. In the request to the rear admiral, I wrote that I would be a good scout, but I was beginning to have doubts. Good scouts returned from missions and slept. Motovilin and Kharabrin, Radyshevtsev and Damanov were sleeping. Having put aside their troubles, in the morning, fresh and rested, they would be ready for a new mission, for new battles. And I was pondering my own experiences. True, for me this was the first battle, and I still did not know how I would feel after the second or the third.

I buried my head in the pillow but for a long time was unable to sleep, and so this time I quietly went over each detail of the day's battle in my mind.

There were twenty-two scouts.

Armed with two machine guns, we loaded up on the boat and took a course to the mouth of the Great Western Litsa River.[13] Along the way, Lebedev told us that in the landing area we were to attack an enemy strongpoint. Our mission was to destroy the position and, if possible, capture a "tongue."[14]

The sea was calm. It was also quiet on the shore of Motovskiy Bay, covered by rocks and boulders, where the boat pulled up almost to the water's edge. We disembarked over a gangplank onto the shore, and three scouts immediately went forward. We walked in a file behind them.

The strongpoint was located on Hill 670, approximately eight kilometers from shore. Lebedev ordered Motovilin (I was in his group) to go around the hill from the south. Petty Office First Class Chervonyy's group was to go around the strongpoint from the north, after which the twelve scouts led by Lebedev would begin the attack from the center.

Motovilin's group had the longest and most difficult terrain to negotiate. The rocky hill was thickly covered with boulders, and when we finally reached the last stage of the hill, Lebedev's and Chervonyy's scouts were already in attack positions. I did not know that Lebedev was nearby and was sure that we were now alone in front of the dug-in jaegers. I crawled close in behind Motovilin. He raised his left hand just a little and pointed to the right. I understood his signal and crawled to the left, to a large rock.

Sticking my head out a little bit, I saw the enemy—five or six Germans. So those are jaegers! Tall, in dark gray pants tucked into short stockings and in the same color jackets with red buttons on the sleeves. They stood up at full height, with uncovered heads, their hands quietly resting on submachine guns hanging across their chests. It seemed to me that the jaegers looked out over the landscape with curiosity and pride. That made me angry—we were lying on the ground, hiding behind rocks, and they were acting like landlords over our territory!

An officer appeared from the direction of a dugout and said something to the soldiers. They began to disperse, and I held on to my rifle and took aim at the approaching officer.

"Don't shoot!" Lebedev said. I shuddered from the unexpectedness. "We have to take him alive. Get ready!"

Then it became obvious that Lebedev couldn't see the other jaegers from his position. But I forgot about him. More than that, when I rushed toward the officer, I even

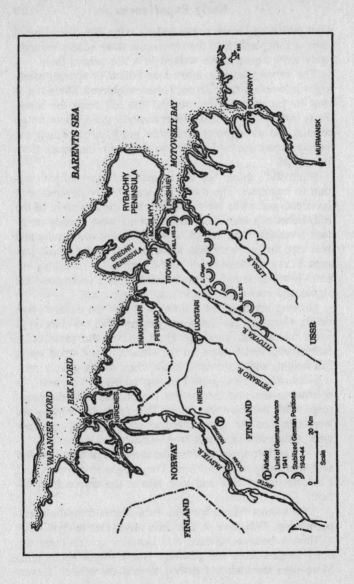

forgot to attach the bayonet to my rifle. The officer pulled out a pistol and fired it but missed. I jumped behind a rock, and firing began all around.

The crackling of gunfire echoed in the mountains. I didn't know who was firing where, and was afraid to stick my head up, but at the same time I knew that I couldn't hide behind the rock forever. What if our men suddenly moved forward or withdrew, and I was left alone? I had to do something, but I did not know what.

"Kolya, over here!" I cried to Damanov, who was lying nearby.

The battle took its course. Taking advantage of the jaegers' concentrating their firing at us, Lebedev successfully led his scouts around the position. Lebedev's and Chervonyy's groups captured a "tongue" and, with two trophy machine guns, were firing along the low ground where the jaegers were concentrated.

And we defended, keeping the pressure on the enemy.

Sailor Nikolay Ryabov was wounded in the stomach. When Motovilin picked him up from the battlefield, he was desperately thirsty. Damanov, Kharabrin, and I covered Motovilin and Ryabov with fire from our semiautomatic rifles.[15] But the Germans were getting within hand grenade range. I threw a grenade, but nothing happened.

"Pull the pin, w-warrior!" I heard Damanov's voice.

Dismayed by my inexperience, I activated the detonator and hurled another grenade. There was no explosion. And two or three seconds later, the grenade came flying back toward me. It fell not far from Damanov and exploded right there. Fortunately, Damanov was fully protected in the rocks.

"Tha-anks, Viktor, you did fine! Sha-ake the grenade. Let it hiss."[16]

I was startled by Damanov's calm and now, not hurrying, hurled two grenades very far. After they exploded it grew quiet. No one was firing.

"Move out?" I asked Damanov and Kharabrin.

We crawled back and joined up with Motovilin.

"I concealed him in the rocks," Motovilin said to Damanov. "The jaegers will not find him."

Can he be talking about Ryabov? Why did he hide him? I wanted to ask Motovilin about this, but the battle was starting up again on the other side of the ridge, and we hurried to the aid of Lebedev's and Chernovyy's groups.

Skirting the perpendicular slopes, we climbed to the crest of the hill and there found the bodies of three jaegers. To one side, face down, lay a scout.

"Senchuk!" Immediately recognizing Sasha, I ran over to him and turned him onto his back. Black strands of hair were scattered along his high forehead. His face was so dark that it was impossible to make out his blackheads. And his mouth was slightly open, as if he were asking, "How could this have happened to me, brothers?"

I don't know why, but I pulled at my friend, looking for his wound. I said something incoherent and then came to myself when Nikolay Losev laid his firm hands on my shoulders. Lebedev had sent him to us.

"These things happen." He pulled me back. "Did you hear me, Viktor? We're withdrawing to the sea. Lebedev's group has already crossed the hollow. Look alive!"

Shots were getting nearer to the crest of the hill, and mortars were firing from neighboring heights. Motovilin, Kharabrin, and Damanov withdrew and shouted something at us, shaking their fists. Only then did I understand that we were to cover the group's withdrawal and could not carry Sasha Senchuk out.[17]

Firing in bursts and moving by short bounds, we approached the depression, which was covered by enemy fire. We crawled one behind the other. Then, without warning, my legs stopped obeying me—they just cramped up. I could barely get up, but, crouching over, moved forward. Motovilin, Damanov, and Kharabrin laid down heavy fire, holding off the jaegers, while I crossed the depression.

When at last we had made it to the boat, lying on the deck we splashed icy water on our flushed faces. Senior Lieutenant Lebedev called me over. He stood behind us, his legs spread wide. His leather jacket, held shut by a belt, tightly outlined his figure. Lebedev looked at me intently. It seemed that he wanted to ask me something, but waved me off. He could see that I was confused and disheveled. It was the appropriate time to turn away and leave, but I just stood there. Lebedev sat me down, sat next to me, and said, "It's difficult to lose a friend. You saw the dead jaegers at the crest of the hill? Sasha climbed up there first and cut down all three. In the heat of the moment he raced forward standing straight up. That was his nature. He cleared the way for us but perished himself. You had a very good comrade, Viktor. I am sorry that we were not able to bury him. Not him, and not Ryabov. Poor Ryabov. They should have lived—the Three Nikolays were friends. Shipmates. All from the same cutter, they played on the same soccer team. And now two are returning to base. What can you do? It's war, we have to get used to it."

And we got used to it.

Not all at once, but each in his own way, we became accustomed to danger, and in spite of this (and, possibly, because of it), began to like service in the naval scout detachment. We tried not to think about the danger—where is there not danger in war?

Three days later the whole detachment was again prepared for a mission. Half of the detachment consisted of beginners, unlike us "veterans," who had been on one or two raids.

Major Dobrotin, a senior officer from the intelligence section of fleet staff, commanded this raid.[18] It was the same Leonid Vasilevich Dobrotin who had selected the scouts from the Murmansk Komsomol organization. Although we did not yet know the major, we had heard much about him. Dobrotin had fought on the fronts of the civil war against Yudenich, Denikin, and Mamontov. He had commanded a squadron in Budenny's cavalry.[19] He had been awarded an honorary weapon by the All Russian Central Executive Committee. He had finished the naval faculty of the engineering academy.

Lebedev said that the major "sees through every scout. Keep this in mind!"

Dobrotin showed up in the detachment on the eve of the operation. He wasn't young, but a tall, erect officer with light crew-cut hair. The major's face was long, with teeth set closely in a small mouth. He looked stern, but after Lebedev's report, Dobrotin gave the command "Stand at ease" and chatted freely with those scouts he had assigned to the detachment. Then the major was introduced to us sailors from the submarine fleet and, finally, to the "artists," as we called the volunteers who had arrived in the detachment from the fleet song-and-dance ensemble.

"Those who have not yet smelled powder," Dobrotin said, "and those who are looking only for romantic adventure," and he paused, looking at the group of artists, "I want to warn: no kind of special romance should be anticipated. Having penetrated into the enemy's immediate rear area, we will draw off part of his troops from the forward positions. The more difficult it is for us, the easier it becomes at the front. That means that it has to be difficult for us! And that's your romance."

He didn't say another word about reconnaissance. Major Dobrotin talked about enemy intentions, the Germans driving toward Murmansk without regard for casualties. If Hitler managed to capture the Murmansk port and the Kirov rail line, we would lose important lines of communication that connected us with our allies and be deprived of the enormous natural resources of the North. The defenders of the Far North would fight selflessly for each hill on the far approaches to Murmansk, for each boulder on each hill. Especially fierce battles were unfolding on the Great Western Litsa River. We would be operating in the enemy's rear area, on the river's west bank.

Senior Lieutenant Lebedev and Captain Inzartsev commanded two groups of the detachment. We knew the captain well. The submarine brigades physical training director,

Nikolay Arkadevich Inzartsev, had, not long ago, won the title of fleet weight-lifting champion. But those who didn't know Inzartsev would be surprised by this. Of average height, round-shouldered and lean, Nikolay Arkadevich hardly resembled a shot-putter. He was very strong, a weight lifter, soccer player, skier, and sailboat racer.

Major Dobrotin named sailor Viktor "Vityek" Tarzanov as his orderly.[20] Small and nimble, Tarzanov had a button nose and always wore a smile on his face. He was a very alert, clever, and smart sailor. After his appointment, Vitek proudly thrust out his chest and gleefully proclaimed in the barrack, "Clear the road! The commander's orderly is coming!"

We only smiled, having decided not to react to him. We knew that he would have a quick answer. But Belov, a sailor who had volunteered from the fleet dance ensemble, did not know this.

"Vitek!" Belov blocked the orderly's path. "How did you get into reconnaissance? They say that you served as a cook's helper on a fishing trawler. Is this true?"

"That's right!" Tarzanov said, though he really came to the detachment from a submarine chaser. "So what? A cook's business is an intellectual occupation. It's not like jumping about on a stage, like you."

Everyone laughed. But Belov, standing almost six feet tall, looked scornfully down at Vitek, stood out of the way, and only said, "Hmm! You've got a smart mouth, sailor boy, but you blow air like a whale."

Tarzanov grabbed him. "You wait! Wait until we go on patrol. Stay close to me, don't get lost, and I'll teach you how to catch fish and cook supper."

"Go to hell!" Embarrassed, Belov finally broke free. "What kind of teacher are you? You stay by me, and don't let them run over you! When you're out of breath, I'll put you in my rucksack, kid, and carry you out."

"Really? Great!" Vitek turned to us. "The major says that in mountain war there's no better transport than a pack—on a donkey. So I'll tell the major that thanks to the fleet ensemble, we don't need donkeys."

At first the battle in the Great Western Litsa area went well for us. The Germans, startled by our appearance behind their lines, abandoned first one hill and then another. Having destroyed their combat outpost security, we gained the dominating height. But below, in ravines covered by moss, the enemy concentrated forces for the counterattack. Major Dobrotin ordered Lebedev to reconnoiter the neighboring hill.

The major had foreseen the course of events. The dominating height is not always the best for combat, it turns out. We were sitting on top of flat, smooth granite. We couldn't dig in, there was no place to hide, and the enemy, most assuredly, would call in air support. The neighboring hill was significantly lower, but its broken, boulder-covered crest was suitable for defense. It would not be easy to knock us off that hill. But the major had even more in mind. He wanted to create the appearance that we were withdrawing. And when, under the intense pressure of superior forces, we began the retreat to the shore and toward the front line, the jaegers, to cut us off from the sea, would call in additional forces. And we would evade them along a route already reconnoitered, the narrow ravine.

In the final analysis, the major was able to impose his battle plan on the enemy. We defended for an entire day, inflicting great losses on the enemy, drawing a part of the enemy's forces away from the front line, and helping our infantry units to counterattack the enemy and occupy more favorable positions.

The mission was accomplished, and our losses were not great. Why did we return home with a feeling that we had suffered some kind of misfortune? We arrived at our dock. We got off onto the shore and waited in exhaustion, knowing that the command "Dismissed!" would not be given.

Four weaponless scouts stood among us. The detachment petty officer, Grigoriy Chekmachev, checked four rifles against a list of serial numbers to determine whose they were. Standing next to the petty officer, Vitek spun around and swung a boot—a single soldier's boot, the ownership of which was not in doubt. On his right flank stood sailor Belov, with one bare foot. Weaponless and barefoot.

What had happened?

Before noon we had beaten off several attacks, and when the enemy received reinforcements, we began a gradual withdrawal to the neighboring hill. The first group already occupied the new line, and ours was still holding the dominating height. The German attacks grew in intensity. The jaegers were so close that we could hear their shouts and the clatter of their cleated boots. Then only two covering squads remained on the hill—Losev's and Damanov's. The major and the captain were with them.

As the battle grew hotter, Belov became more frightened. Glancing around, he shouted, "Everyone's already withdrawn!" and ran off. Three other scouts followed him. They made their way down, and, to take a shortcut to the hill, turned straight toward a lake. We were defending fiercely on the crest, and our fire was growing stronger, but the fugitives believed we were the enemy, firing at them. Having thrown down their rifles, they jumped into the water, and Belov lost his boot.

Major Dobrotin blew up at Petty Officer Losev. "Where are your troops? Half of them are lost? Oh, you are poor excuses for scouts!"

Dobrotin and Inzartsev lay on the hill, and we beat off still another enemy attack.

I saw the major in battle. He was calmly aiming and firing his submachine gun. Inzartsev fired the machine gun with short bursts. Infrequently glancing to the sides, Grisha Kharabrin, Nikolay Losev, Aleksey Radyshevtsev, and other scouts fired with determination, but without fear. In preparation for the close-in battle, they placed hand grenades nearby. Kolya Damanov fought spiritedly, with a kind of mischievousness, and it was easy for me to be near him. I even wanted to wink at Nikolay and shout something silly.

In the morning, when the jaegers showed themselves in the distance, the mood had been quite different. The unknown and a kind of vague unease tormented us: How is the battle unfolding? All this happened. Even in the critical moments of the enemy attack there was no fear. Our commanders and comrades were nearby. And if two of our squads with one machine gun can hold off an entire company of jaegers, then one man can feel invulnerable.

On the major's command we withdraw to the lower hill and joined Lebedev's group. Inzartsev, Losev, Kharabrin, and Tarzanov clambered up the slope with the others. Losev and Kharabrin carried the rifles dropped near the lake.

"Trophies of a heroic covering screen!" Kharabrin declared. "I order that they be carried back to base under guard."

And Vitek, shaking the boot, had already moved toward the pale Belov.

"Now you'll have to pay for this!" Tarzanov declared, but then froze under the major's stern reproach.

"Stop!"

So here we stood in formation at our base, waiting for the arrival of Major Dobrotin, who had been delayed on the boat. What would he say? How would he judge the battle we had just fought? What punishment awaited our panic-stricken soldiers?

Seeing the major, Captain Inzartsev was preparing to report, but Dobrotin waved him off: "It's unnecessary, be quiet!" He came up close to us and spoke softly—quietly and softly. But each of his words stuck in our ears and in our hearts.

"Cowards are judged by a court-martial,[21] and they are judged harshly, according to wartime standards. I am sick and ashamed that among the volunteers of this detachment—among you who were hand-picked and screened—there turned out to be such as these, who should be judged by a court-martial. It's a disgrace! I was with you in battle. I know that it was the first experience for many of you, and therefore I will not formally charge you. Given this second chance, I hope that those who are guilty will cleanse themselves of this disgraceful blemish. But never—are you listening?—never will we in the detachment cast suspicion on anyone who fights bravely. Let anyone who remains in the detachment, who becomes a genuine naval scout, be proud of this title. And now, my friends, rest."

In the barracks that evening there was talk only about the first fight. Senior Lieutenant Lebedev talked to us about the calling and duty of a scout, about the genuine and mythical romance of naval service. To those of us who had left the ships for combat duty on land, Lebedev drew a picture that repelled some and excited others. This was a unique experience for each volunteer who had come to the detachment.

"Here in the North, we are fighting a very powerful and dangerous enemy. Hitler's jaegers are trained in mountain warfare. Regiments and battalions from General Dietl's corps, which threaten Murmansk and the entire Kola Peninsula, have gained experience in many battles in the mountains of the South—in the mountains of Greece and Yugoslavia—and in the mountains of the North—in Norway.[22] The jaegers know how to fight. To defeat such an enemy, one has to be stronger than him. Strength meets strength.

"If you want a victory, then you must not only be more skillful and brave than the jaeger, but also overcome him with your mastery, cunning, and quickness. This will not come to you immediately. There will be no easy life for the Northern Fleet scout. Danger will threaten you both on the sea, when the assault is just nearing the enemy shore, and on the shore itself. There will be difficult and continuous battles in the near and deep enemy rear areas.

"Autumn will be here soon, and right behind it everything will be hidden in the darkness of the around-the-clock polar night. Then your busiest time will begin. You will have to fight and sleep on the rocky soil, under the icy wind, in snowstorms and blizzards. There'll be no hot food for days, possibly a week, because you can't build a fire during a raid. It will be difficult to move up the steep cliffs, or even a single kilometer along the marshy tundra, and across mountain streams and swamps without a battle. But you will have to conduct battles on the march for tens of kilometers, climb up into still steeper mountains and hills, which, as we have already seen, are laced with ravines and precipices.

"It is difficult to fight on rocky shores but even more difficult farther inland. But if you decide to become a scout—a naval scout!—there should not be any timidity in your heart in front of the strong and clever enemy, or fear of severe trials. In your heart you should carry fear to the enemy and unquenchable hatred toward the occupiers!

"You will be operating with the detachment as a whole, in a small group, or perhaps by yourself. All your hope is in your weapons. Hold onto them to the very end. But the most powerful weapon of a Soviet scout is his clear conscience and high duty to the Motherland."

We listened to Senior Lieutenant Georgiy Lebedev without interrupting. No one asked about anything. It was all completely clear, and the choice—to remain in reconnaissance or return to base—was still open to each sailor. But my choice was already made.

After the second raid I had trouble falling asleep again, this time not because doubts troubled me, but because I kept remembering the formation on the dock and barefoot Belov on the right flank. I felt unbearable shame for what he had to experience. It would have been better to die honorably like Sasha Senchuk—better, even, to die in agony, like Nikolay Ryabov—than to be like Belov, healthy and unscathed but unable to look his commander or his comrades in the eye.

The trials were only beginning. The second raid was by far not the same as the first. But I looked into the future calmly and confidently.

2

Strength Meets Strength

IN THE HISTORY of the Northern Fleet reconnaissance detachment one encounters the names of many capes and fjords. Cape Pikshuev on the shore of Motovskiy Bay, near the mouth of the Great Western Litsa River, comes to mind more than any other. This sloping cape with a spit juts out into Motovskiy Bay. Since the supplies of our troops who were defending the Musta-Tunturi Range passed through this bay, the significance the enemy attached to Cape Pikshuev became clear.[1] Here were his observation posts and bunkers. A permanent garrison of mountain infantry and artillery defended the cape from both land and sea.

On the eve of our first raid against Cape Pikshuev, Olga Paraeva arrived in the detachment.[2] Olenka [Little Reindeer], as the scouts quickly named her, was a small, shapely, attractive blond, Karelian by nationality.[3] They assigned Paraeva to the detachment as a medic and interpreter. She knew Finnish, and according to intelligence there were Finns defending Cape Pikshuev alongside the jaegers.

The appearance of Olenka generated unusual excitement among the scouts, and several sailors recalled the ancient omen about the unenviable fate of a ship that allowed a woman on board. "But this young girl is some kind of *woman*!" argued those who with particular zeal began to judge her by her appearance. They caustically fussed over imaginary patients, who had come to the "doctor" with high cheekbones, rosy cheeks, and mischievous gray eyes with unusually long eyelashes.

I was openly indifferent to our "scout in a skirt" and spitefully made fun of her patients. For this I unexpectedly became the object of Olga Paraeva's attention; she disliked my splendid head of hair. In the presence of other scouts, Paraeva criticized me and advised me to become a monk.

"What are you saying, Olechka!" Vitya Tarzanov said. "Leonov's strength is in his hair, just like Chernomor had his in his beard. Haven't you read *Ruslan and Lyudmila*?"[4]

Paraeva looked at me seriously and blinked. "Perhaps you want a haircut?" she asked, clearly unhappy that it was just the way I liked it. "That forest is thick! And it is also unhygienic! Would you like me to cut it, Leonov? *Very* neatly."

"Of course he would! What kind of question is that!" Vitek said. "Did you bring a pair of scissors? We can transform him from Chernomor to Belomor in an instant."[5]

I got annoyed and told Paraeva to leave me alone, which seemed not too much to ask. I told her to busy herself with salves and pills for her patients. She had more than enough to worry about without me.

Two days later, in completely different circumstances, Paraeva reminded me of this conversation.

In the first raid on Cape Pikshuev I observed the battle more than I actively participated in it.[6] I was wounded immediately after the landing, when a shell splinter pierced my right foot.

A soldier who has been wounded in the enemy's rear area feels his helplessness very acutely. He sees how difficult it is for his comrades, who are not able to help him, and he is a burden to them if there is not a medic nearby. I was in the small group of Senior Lieutenant Klimenko. The platoons of Senior Lieutenant Lebedev and Junior Lieutenant Batskiy, with Major Dobrotin leading, were moving from the shore toward Pikshuev. The medic

Paraeva was with them. Klimenko's scouts were to block the road to the rear of the enemy while the main group attacked the position on the cape. So as not to weaken the group, I refused an escort and requested that the lieutenant leave me alone—let everyone follow his own path.

Having cut through my boot top, Stepan Motovilin pulled the boot off and bandaged my wounded foot. Klimenko, leaving me a spare ammunition drum and two grenades, said, "This is just in case. Hide yourself in the rocks and wait. We will come for you after the battle."

"Don't worry, Viktor, we'll be back," Stepan said before running to catch up with the other scouts, who had already moved out.

I remained alone and soon realized that solitude weighed more heavily on me than my wound. It was quiet all around me, and this quiet so tormented me with its uncertainty that I was glad when shots thundered in the mountains. First they seemed to come nearer, then they faded away. The sun was warming me. The reindeer moss gave up to the sun the dampness collected during the night, and invisible rivulets babbled still stronger. The shots became more infrequent and were muffled, but they were not from the direction where I had expected them. I knew that sound is deceiving in the mountains and believed that an experienced pathfinder like Motovilin would find the way to me; just the same, nothing could quiet the worry that had taken hold of me.

Suddenly I decided that my wound was superficial and I could move. I got up, tried to put weight on the toes of my right foot, and at the same time gritted my teeth so as not to cry out. Carefully looking all around, I crawled. My foot hurt unbearably; my neck ached. Then I became dizzy. Realizing my weakness, I already was sorry that I had left the place where they would look for me. Now I could not find the place myself and could become lost. When the firing stopped, I had nothing to orient me. I imagined an ambush behind every stunted bush, behind each rock. Desperation gave me strength, and, jumping on one leg from boulder to boulder, I made my way forward and upward to the crest of the cape.

I caught up to the scouts so that I could leave with them. Having killed the enemy sentries, the platoons had gone forward and were assembling for the attack on the bunkers of the garrison of the cape. Major Dobrotin ordered Paraeva to remain with me and, if danger threatened us, give a signal.

"What's wrong with you?" Paraeva asked resentfully when we were alone.

I lost control of myself when she spoke in this manner.

"Nothing!" I rudely answered and turned away. "I'll rest and then go on. You can go now; I won't hold you up."

"Listen, Leonov, you are not at the base, and we are not arguing about a haircut. Why are you angry?"

I was embarrassed and therefore quiet.

We sat on a single rock, back to back. It was not any easier for me now that there was a medic nearby. Paraeva was nervous: somewhere up ahead shots rang out and a machine gun barked.

"Do you hear it?" Olga worriedly looked at me.

I could not stand it and shouted: "Why are you sitting here? The battle is over there. Go! Run!"

"But the major ordered me—"

"Olga," I said, calling her by her name for the first time, "we'll go together. Okay? Together is better, but you'll have to help me a little bit." Leaning on my weapon, I got up. Olga placed my left hand on her shoulder. And without any more arguing, we moved to where the battle was heating up.

Ten minutes later I was lying in a position next to a machine gunner and pointed out targets to him while I fired my own rifle.

Olga Paraeva joined up with the scouts who were attacking the bunkers.

In each skirmish there is a critical moment that decides the outcome of the battle.

Motovilin, Damanov, Losev, and Radyshevtsev, all from Klimenko's group, skirted around the large dugout on the top of Pikshuev. From the embrasure of the bunker the jaegers poured leaden rain on the rocks where Lebedev's scouts were seeking cover. Motovilin and Damanov each hurled two antitank grenades, blinding the apertures of the bunker for several seconds. This was enough time for Lebedev's scouts to dash forward in the attack. The large bunker fell.

Having hopped up to the destroyed bunker, I saw the twisted machine gun barrels in the embrasures made rubble by explosions. Major Dobrotin, Lieutenant Klimenko, Olga Paraeva, and five scouts were already in the spacious bunker. A dead German officer lay on the floor next to the threshold. The other officer, a tall Finn, stood at attention in front of little Olga and was talking rapidly. Six unarmed Finnish soldiers were lined up against the wall and were looking at Paraeva. On the table lay Finnish submachine guns and one rifle with telescopic sights. And there was a telephone on the table.

Olga glanced nervously at the telephone while she interpreted the speech of the Finnish officer.

"This is a *fendrikh*, equivalent to our warrant officer. His name is Heino," she told the major. "The *fendrikh* says that the German *Oberleutnant*[7] came here from the headquarters, which is in Titovka, to discuss the rotation. The Germans were to replace them in two hours. The *Oberleutnant* reported by telephone to his headquarters that our attack was beaten off and that they were counterattacking to throw us off the hill."

The major turned to the *fendrikh* and asked him in German, "Have you been observing the bay?"

"Yes, the *Oberleutnant* took the notebook with our written observation reports," the *fendrikh* answered in somewhat garbled German, "but I can recite the latest data from memory. Do you want me to repeat it?"

"It's not necessary, we already have it. To whom were

you subordinated? With whom are you now maintaining communication with this telephone?"

"With the commandant of the Titovka fortified region. We are directly subordinated to him."

The major did not take his eyes off the Finnish warrant officer, who, having pressed his hands to his hips, stood motionless and quiet. "What was the last report you gave to the commandant in Titovka?"

"An hour ago I reported about your attack on the strongpoint and then went out to the forward position."

"Hey, who's in there? Where is the major?" someone shouted outside.

Seaman Kupriyanov from Lebedev's platoon came down into the bunker. Spotting the major, he came up to him and in a muffled voice said, "The senior lieutenant was killed, a round right in the head. It killed him instantly."

Dobrotin turned pale and spoke quietly: "This cannot be." Then just as quietly he turned to Kupriyanov: "Run back to the platoon and tell them that I will be there shortly."

Kupriyanov ran out of the bunker.

Dobrotin turned to Paraeva. "Tell the *fendrikh* that he and his men have nothing to worry about. They can lie in the hollow behind the bunker. And to guard them. Can you?" He looked at me and, not waiting for an answer, commanded: "The rest of you, follow me!"

But then the telephone rang. The major went over to the phone, picked up the handset, and, imitating the voice of the *fendrikh*, said in German, "This is Heino. I hear you. No, it's not necessary to open fire. We beat off the attack. The *Ober* is in the bunker next door. You will soon arrive? Thank you!"

We stood waiting, guardedly listening to this conversation, and breathed easier when the major put down the handset.

Hardly containing a smile, the major turned to the *fendrikh*. "The Titovka commandant thanks you, Heino!" Then he said to us, "He promises to send reinforcements and is coming here himself. Fine! We will greet our guests."

The major left the bunker, the scouts following behind him.

The prisoners remained very still but nervously glanced to one side. As near as I could figure out, they were indicating the direction from which danger could be anticipated.

Seaman Voloshenyuk, who had been wounded in the hand, came to the bunker—Klimenko sent him—and told me that Senior Lieutenant Lebedev had been suddenly cut down by a bullet as he was leading the platoon in the attack.

"Perhaps a Finnish sniper shot him," Voloshenyuk said.

Sniper? I recalled the rifle with telescopic sights.

"Voloshenyuk, check to see if the rifle on the table in the bunker is loaded."

Voloshenyuk scowled at the prisoners and went down into the bunker.

The rifle turned out to be unloaded. Having removed its scope, Voloshenyuk was getting ready to leave when the telephone rang again. Hearing "Hello! Hello!" I ran to the bunker to warn Voloshenyuk, but it was already too late.

"Why are you barking like a yak dog?" Voloshenyuk snarled into the receiver, and only after my vain shouts did he pull it away from his ear and throw it on the table. "How the hell was I supposed to know?" he excused himself when I told him what he had done. "Should I run and tell the major?"

While the scouts were destroying supply caches, the bunkers, and fixtures of the observation posts, a column of jaegers was moving from Titovka toward the cape.[8] The Finnish prisoners saw the Germans from some distance and brought their approach to my attention. Voloshenyuk ran to the major to warn him of the danger. Then guns and mortars from Titovka fired on Pikshuev. Our radio operator was wounded and his radio destroyed, but by then two of our subchasers and the major's motor launch *Kasatka* [Swallow] were already coming to shore from the sea. Climbing up to the crest of the cape, Kolya Damanov signaled the vessels with semaphores: "Support us with fire!" The sailors fired with cannons and machine guns, preventing the jaegers from coming around to our seaward flank.

The wounded moved to the shore first. Four scouts carried the dead Lebedev on a poncho. Voloshenyuk and I accompanied the prisoners. Behind us the scouts fought an unequal battle with the pursuing jaegers. The scouts from the squads of Motovilin and Radyshevtsev loaded up last on the commander's motor launch.

The *Kasatka* fell behind the cutters, and halfway back to base the Messerschmitts caught up with it. The machine gunner on the *Kasatka* managed to beat off the enemy fighters, even shooting down one aircraft. But there were already dead and wounded on the deck of the *Kasatka*.[9] Not far from the shore the heavily damaged motor launch began to sink, and the major ordered everyone to swim to shore.

The wounded Dobrotin was the last to abandon the boat.

After three days in the hospital where we were taken for treatment, Radyshevtsev and Damanov dropped by. I learned from them that Olga Paraeva had helped Major Dobrotin swim to shore and that our cutters picked up all the survivors from the *Kasatka*. Dobrotin was now in the naval hospital, and his orderly Tarzanov, seriously wounded in the chest, had been sent to a hospital in the rear. The detachment buried Lebedev with full honors. His grave was located on a high cliff facing the sea.

Captain Inzartsev was named commander of the detachment, and he sent Radyshevtsev with Damanov to check on us. "We're waiting with a large number of replacements" was the last news given to me by my friends.

Motovilin and I were in the same tent.[10] Motovilin had a light wound. Disheveled and unshaven, in a robe that hung to his heels, he paced from corner to corner and mercilessly cursed himself for agreeing to be evacuated to a hospital. It was obvious to me that Stepan would be discharged from the hospital before me and I would remain there alone.

I also had not shaved, hadn't even combed my hair. Angry at myself for something, I was telling Stepan how it was possible to be mistaken about someone and, for example, how nice a girl Olga Paraeva turned out to be. Stepan, of course, did not understand me. The entire time we were in the hospital, he repeated his own "diagnosis." "Viktor, you're beginning to deteriorate. Confinement to bed is hurting you. As soon as they discharge me, put salve on your wounded heel. I will wait for you by the hospital gate."

Time dragged on endlessly, and life was not great for us. If, remembering this unpleasant time, I decide to talk about the days I spent in the hospital, it is only because they are connected with Dobrotin, whom they quickly brought in. We passed many hours in conversations with the major. I will remember them for a long time.

They placed the major in the tent with the seriously wounded. Having learned this, Motovilin and I evaded the careful eye of the nurse and quickly made our way to his tent. But there we ran into the doctor on duty. "What is the meaning of this?" he asked sternly. "Who are you looking for?"

"Major Dobrotin!" Stepan blurted out, and that saved us. The major heard the scout's familiar deep voice.

"Let them come in, doctor," the major called out.

"Five minutes!" the doctor said and, glowering at us, left.

We hustled into the tent. The major was half-reclining on fluffed-up pillows. He looked somewhat surprised at our presence. Threateningly, he pointed his finger. "Sit down, it's been a while! How are you?" he asked Stepan.

"It's nothing, just a scratch, but I'm afraid, Comrade Major, that one could become genuinely sick here."

"You're right. How is your foot, Leonov?"

I smiled and said that the doctor threatened to hold me in the hospital for two months.

"Ouch!" The major breathed easier. "And I was worried when I saw you!"

Stepan and I glanced at each other in bewilderment.

"Why the looks?" the major asked sternly. He gave us a condemning look. "Unshaven, disheveled! How can I tell the doctor that you are naval scouts? He won't believe it. You want to be discharged quickly—look after yourselves! Don't mope around. So as not to anger the doctor." He looked at his watch and—though the prescribed five minutes were not up—said firmly, "Let's stop now. This evening come back again. Will you?"

We eagerly agreed and hurried toward the exit.

In the evening, having carefully shaved and freshened up with cologne, and with our robes buttoned up all the way, we went to the major's tent and didn't leave until retreat. After that we called on him every day. The major knew that he would not return to duty any time soon, and in any case he would not be leading any scouts into the enemy rear. Perhaps that was why he talked with us so freely about what he considered most important.

"Why did I not punish Belov and the other panic-mongers?" He repeated the question put to him once by Stepan. "Indeed, why not?" He seemed so sincerely surprised at this that I decided to scold Stepan for bringing up this unpleasant event in the life of the detachment. "Well, listen."

The major adjusted his pillow and closed his eyes a little bit, as if trying to recall something. "At your age I had already fought some but had never gotten cold feet. But there came a time when I learned the true price of self-control in battle, something especially important for scouts.

"They had sent me on reconnaissance with a platoon of cadets—Yudenich was attacking Petrograd.[11] After a night patrol we were settling down in a small grove for a rest. We had taken off our saddles, were feeding the horses, and were beginning to eat. And then a lookout, who had been sent out to the edge of the grove, galloped in yelling, 'Whites! A whole squadron has come from the village.

They are surrounding us!' The cadets raced to their horses. One, having forgotten to cinch up his saddle, was bouncing in it under the horse's belly. Such laughter and grief! I could hardly tear myself away from the spot where I was standing. And even today I can't forgive myself for that 'hardly.' We would have rushed out of the grove in all directions, like rabbits before greyhounds! But I got myself under control and ordered everyone to dismount.

"I have to tell you that the village was five kilometers from us, and the enemy couldn't have known of our presence in this particular grove—there were many such groves all around, and it would not have been easy to encircle us. When you lose self-control, thoughts come into your head at random. 'Did you start this panic?' I shouted at the lookout. 'I saw them with my own eyes!' he said.

"At full combat readiness we moved toward the edge of the grove and there established that not a squadron, but only a platoon, was leaving the village, and they knew nothing about our location. We attacked it suddenly, defeated the forward element, and even captured some prisoners.

"Now, back to Belov," the major continued. "The whole time that I was walking toward you from the dock, I was thinking, how should I treat Belov? And then I recalled the incident with the lookout, so long ago. I have forgotten his last name. After that we called him Panic-man, and he was known as Panic-man until he earned a medal for bravery. Oh, how he tried! But in his first battle, as you have seen, he failed. It happens."

"Exactly, Comrade Major!" I couldn't restrain myself. "I know through you!"

Major Dobrotin spent nearly a month with us in the hospital, then they sent him to the rear for final recovery. On his last evening, the major showed us two letters that he had saved in the same envelope. The first letter was from the wife of Senior Lieutenant Lebedev, and it had arrived from Baku. Lebedeva thanked the major and all the scouts for their concern and attention to her.

"You asked me to be brave," she wrote. "Zhora encouraged me about this in his last letter: 'We are now in the second month of war. I believe in life and in our victory. You are the wife of a Soviet scout. You must have a calm and brave heart. And our little boy must never see tears in your eyes. Remember when we had just met, and your hero was Ovod.[12] You delighted in his determination and loyalty. And you often repeated the lines with which he finished his last letter to his favorite woman: 'I am a happy butterfly, I will live and I will die.' "

The major stopped reading.

Afraid they would notice my emotion, I couldn't lift my head. I remembered the novel *Ovod* and those lines. And I had still not forgotten what Lebedev had said to me after the death of Sasha Senchuk.

"He was such a man, our Senior Lieutenant Georgiy Lebedev," the major said. "And here is another letter, never sent. The German *Oberleutnant*, the same one who was killed in the Finn's bunker on Pikshuev, wrote it. It is also addressed to his darling. And here is a verse, see here, the *Ober* himself composed. It translates like this: 'By the will of the *Führer*, they dropped us in this cold land. Pray for me! I already sleep a horrible sleep. The polar night and the blizzards. I am still alive, but they consider me dead. And I can't tell anyone that they have buried me alive. Only the wild reindeer visit my grave and trumpet their melancholy song.' "

"A sentimental German!" Stepan exclaimed. "And this *Ober* was desperate! The bastard was firing his machine gun while we were crawling up to the embrasure. Reindeer trumpet?" Stepan smiled ironically. "Perhaps, Comrade Major, it was my antitank grenade that trumpeted his last song?"

"Possibly," the major answered slowly, thinking, perhaps, his own thoughts, because then he spoke fervently. "The enemy speaks with German precision about how much superiority they have in aircraft and weapons; they measure the strength of the blows of their mountain divisions, bri-

gades, regiments. According to the calculations of their
staff officers, they should gain the upper hand over us in
the shortest time. But this"—the major held up the letter—
"this they didn't consider. This did not enter into their calculations! It seemed like some kind of devilry to their
Oberleutnant to die behind the granite wall of the strongpoint. He fought desperately?" The major turned his head
toward Stepan. "Desperate is not the same as brave. Our
Senior Lieutenant Lebedev went into battle and assaulted
the bunker, believing in life and believing in victory. To his
last breath he believed! Don't ever let this belief leave you.
And strength? Our strength is still to be told!"

[In late August–early September, the detachment attempted
to mount an operation in cooperation with an army reconnaissance element against the German airfield at Luostari.[13]
The army reconnaissance force was totally unprepared for
such a mission. Men had been taken from jails in Murmansk and promised pardons for participating in the raid.
Operations security was nonexistent within the army group,
and their physical conditioning was not adequate to the
task.

Despite all these problems, the compromise force managed to penetrate on foot into the objective area and was
several kilometers from the airfield when one of the army
personnel deserted to the Germans. Having lost the element
of surprise, the commander of the composite force ordered
withdrawal and return to base.[14] Although not all joint operations conducted with army or naval infantry units ended
so disastrously, the fleet reconnaissance detachment pre-
ferred to operate independently.]

The calendar showed autumn, and in the North, winter was
beginning.

A violently mad wind drove hard snow in from the sea,
piling up drifts and stripping the rocks. After my long stay
in the hospital tent, the wind seemed especially fierce.[15]
Hiding my head in the turned-up collar and leaning on a

walking stick, I stepped carefully, limping a bit. In the pocket of my field shirt lay a directive describing me as "temporarily not fit for duty." Because of that, I changed my route and went straight to the detachment rather than the fleet headquarters.

Captain Inzartsev asked, "How are you?" After reading the directive and recording it in the sick register, he said, "We can arrange something for you here at the base. But I can't include you in the combat group. Where can you go with a walking stick?" But suddenly the ski pole that I was holding gave the captain an idea. "My friend, why don't we send you to the ski base? Find something to do there, and then we will see."[16]

Thus, I remained in the detachment, and by the end of winter, when my wound finally had scarred over, I was already participating in raids in the enemy rear.

By then scouts who were steeled in battle and united by the strong bonds of sailors' friendship were being sent out on operations. At the ski base I had heard and read much about them in the front newspapers and leaflets.

Brave new pathfinders of the Far North had developed alongside the detachment veterans. There were sailors of various ages among them. Warranty officers, chief petty officers, and petty officers called up from the reserves, Aleksandr Nikandrov, Anatoliy Barinov, Andrey Pshenichnykh, and others, were commanding squads. Komsomolists Aleksandr Manin, Zinoviy Ryzhechkin, Evgeniy Ulenkov, and many other youngsters, just recently drafted, were also acquitting themselves well. People who had learned by everyday experience, like Murmansk engineer Florinskiy and Leningrad machinist Abramov—both masters and craftsmen who knew not only our own but also enemy weapons and field equipment—enjoyed great authority among the sailors. There were outstanding athletes among us—students of Leningrad institutes such as Golovin, Staritskiy, and Sheremet. In the ski base I became friends with Vasiliy Kashutin, who arrived in the detachment from the border troops. Sergeant Kashutin was a former scout and outstanding rifleman who zealously taught his squad rock climbing, camouflage, and observation in the mountains.[17]

The veterans in the detachment greeted the new personnel warmly, especially those who came from the fleet. We took seven old acquaintances from the base into our ranks—among them electrician's mate Pavel Baryshev, machinist's mate Ivan Lysenko, helmsman Yuri Mikheev, and Semyon Agafonov, the submarine's cook, who for some unseemly deed had been assigned to shore duty.[18] Agafonov was the only sailor for whom Captain Inzartsev made an exception, accepting him into the detachment under his personal responsibility. If the normally strict Inzartsev would go so far, then, it seems, he highly valued that coolheaded and endlessly clever native of the White Sea coast. As events later proved, Inzartsev did not err with Agafonov.

There were now party and Komsomol organizations in the detachment. The political section of the fleet sent an experienced political instructor, Dubrovskiy, to the position of commissar. I went to him with a request to permit me to go on the next raid and, if possible, in Kashutin's squad. The commissar advised Inzartsev to make me a runner in his headquarters section.

"After a long break from combat," the commissar said to me, "you must be closer to the commander. Kashutin's squad will be bringing up the rear."

On a dark snowstormy night [in early November 1941] we landed on the rocky shore and began a march across the mountains toward the enemy base.[19] The indefatigable Motovilin, Radyshevtsev, and Agafonov cleared the route for the detachment. Those moving at the front of the column were delayed for a while by an obstacle. The rear guard was just overcoming the obstacle when the lead elements were moving far forward. The commissar walked with the rear guard—Kashutin's scouts—at a pace that everyone could maintain and that would leave no one behind.

It was midnight, and a snowstorm raged in the mountains. One could not even see the scout walking five meters ahead, and, so as not to lose contact with each other, we moved in a close file almost to the objective itself.

Not far from the enemy base everyone lay down. Then Aleksey Radyshevtsev and Nikolay Damanov went forward to climb to the area near the plateau where sentries were posted. We waited with anticipation for the outcome of the short, dramatic fight, which in the language of the scouts was called "quietly taking out" the guards.

Two jaegers in full-length capes with high turned-up collars were walking to meet each other. They did not see the scouts outfitted in white camouflage smocks, lying prone in the snow. And even the scouts saw the sentries only when they came together at the center of the plateau. Then the jaegers disappeared into the darkness of the night, reappearing at the same place two or three minutes later. It was necessary to "take out" the jaegers simultaneously; otherwise, the first sentry would notice the disappearance of the other and raise the alarm.

When the jaegers separated, a scout was crawling behind each of them. Radyshevtsev concealed himself behind a bush near the path used by the sentry and remained still. When, having turned around, the jaeger, stooping down and looking under his feet, passed by the bush, Radyshevtsev overtook him with a single leap, knocked him out with the buttstock of his rifle, and then drove a fist into his stomach. Only then did he tie the jaeger's hands behind his back.

While Radyshevtsev was doing all this, he heard the muffled death rattle of struggling men. He ran to the opposite side and didn't find Damanov but saw tracks and signs of a struggle, where Damanov had jumped the jaeger and knocked him down. Apparently, the German had resisted when Damanov was tying him up. Tracks in the snow indicated that the two had fought desperately, rolling on the ground and over to the precipice, where the track came to an abrupt end.

Hearing a rustling noise below, Radyshevtsev flinched and jumped back, clutching his submachine gun. In the darkness of the night he could not see who was clinging to the rock, clambering upward. Then he saw first the fingers of a left hand, then a knife clenched in a right fist, and, finally, Damanov's ski cap.

"Kolya!" Radyshevtsev called under his breath.

Damanov climbed up, sweat pouring off his face. "S-sign-nal!" he breathed.

Radyshevtsev signaled us with a flashlight.

Leaving each other behind, we climbed up onto the plateau.

Inzartsev led his group to a column of vehicles parked under an awning, and Dubrovskiy led his scouts to the barracks and supply dump.

By the time flames soared above the supply dump, Inzartsev's group had already destroyed the vehicles and set fire to the fuel storage area. Illuminated by the flames, jaegers rushed between their barracks and the supply dump and were cut down by well-aimed bursts from our submachine guns.

We departed the area. Shells in the ammunition dump began to explode and enemy artillery opened up on its own base.[20]

Though our assault landing cutters were already far away from shore, we could still see the billowing flames above the hill where we had been not long ago. And the explosions of the shells bursting in the fire rent the air longer still.

The operation was conducted boldly, suddenly, and swiftly. Most of all, I remember how I was struck by the calm certitude of the scouts during the battle. It could not be any other way!

Yes, this was already a different detachment, and a different strength—one that overcomes the enemy's strength, that in which Major Dobrotin and Senior Lieutenant Lebedev ordered us to believe and themselves believed without limit.

* * *

[In November 1941, another attempt was made to reconnoiter the Luostari airfield, this time by the detachment's ski teams.[21] They were to examine the approaches to the airfield to discern the nature of its defensive system. If all went well, the ground force would initiate an attack, followed by air strikes by fleet aviation units. The ski group was accompanied in the initial leg of its march by reindeer pulling sleds, on which were carried ammunition, heavy machine guns, and extra provisions. On 11 November they left Soviet lines and crossed the Titovka River a few days later south of Lake Chapr. On 14 November they reached the target and conducted detailed reconnaissance, including drawing sketches of airfield defenses and installations. On 15 November they began the seven-day trek back to friendly lines, carrying one of their men who had suffered an acute attack of appendicitis. It was probably his illness that caused the cancellation of the joint air and ground attack.

While the ski troops were reconnoitering the airfield, Captain Inzartsev led a platoon-strength group on a mission to locate a German strongpoint overlooking the mouth of the Great Western Litsa River.[22] The group landed from two small subchasers and moved up into the snow-covered hills. After some hours of movement they followed a telephone wire to a German guardpost. Without carefully observing the surrounding landscape, they attacked the guard and an adjacent shelter. Several other Germans returned fire from nearby positions, forcing Inzartsev and his men to make a hasty retreat to the shore. They had located the German position, but at the price of four dead.

Sometime later, the army informed the reconnaissance detachment of a captured Finnish lieutenant who was willing to lead a patrol to an unoccupied "winterized" German strongpoint.[23] Accompanied by an army detachment with the Finnish officer and an interpreter, Vizgin sent seventy scouts on two boats from Polyarnyy to Cape Pikshuev. Delayed by a winter storm, the composite detachment arrived at the target area on the second day and moved directly from shore to the strongpoint. There, buried under the snow, they found two small antitank guns with over three hundred rounds, other weapons and ammunition, and over seven kilometers of telephone wire in rolls. The men moved all the captured material to shore and then to their base. The detachment now had enemy guns and ammunition for use in operations behind German lines.[24]

In January 1942, a group of twenty-five men attempted to penetrate into the Nikel area, the site of an important mine- and airfield, seventy kilometers behind the front line and over fifty kilometers from the coast.[25] Admiral Golovko was not eager to permit an operation so far inland, but he allowed it to go ahead only because the army had requested assistance. The mission was to determine how much ore was being extracted and by what routes, means, and schedule it was being taken to Kirkenes for loading onto ships. The one-way distance to the objective area was over 150 kilometers, on extremely difficult terrain, in the coldest month of winter.

Accompanied by reindeer-pulled sleds, the group departed Soviet lines on 4 January 1942, in temperatures below -30 degrees Centigrade (-24 degrees Fahrenheit). To avoid observation by German aircraft, they had planned to move only at night. But the patrol leader soon discovered that the men could not lie still for long periods of time without suffering from frostbite, and so they had to move during daylight also. It was during one of the daylight movements that a flight of German aircraft observed and strafed the group, wounding ten men.[26] The patrol was forced to return to base.

At the end of February 1942, nearly three months had passed since the detachment had taken a detailed inventory of German activity on the south shore of Motovskiy Bay. On 3 March three small subchasers departed Polyarnyy, arriving in the landing area near Cape Pikshuev late that night.[27] One platoon went ashore to clear the immediate area, while the remainder of the force waited on the boats. When the lead platoon reached the rocky plateau above the landing site, it made contact with a German outpost of undetermined strength. The Soviet force quickly put the Germans to flight, while the other platoon rushed from the boat to their aid. The Soviets hurriedly gathered the documents from several German bodies and took with them back to the boat a wounded German soldier, who soon died.[28] Vizgin was present on one of the subchasers and, after consultation with the platoon leaders, decided not to continue the operation. The element of surprise had been lost, and pursuit of the small German force could result in unnecessary casualties.

Another patrol of one or two platoons went to the same area on 13 March on two subchasers.[29] Sometime after midnight, one group went ashore south of Cape Pikshuev. Another dozen men landed at Cape Mogilnyy to the west. A storm quickly obscured the entire area, preventing signal communications between the forces ashore and the boats. The leader of the smaller of the two forces, moving by dead reckoning in a blinding snowstorm, halted his men in what he believed would be a safe shelter. At dawn, however, with the storm subsided, the group found that they were in the middle of a German position that contained approximately ten shelters.

The naval scouts lay in the snow the entire day, observing the activities of this heretofore unknown German position. German aircraft en route to bomb the Rybachiy Peninsula flew low overhead twice. German soldiers were constructing fortifications with rocks, apparently developing the position into a strongpoint. After dark, the scouts quietly moved back toward their landing site, pulling behind them on a makeshift sled one of their men who had suffered frostbite. After waiting some three hours, they were picked up. Unable to find the other patrol, the boat commander returned to base at dawn.

Several unsuccessful attempts were made over the next five days to extract the remaining patrol. Some were turned back by stormy seas and one by German shelling and strafing. Admiral Golovko ordered Vizgin to lead the search personally. On the sixth recovery sortie, late on the evening of 19 March, Vizgin—with two boats and naval air support—extracted the patrol.

Five of the men were taken straight from the dock to the hospital, suffering from serious frostbite. For six days the group had contended with the weather, German ground troops, and periodic German air searches. Their provisions ran out on 15 March, but they found a large dead codfish on the shore and ate it. Late on 18 March they observed a thirty-five-man German search party, and the next morning German artillery began to fire methodically into the area. German ground forces supported by aircraft were closing in on them from two directions. As the patrol was about to be overrun, Soviet aircraft arrived on the scene and suppressed the German pursuers. The exhausted patrol was safely extracted.]

3

On Hill 415

THEY JOKINGLY CALLED US scouts "dry-land sailors."

The sea accompanied us down a difficult and dangerous path. During a landing, the noise of the surf muffled the footfalls of the assault troops jumping off on an enemy shore.[1] We frequently fought far from the sea, in the hills and in the moss-covered tundra, on the tops of mountains, and in the clefted rocks.[2]

When we returned to the shore, to the cutters, the dark night coming in from the Barents Sea covered us from pursuit. The sailors from the cutters remembered how many of us had landed and saw how many of us came back. Sharing our grief, they never asked about those who remained in the mountains.[3]

Each sortie in the enemy rear had its own peculiarities. Thus it was with that memorable operation, later named the May Raid in the history of the detachment.

The operation began on the eve of the first wartime May Day, in 1942. By that time, as a petty officer second class, I was commanding the headquarters group of ten scouts.[4]

We were sitting in the barrack, unhurriedly preparing our equipment for the mission. Most of the concern fell to Semyon Vasilevich Florinskiy. He was checking the machine guns, both ours and the captured weapons.[5] As usual,

Florinskiy was meticulously inspecting the weapons, but suddenly, turning away from his work, he said, "Last year, at exactly this time, I was sitting with my wife, Elena Vasilevna, at a May Day concert in the Murmansk theater. My wife was in a holiday dress, and I was wearing a new suit with vest. And tie. And a necktie, guys! Strange."

I imagined Semyon Vasilevich in civilian clothes, a dark blue suit with a vest. Next to him, his neatly dressed wife. A normal enough picture, but back then it seemed strange indeed, and so far away.

"You fo-found something to remember, your wife in a f-fa-fancy suit." Nikolay Damanov chided him. "You are dreaming!" Then Damanov suddenly realized that he might have offended the detachment's respected armorer and, changing his tone, added, "We will not rem-member the past. We will look ahead. Ten years will go by, we can s-say, and you will tell your grandchildren, Semyon Vassilevich, how on a night around May Day we pu-pulled off a visit on the jaegers—the Laplanders. That would be interes-sting for them."

There was a pause.

"It would be nice," Florinskiy answered quietly. "It would be nice, Kolya! I'll say that there was an electrician's mate from the submarine in our detachment, a dashing scout, a courageous petty officer second class by the name of Damanov. A desperate soul! And one time—"

"In the deep polar night!—" Evgeniy Ulenkov added.

"He we-went out to hunt!" Damanov good-naturedly cut Ulenkov short.

It was not customary to talk much about upcoming operations. During the day Captain Inzartsev, the detachment commander, had learned the details of our mission. It soon became clear to everyone that this time we were not going on an ordinary raid. In the evening the detachment commissar (Dubrovskiy) talked with us. He recalled the enemy strongpoints we had destroyed, the capture of tongues, and then said, "Our operations last a night or a day. No more. But what if we did not return to base right away? That hasn't happened yet. But—suddenly the situation changes and we have to operate in the enemy's rear for several days—what then?"

Though we had thought about that, it was not a theme we wanted to dwell on. "The command knows what to do in such circumstances," one scout suggested. "The sailors wouldn't abandon us—they'd come to our rescue!"—everyone firmly believed.

But the commissar was not about to leave any doubts on this score. "Surprise and unexpectedness—you scouts have become accustomed to them. However, you must also be prepared for long and fierce battles. On this mission a naval infantry unit will follow behind you in the amphibious assault.[6] They have their own assignment. And we scouts will land first—not noiselessly, not under the cover of night, but in the open, fighting to draw the enemy's attention.[7] That way we'll help the infantrymen. But this will not be the concealed, short, and stunning blow that is so familiar to many of you."

The commissar emphasized one word several times: "Determination!"

Recalling the May 1942 raid, we now know full well the real price of that determination about which the commissar spoke. But that was later. Meanwhile, we carefully packed our rucksacks, checked our weapons, clothing, and footgear, and finished the preparations only after the cheerful command of the petty officer:

"Form up! Today there's a holiday supper."

Night. May Day night.

Motors racing, two cutters plowed the waters of Motovskiy Bay. At full speed they headed for the familiar shore of Cape Pikshuev.

German combat security was on the alert; the observation posts picked us up, and the shore battery on Pikshuev opened fire. The sky was lit up by flares, and fountains of water grew nearer all around us.

On our seaward side were several additional cutters,

moving slower. Their captains opened fire on the coastal ridgeline of the cape, firing with precision, and soon the hill was enveloped in flames that covered it with a blazing red cap, blown about by the wind. Clinging to the running lights, we looked out, shouting, "Go-go-go!"

As if in obedience to this command, the cutter crews answered with salvos along Cape Pikshuev.

An artillery duel unfolded above the sea, and our cutter, not slowing down, was coming about for the landing of the first assault.

Enemy machine gunners fired from the height of the cape.

Not waiting while the second gangway was lowered, Seaman Sheremet and, behind him, Damanov and our detachment Komsomol organizer, Sasha Manin, jumped into the water. Across the gangplank, balancing a machine gun, ran Florinskiy and Abramov. We stormed the first hill, and Sheremet threw a grenade on the run. It exploded behind a big boulder, and Damanov and Manin rushed forward in its wake. Wounded, Sheremet stumbled over the body of the enemy machine gunner and took on the assistant gunner, an enormous jaeger, in hand-to-hand combat. But Damanov had already grabbed the German machine gun. He clambered higher up the hill, set the machine gun up on the very edge of the cliff, and fired a long burst, which cut short the explosions of incoming grenades. Then, mortally wounded, Kolya Damanov slowly slipped to the ground, almost falling away from the rocks. Hurrying, Florinskiy caught him. "A-a-a-a! Ba-a-astards!" Florinskiy cried out.

Abramov and Florinskiy, clinging to the machine guns—ours and the trophy—hosed down the fleeing jaegers with fire.[8] Sailors' shouts of victory rang out to the right and left of them.

We rushed into a bayonet attack and, destroying small pockets of enemy on the move, took the crest overlooking the bay.

* * *

Soon it would be light, but in the meantime it was very dark.

Deep, sticky snow lay in the low areas, and it was incredibly difficult to walk in them, especially with our load. During the daytime, ponds appeared everywhere in the hills, during the night they froze, and in the morning they were covered with a layer of treacherous ice. Up ahead and off to the flanks, jaegers occupied the dominating heights. Of course, they saw our landing, calculated our strength —no more than two platoons—and now, having cut off the path to the sea, were following us, firmly convinced that we had fallen into a trap and were doomed. The jaegers knew that scouts did not allow themselves to be captured.[9]

Winding our way through ravines, we moved forward toward our final destination, marked by the number 415 on our commander's map.[10] But it was still a long way to the hill, and Captain Inzartsev was concerned about stragglers—young scouts from Warrant Officer Nikandrov's squad. They could become a light snack for the pursuing Germans. He said, "Leonov, Kharabrin, and Manin—bring in the rest of the column. In case of any trouble, delay the jaegers. If you have to withdraw, signal with a rocket."

Morning was breaking. Now we could make out the crest of Hill 415. On the crest, figures in long capes were hurriedly constructing a position in the rocks and setting up a machine gun. Scouts Kashutin and Radyshevtsev maneuvered around Hill 415 to attack the enemy from the rear. Then firing broke out, inspiring the straggling scouts to pick up the pace. Kharabrin, Manin, and I ran back to the rear of the column and hurried forward with our comrades.

Two scouts were carrying Vladimir Sheremet on a poncho. He was wounded in the leg and stomach. He was breathing heavily and cried out to Medical Service Lieutenant Zasedatelev, who was walking next to him:[11]

"You can't do this! Get the commissar! Call." Then Sheremet noticed us and asked to be put down. He stretched a hand toward Kharabrin. "Grisha, Grish. Give me a pistol! Grishenka, it would be better if you would. I'm asking you as a friend!"

Kharabrin moved over to Sheremet and tried to quiet him, but Sheremet only gritted his teeth and shook his head. "You're no friend of mine. Remember! You know I'll be a burden. I'm begging you."

Kharabrin turned around and said to Zasedatelev, "The jaegers are right behind us. Carry him quickly."[12]

Baryshev and Kolikov were bringing up the rear of the column. Kolikov was limping and leaning on Baryshev's shoulder. We hurried them off and lay in the rocks.

We didn't have to wait long.

"They are coming!" declared Kharabrin.

"Look!" Sasha Manin said. We heard his Vologda accent.[13] "Jaegers! Along the lake, straight ahead, coming into view."

Manin looked in my direction in surprise. Trying to speak calmly, I told him, "They're hurrying because they want crosses for their chests."[14]

An officer walked confidently at the front of the file of jaegers. We could have taken him out with a machine-gun burst, but Kharabrin did not fire until the jaegers got closer, and we then fired simultaneously from the machine gun and our submachine guns. The file was cut apart. The Germans scattered and went to ground. Only the officer, as though hypnotized by the bullets, did not even crouch down. Pulling out his parabellum, he shouted something at his soldiers, got them up to attack, and, turning his side to us, advanced again.

"He is strong!" said Kharabrin. "He knows that my bullets can't find him, but I'll get him, that shit." Then we heard a burst of strong language, spoken from the heart. But his outburst did not prevent Kharabrin from aiming and firing a short, accurate burst. The officer threw up his arms, then fell down and rolled over on his side. The jaegers had been waiting for that; they ran back into the bushes and from there began firing wildly. We lay behind solid cover and listened to the firing behind us in amusement. By then grenades were already exploding on Hill 415. I gave the signal to withdraw.

When we caught up to the detachment, we almost ran into Pavel Baryshev, who was carrying the lanky Kolikov. At first I thought that Kolikov was wounded, but it turned out that the "ski champion," as he had called himself when he first arrived in the detachment (Kolikov was considered one of the best skiers of the Northern Fleet), had simply turned sour. In cross-country competitions, Kolikov left Pasha Baryshev far behind, but on his first sortie through the mountains and cross-country, with full kit, he ended up exhausted and draped across the broad back of the shorter Baryshev. Now, with his legs broadly spread and sweating profusely, Baryshev groaned but carried the "champion" on his back.

When he saw us, Baryshev threw Kolikov down.

"A wooden log! Now what do we do with him?" he exclaimed, turning to face us. Warrant Officer Nikandrov said, "Well, don't just leave him here! The battle is over there, and I'll deal with him later."

There was a lot of anger in Baryshev's voice, and we were staring at Kolikov when Kharabrin looked around apprehensively and reminded us that the jaegers were right on our heels.

"Brothers!" pleaded Kolikov. "I'll walk, really, I'll walk on my own! Just don't leave me here alone."

"Get your ass up the mountain! We'll cover you!" Kharabrin said.

And, indeed, Kolikov began to hobble so quickly that we could hardly keep up with him.

"You see that?" Kharabrin asked Baryshev. "You carried him on your back for nothing, Pasha. What did it accomplish? He's a champion, but he took the wind out of you. That's wrong! But now even God will remember. You'll see justice!"

After an hour's fighting we took Hill 415.

From the crest we could see two roads that led from

Titovka toward the Great Western Litsa River and toward the sea—to Cape Mogilnyy. But we had more important targets to observe. Jaegers, attempting to encircle Hill 415, were assembling on nearby hills. There were a lot of them, but Vasiliy Kashutin told the new troops: "We can defend this hill; they can't crawl up it without being seen. Just let them try to stick their noses in here."

But the jaegers did not hurry to attack and were busy with some incomprehensible maneuvers—they would lie down in one place, then get up and move to another. "They're choosing an attack position," Kashutin explained.

A cutting wind with sticky snow blew in from the sea, and visibility was sharply reduced. Finally, there was gunfire, and the first attack was made against our left flank. Then a group of enemy submachine gunners, who had infiltrated between the rocks and bushes, threatened the right flank. The jaegers stubbornly crawled upward, hiding behind each rock.

The groups of Barinov and Nikandrov came down the slope to hold off the submachine gunners. Just about then a runner arrived from the right flank with an alarming report: "The Germans are piling on additional forces! They are preparing for a new attack."

"Don't wait for them, counterattack!" Inzartsev ordered. "Machine gunners Florinskiy and Abramov, change positions."

Unexpectedly, as is often the case in the North during spring, the snowfall subsided. The sky cleared and the wind dropped off.

Night came. The naval infantry battalion that had landed in the area of the Great Western Litsa River was pushing toward the road to Titovka, but the enemy hadn't yet decided to deploy his forces against this new assault because he feared a counterattack by our detachment. But the jaegers increased the attacks on Hill 415 so the battle entered its second day.

A difficult movement, two sleepless nights, a piercing cold wind with snowfall, and uninterrupted battles tired several of the scouts so much that they literally were ready to drop. We had never before touched wine on a mission, but now, when a cloudy dawn was beginning to break, Lieutenant Zasedatelev treated some of the nearly frozen scouts with measured doses of alcohol.

Those hardened by experience only griped at the nuisance when the "doctor" came around to them. Semyon Agafonov asked the doctor to let him smell the empty measuring glass.

"What'll you have?" he asked, rubbing the end of his nose and turning to Manin. "Now it's your turn for some of the fleet's soup!"

"Tsaiky s kolistratom!" Manin declared with a blissful look. He wanted tea with cranberry extract, a brew for which he had a great weakness.

"Goose with apples! *Shashlik*, like in the Caucasus![15] Cutlets from Vologda!" Manin added. Then I saw the observer's signal.

"In your places!" I commanded.

And fighting again broke out that did not subside until nightfall.

We beat off twelve attacks that day. Perhaps the jaegers had a special score to settle with us. They seemed resolved to destroy the detachment at any price.

The following morning began in an overcast, and thick flakes of snow were falling.[16] The commander decided to make contact with the naval infantrymen and coordinate for mutual support.

Inzartsev ordered me, Nikolay Losev, and Stepan Motovilin to assemble on the road. We had to infiltrate between the enemy hills and move about six kilometers to the hill where the battalion headquarters was located.

The snowstorm had covered the whole area with a sheet of snow, making the footing treacherous, and we fell head over heels down the steep slope and into a rock crevice.

"We can crawl through here!" Motovilin said.

The blizzard whipped up a whirlwind above our heads. But the battle grew more intense.

We wanted to move from the crevice as quickly as possible, but when the blizzard stopped and we could see, it became obvious that our objective was still far away.

The mountains concealed the distance. You walked and walked, and it seemed as if you kept tramping past the same hill. Eventually, even a skilled, conditioned walker like Motovilin could hardly move his legs. Finally, we got close to the hill where the naval infantrymen were supposed to be. Motovilin decided not to skirt it but to go straight across the low ground. We paid a price for this decision— the naval infantry greeted us with fire. I dug into the snow, shrinking under the whistle of the bullets, and cursed Motovilin for his foolishness. To make amends, Stepan got to his knee and shouted, "You idiots, you're shooting at your own! Hold your fire!"

"Who can hear you, agitator? Lie down," Losev said.

But then we realized that though the machine gunner could see us and continued to fire occasionally, the bullets were way above our heads. It was as if he was holding us in his sights just in case.

There was nowhere to hide so we went forward at a crouch.

"They can shoot us like rabbits," Stepan angrily grumbled, stepping up the pace.

An unexpected cry of "Halt, hands up!" stopped us.

Motovilin's eyes flashed fire. Afraid of what he might do, I stepped forward. "I wasn't trained to raise my hands!" I shouted to the invisible machine gunner behind the rocks.

"Okay! Who are you?" the same voice asked.

"And who are you!" Stepan could not restrain himself and rushed forward. "Are you blind? Is this the way you shoot at jaegers, too, eagle?"

The machine gunner stuck out his head: "All right, come this way. There they'll sort out what kind of eagle you are."

"Plucked chicken!" Stepan muttered.

But the war of words was broken off immediately—a lieutenant appeared. Recognizing us, he began to laugh. "You looked very suspicious. Not German, not Finnish."

We were wearing cloth ski caps with long visors, fur jackets, and pants of inside-out reindeer hide.[17] It really wasn't surprising that, seeing us from a distance, the machine gunner opened fire.

The captain arrived. He was deputy commander of the battalion, and I reported the situation to him.

The naval infantrymen knew that our actions on Hill 415 were siphoning off the German forces to help their assault force carry out its mission in the German rear. But the battalion headquarters had only a platoon of security at its disposal. The other units hadn't come back from their missions. As soon as a mortar platoon arrived, he would immediately send it to help us. The captain asked me if we could hold out on the hill for another day.

"If we have to," I said, "we'll hold out."

We began to discuss the mortar platoon's march route, adjustment of its fires, and other means of communication.

The battalion staff suggested that we take a break. After eating a full meal and finishing off one of the lieutenant's cigars, we assembled for the return trip. As we passed by the friendly machine gunner, Stepan said, "Hey, great marksman, keep your eyes open! If you transfer to the scouts, we'll teach you not only how to raise your hands but also to crawl on all fours."

The machine gunner wasn't offended, and followed us with a sympathetic glance.

Carrying good news, we were able to overcome our fatigue and hurried back to our unit's position.

The day was clear, and the snow had melted from the hills. But it still lay in the low ground, which the jaegers were watching and covering with fire. So that we could slip across the low ground toward the base of Hill 415, the scouts organized a false attack, drawing the enemy's attention. Meanwhile, Vasiliy Kashutin, Semyon Agafonov, and Zinoviy Ryshechkin came down to meet us and helped us cover the distance more quickly.

While I reported to the commander about coordinating

with the naval infantrymen, my cohorts were already lying down to sleep. I squeezed in between Motovilin and Losev. Pressed together, warming each other with our bodies, we slept until morning. No one disturbed our sleep, even when the jaegers furiously assaulted Hill 415 and penetrated almost to the crest in a few places.

Our fifth day in the enemy's rear passed.

With each hour the pressure grew. At times it seemed that the limit of our endurance had been reached. We conserved our ammunition and divided the last dry rations. The snow had melted, so we had no water. Kashutin woke me in the morning and, licking his wind-dried lips, asked: "Viktor, you walked all around the area yesterday—did you notice a brook?"

"You know, there's a small lake nearby."

"The jaegers are already drinking the water there. Things are bad, Viktor!"

Suddenly, he turned his head, and I followed the thirsty stare in his eyes. Near us, on a large flat rock, was a small puddle. Vasya looked at it as though he was hypnotized. "It's very dirty," he said.

Pavel Baryshev came over. He was also dying of thirst, but he knew the find belonged to Kashutin, so Baryshev decided to kid around. "Leave it, Vasya! There wasn't a drop of water there yesterday. Maybe Kolikov pissed there from fright during the night."[18]

"Ah, here goes!" Kashutin got up on his knees and closed his eyes. A minute later the only thing left on the rock was a damp spot.

A battle flared up again, this time quite near to us. The jaegers were firing almost point-blank, but we couldn't see them. Clinging to a boulder, Manin thrust the edge of his hat outward, and a machine-gun burst cut cleanly through it. I crawled over to Manin, ordered him to report the situation to the commander, and took over observation myself.

Carefully examining the terrain, I noticed mounds of rocks that had not been on the slope the day before. Then, as one of our sailors was running toward me, a short

machine-gun burst from nearby cut him down. I noticed
that the firing was from one of the mounds, but I wasn't
able to maintain my position. The firing was so close that
I instinctively flinched. Then, stunned by a blow to the
head, I lost consciousness for a moment.

Fortunately, the jaeger was not accurate. The machine-
gun burst was very close, but only one bullet, ricocheting
off a rock, hit me and penetrated my left cheek. The end of
the bullet protruded into my mouth.

"It happens," Medical Service Lieutenant Zasedatelev
said with surprise, trying unsuccessfully to remove the bullet from my cheek. He wrapped my head with bandages,
leaving me only two openings, one for the mouth and the
other for the eyes.

I ran over to Inzartsev and told him where the enemy
machine gunners and submachine gunners were concealed.

"An old trick," Inzartsev mused. "During the attack last
night, they left some men close to us, covered with ponchos
and rocks. We'll have to burn them out."

Semyon Agafonov fired on one mound, then another,
with his sniper rifle.[19] Submachine gunners jumped up, began to yell, and ran away. He "lit up" other mounds as
well, and the jaegers were driven back down the hill.

Just then a red rocket burst upward over one of the hills,
and we heard many voices shouting "Urra." With the help
of the rapidly approaching naval infantry platoon, we
cleared all the slopes of the hill. But the jaegers dug in on
a neighboring hill and began harassing us with mortar fire.

We received a resupply of ammunition and food, and the
infantrymen dug in on the flanks of Hill 415. Now we
could fight. But I had a splitting headache and couldn't
open my mouth, even for a sip of fresh lake water.
Zasedatelev demanded that they send me to the medical station with an escort, but I remembered my wearisome stay
in the hospital after my first wound. Putting on a brave
face, I told the commander that I would go by myself to the
shore, where the medical boat was patrolling, and report the
situation once I got to the base. Inzartsev agreed.

After I got there, I sat on the shore a long time, waiting for the medical boat to appear. Finally, it seemed to notice my signal and approached the shore. But suddenly the boat turned around and showed its stern. I couldn't shout—my mouth hurt so much that it was difficult even to make a noise. I angrily threw up my hands and then fired a burst from my submachine gun into the air. The boat speeded up and took cover under a rock overhang on the other side of the bay.

I felt much worse off than I had when I was being fired at by the Germans. My only chance was to use my remaining strength and climb up a cliff to get their attention so they'd pick me up. Somehow I got over the ridge and saw the sailors, who were picking up the gangplank. Pointing to me, they shouted, "There he is! There he is!"

I turned around. There was no one behind me. Was I imagining?

Fortunately, a wounded officer on the boat, a sailor, recognized me. "Heave to! What the hell's going on—did you think he's a fascist? It's Leonov! From the naval scout detachment."

I was saved!

Exhausted, stumbling with each step, I walked toward the shore.

"Who can figure out these scouts!" the captain of the boat grumbled. "They take in any kind of garbage." He even shook his finger at me. "I mistook you for a jaeger; I thought that the Germans were in ambush by the shore, and you were the decoy."

I was the decoy! The crew and the other wounded shouted with laughter.

I would have laughed too, but it hurt me even to smile. Instead I shook my bandaged head.

In four hours the boat was in base, and two days later the detachment returned.

The medical unit was filled up with scouts who had received light wounds or frostbite during the May Raid.[20] May could be cold in the Far North!

The doctors quickly treated us. Losev, Manin, Motovilin, and I were discharged at the same time. We cheerfully marched into the detachment, and Manin said, "We fought day and night, in situations like we've never seen before! Seven days we fought in the defense. Seven days! From now on nothing will surprise us!"

Of course, we agreed with Manin; we had survived the most difficult test. We thought the devil himself couldn't overcome us!

If the first mentor of the detachment, former scout Major Dobrotin, had overheard us, he probably would have smiled and, perhaps, hinted at the carelessness, lightheartedness, and even a certain self-sufficiency of youth. Yes, we were young and inexperienced. We didn't think that much about the unexpected and dangers that lay in wait for scouts in the enemy rear. Of course, our most difficult trials and heaviest battles were still ahead of us.

[In the early summer of 1942, the detachment conducted another patrol to the Luostari airfield.[21] The mission was the same as before—observe German activity there and determine the nature of the defensive system. The four-hundred-kilometer round trip was expected to take three weeks. Each of the fifty men carried not only his own supplies, but also common items such as extra ammunition drums, radios, and batteries. Five radio operators accompanied this patrol, far more than normal.

The detachment walked for several days, crossing the Titovka and Petsamo rivers, photographing and noting locations of suitable fording sites. When the scouts finally arrived at an observation position near the airfield, they drew sketches of it and took more photographs. Six days later they crossed back through Soviet lines, where they organized for a short excursion to Lake Chapr. This patrol was brief, lasting three or four days. The group found evidence of German patrolling activity but no positions or forces until they reached Hill 374 (Bolshoy Karikvayvash). There they noted a German observation position of at least a half-dozen men. The scouts returned safely to their base in Polyarnyy.]

4

A Rookie Arrives
in the Detachment

PETTY OFFICER FIRST CLASS Makar Babikov, former clerk in a coastal artillery battalion, whom I had earlier occasionally met in the political section, arrived in the naval scout detachment with a small group of new personnel. Babikov was assigned to my squad.

The detachment's senior petty officer, Grigoriy Chekmachev, had known Babikov well in the training detachment of the Northern Fleet's Combined School,[1] where they served together. He told me everything a squad leader would want to know about one of his men.

In the past, refugees from the tsarist persecution of Old Believers had settled on the shores of the Pechora River,[2] where they became farmers, hunters, and fishermen. This severe but rich region rewarded the hardworking newcomers, who rigidly preserved the ancient rituals of their way of life.

In Ust-Tsylma village,[3] where Babikov was born, far from the nearest railroad, the breakdown of the Old Believers' way of life began only in the 1930s. The new conflicted with the old. The young were pulled toward education and, disobeying their fathers and grandfathers, frequently left for study in Arkhangelsk or even in Moscow. They built their own schools and technical school. The children also resisted their forefathers' iron-clad traditions. When nine-year-old Makar Babikov entered the Pioneers, he openly tied the red scarf around his neck and boldly looked his grandmother in the eyes. The old lady crossed herself, groaned, and waved her hand at the boy.

His father died early, and Makar shared with his mother the care of the four children in his family. During the winter evenings, Makar harnessed horses and carried the mail by relay for thirty-plus kilometers, returning after midnight. The horses trotted home on their own while the twelve-year-old coachman slept in the sleigh, wrapped in his father's reindeer-fur coat, in the secret pocket of which lay an earned "five."[4]

In the morning, lessons prepared, Makar ran to school.

When summer came and the Pechora River spilled out over tens of kilometers, Makar equipped himself with a flat-bottomed boat, selected a bank densely covered by undergrowth, built himself a camouflaged lean-to, and, placing a duck decoy in the water, patiently waited for dawn. A wild flock, flying over the Pechora River, circled over the decoy, landed on the water, and, not frightened away by any strange noises, swam over to the shore. After gathering his harvest, Makar again returned to his schoolbooks.

At fourteen he entered the Komsomol. Books, meetings, and parties with other young people opened a new world to him, a world full of alluring horizons. Military veterans arrived in Ust-Tsylma from those faraway places and told stories of the large cities in which they had lived and served, about seas and oceans on which they had sailed. Makar's uncle, an officer in the reserves, also returned to his native village, where he headed up the Osoaviakhim organization and began to teach the young men rifle marksmanship. Invariably, the Osoaviakhim commander's assistant was his nephew.

At seventeen, Makar finished the tenth grade. Though many of his classmates intended to depart for various institutes, Makar Babikov, who had earned a certificate of excellence, agreed to teach in the lower grades so he could take care of the younger children in his family and give them the opportunity to finish school. In the evenings he worked on his own correspondence courses.

A year later Babikov was accepted as a candidate for membership in the party, and a year after that he was drafted into the army.

The military commission of Ust-Tsylma, which had recommended the young teacher to the party, knew that Makar was eager to serve in the navy.[5] But could they put together a detachment for the navy in Ust-Tsylma? Young men have an unquenchable thirst for the sea. No uniform attracted the young men of Ust-Tsylma like a sailor's uniform or a sailor's cap with ribbons flapping in the wind.[6] And there were no great heroes like those from the movie *We Are from Kronshtadt.*[7]

On the day before departure from Ust-Tsylma, Babikov sat in the office of the regional military commission sporting a short military haircut. The senior political instructor, who had vouched for Makar Babikov to the party, now spoke with him about such important events as the Soviet Union's struggle with the Japanese at Khasan and Khalkhin-Gol,[8] the growing danger of Nazi fascism, and his patriotic duty to the Motherland, which was on the mind of every Soviet citizen—communists most of all.

The draftees traveled down the Pechora River, then went by sea to Arkhangels'k, where commanders from various branches of service awaited them. A naval officer approached the formation, on the left flank of which stood Makar, and the faces of these future sailors lit up. Another thorough medical examination was begun, after which the selection commission distributed the inductees to their training units. While Makar was musing about what he would be, they assigned him to the Combined School, to the training company for clerks and a platoon which at that time was commanded by our detachment senior petty officer, Grigoriy Chekmachev.

The war began and Chekmachev was sent to the detachment of naval scouts. Petty Officer First Class Makar

Babikov, by then a clerk in a coastal artillery battalion, for an entire year petitioned and wrote requests to be assigned to our detachment. Eventually, his request was approved, and the rookie crossed the threshold of the two-story house where we were billeted.

Short and thin, with light hair and gray eyes and a clever, sometimes piercing glance, Makar Babikov immediately attracted attention. He did not enter into the conversation, and inquisitively and carefully looked at his new surroundings.

Petty Officer Second Class Ivan Polyakov noted the arrival of Babikov with a caustic joke. "Stand clear! A clerk has arrived for reconnaissance—Death to the jaegers!" he said, without even glancing at Babikov. Contemptuously shrugging his broad shoulders, he left the room.

Babikov did not laugh. He threw a sharp stare at the back of the departing Polyakov and slowly looked around at us with a bewildered face. The departure of Polyakov left everyone uncomfortable. But then Pavel Baryshev got everyone to laughing. "Don't pay any attention to that big mouth Polyakov," he said affably as he turned to the new man. "You and I aren't exactly giants, but a small ax can chop down a large tree! You served with the clerks—that's important. Look at Semyon Agafonov here—he was a cook. Well, so what? This cook went on a patrol and brought back two prisoners. Thus, you shouldn't be offended."

"I'm not upset."

"Good!" Baryshev smiled. "And then there was Kolikov—"

A burst of laughter cut him off, and now Babikov laughed. He didn't know that Pasha was just getting warmed up, recalling how he had carried the "champion" Kolikov on his back in the May Raid. Pavel was glad for the arrival of Babikov mainly because the rookie was the same height as he and might replace him on the left flank of the formation. Baryshev even measured himself against the rookie and sputtered in annoyance: Babikov was just a bit taller.

I don't know about anyone else, but scouts knew how to judge the value of a soldier by something other than his external appearance. We knew that Ivan Lysenko, Aleksey Radyshevtsev, and other strong and tall soldier-athletes emerged victors in single-handed combat with the enemy, that athlete Vladimir Lyande,[9] though unarmed, took on an armed jaeger. And we knew many others just like them. Semyon Agafonov, a former submarine cook, was stocky, short, and awkward in appearance. But he fought fearlessly, with inexhaustible energy and satisfaction, and at the same time with such a cool head that everyone considered him the best scout in the detachment.

And Pavel Baryshev? And little, curly-haired Zinoviy Ryshechkin? Our Ryzhik was probably a head shorter than any German he faced, but in hand-to-hand combat he'd knocked a jaeger down and disarmed him. And the detachment's Komsomol organizer, short Sasha Manin? When we were in base, the correspondents couldn't get him to say two words about those combat episodes in which he was a hero—Sasha literally was transformed in battle, fought happily and skillfully, and encouraged his comrades by his personal example and humor.

No, most of us didn't hurry to judge a new scout by external appearances or information from his personnel file. Though he was a clerk, Makar Babikov had already served in the navy; our Komsomolist Boris Abramov knew nothing about military service in general when he joined the unit. Perhaps none of us imagined that together with Semyon Florinskiy, Boris would soon become an outstanding machine gunner. Florinskiy chose Abramov for his partner, imparted to him a love for weapons, suffered along with him when he didn't receive a letter from the blockaded city of Leningrad, and helped him get through his first combat operations.

Glancing at them, I recalled how Sergeant Vasiliy Kashutin, member of the party organizational bureau of our detachment, had been just such a mentor to me. His advice was not judgmental and his assistance was not for show; he gave me great support. Later his "patronage" tapered off as subtly as it had appeared. But the friendship remained and grew stronger with each battle. One particularly cold night Vasa and I were lying in a hollow on Hill 415. We were pressed together like jacks on a playing card, toe-to-toe under our fur jackets to cover the ends of our feet, in a short hour of rest after a battle. Down below, laying siege to the hill, the Germans waited for dawn so they could launch new attacks. We were talking in undertones about our most intimate thoughts, sharing that which each man considered his personal, carefully guarded secrets. Later, having successfully returned to base, I was struck by that wonderful feeling, sometimes falsely attributed to human weakness, which in a difficult moment allows one to open his heart up to a comrade. One has no regrets about this if the friendship is strong and unselfish and has been validated in such severe tests as combat in the enemy rear.

Life itself taught us this. It graphically proved the great strength that the personal example of an experienced scout could be for a new man.

We still knew nothing about Babikov, but it turned out he was already familiar with the combat history of the detachment. He'd saved all the newspaper clippings about our raids and hoped to become a skillful pathfinder like Motovilin, Radyshevtsev, and Kashutin. If one of them had uttered a malicious joke about the danger of accepting a clerk into a reconnaissance unit, that would have hurt Makar Babikov!

But that did not happen. Things turned out differently.

We were preparing for a deep raid into the enemy's rear.

Avoiding the enemy, our detachment was to penetrate to an important target in his defenses, reconnoiter it, and return to base. In the meantime we decided to conduct a full rehearsal, which as closely as possible approximated the combat situation. For the newcomers, such an exercise was the first test of their strength. Far from the base, the young trackers gradually became familiar with the new conditions and became more closely acquainted with the experienced scouts, who could watch them and show them the way.

The first halt. The scouts, having camouflaged, sat in small groups, eating and resting. They had just assembled on the path when I heard Stepan Motovilin call for Makar Babikov. Because Babikov was in my squad, I went up to Motovilin.

"Viktor, permit me to teach some sense to the rookie," said Motovilin, "in your presence."

Stepan did not at all mean to offend the newcomer. He instructed him. Babikov ran up but did not know to which one of us he should report.

"Are you leaving?" Stepan quietly asked him.

"We are leaving—"

"And what's this?"

With the toe of his boot, Motovilin pointed at a cigarette butt.

"I didn't smoke it!" Makar protested, turning to me. "And here's the proof—I still have my cigarette."

"That's unimportant! Didn't you put your rucksack down here? As soon as you assembled on the road, you should have inspected the area to see if you or someone else left something—you didn't smoke it and I didn't smoke it! What difference does that make?"

Babikov was quiet.

Motovilin picked up the butt, turned it over, brushed away the tobacco on his palm, smoothed out the scrap of already yellowed paper, and though it was clear to him that the butt had lain there for a long time before our arrival, he reproachfully shook his head. "Imagine, comrade Babikov, that we are in the enemy's rear, and one of us left this butt. A jaeger, also a skilled scout, picks it up." Now Motovilin and Babikov walked together, quietly conversing, and to make his arguments more convincing, Stepan began using "*vy.*"[10] "Let's see what is written on this. *TASS.*[11] And here is the date. The German now knows when the Russians passed by here and will inspect the surrounding area. Do you understand?"

"I understand."

"Now look out ahead," Stepan continued with the same unruffled tone. "Do you see how the patrol goes around the bushes? Why? Let's say that they trample straight ahead and, you see, break a branch. The German scout comes across the bushes and sees that only a man could have broken the branch. He looks at the fresh break and sees in which direction the man passed. Then tracking begins, rounding up, pursuit. The enemy was warned, he increases security, and combs the entire area. He could disrupt our operation. And all because of a broken branch. You aren't tired are you, Babikov? Is your rucksack getting heavy?"

"No, thanks. I can walk far and fast."

"Good. Walk fast and walk carefully!"

I ordered Yuriy Mikheev to stay closer to Babikov to orient him on the terrain.

"One time I almost ran into a jaeger!" Mikheev was telling Babikov on the next break. "We were going toward the 'Valley of Nerves'—we call it that because the Germans so thoroughly observed and covered it with fire. And the hills around the valley were so much alike that it was tiresome to look at them. When God created the Far North, perhaps he did a few things wrong. He piled up rocks, ravines, and boulders everywhere and made these bare hills all look the same."

Mikheev intended to say more about the whims and eccentricities of nature in the Far North, but he noticed the impatience of his listener, who was more interested in the details of the incident itself. "I'll tell you about it some other time. But here's another one. They sent me and Zinoviy Ryzhechkin on patrol. Do you know him? We call him Ryzhik. I was in front. He was a rookie, so he was following. I turned to the right, and Ryzhechkin caught up to me, placed his hand on my shoulder, and motioned that I should turn left. And he was right! He'd noticed the last time we'd slipped through the Valley of Nerves that one hill had a barely noticeable notch. That meant that Ryzhik had acquired an eye and had a good memory. I'd really have been embarrassed if we'd fallen into a German ambush! In our business, Comrade Petty Officer First Class, one must know—look and notice!"

After the exercise I was on temporary duty and couldn't participate in the next raid. I knew that the detachment was breaking new territory and would avoid an engagement. Nevertheless, I was concerned for Babikov, just as, perhaps, other squad and group commanders were worried about their own new men.

The raid was successful. The single small glitch was with Babikov. During the mission his tightly packed rucksack burst open, and all its contents—hardtack, ration cans, ammunition—fell out. There weren't any spare rucksacks so Babikov had to wrap up his cargo in a poncho and continue the march with a parcel on his back. He became tired but refused the aid of his comrades and did not fall behind. The detachment commander said to the rookie, "You have to prepare for the sortie more attentively." But I blamed myself and Agafonov, my replacement on the raid. We should have checked Babikov's equipment more carefully.

But this was just a sortie, not the kind of reconnaissance mission which the new people dreamed about, full of combat and adventure. Meanwhile, the young scouts listened to the stories of the veterans with unusual interest. Stepan Motovilin talked to them about several raids, including the one in which Grigoriy Kharabrin burst into a German hut, mowed down three enemy with his submachine gun, jerked a fourth out from under a table, and the whole way home kept repeating, "A good 'tongue' fell into my hands, brothers!"

"No, there have been no 'tongues' like those delivered by Radyshevtsev—no one has managed to top him!" Baryshev said, interrupting the conversation. "Do you remember the Bavarian brothers?"

How could one forget! But Baryshev knew how to recount the circumstances; the incident was instructive for the rookies to hear, and was itself very remarkable.

This was about six months before Babikov's arrival. We had been walking through the ice-covered hills for a long time, had infiltrated unnoticed into the mountains, and, when the polar night was lit up with the faded northern lights, we lay still on the snow-covered top of a ridge. Then we again probed forward, unable to see the white mounds near the foot of the hill toward which we were moving. These were the snow-covered huts of the jaegers.

Kashutin's group was ordered to capture the positions on the crest of the hill. Radyshevtsev, Agafonov, and Kharabrin crawled like hunting cats toward the guard looming near the outer hut. But Kashutin's scouts had already attacked. A hurriedly dressed officer with a submachine gun at the ready came out of the last hut and collided with Radyshevtsev. There was the chatter of submachine guns, the clashing of barrels, and muffled cries. When this desperate fight began, the surprise and swiftness of the attackers gave the small detachment the advantage over an entire battalion.

Kashutin's group covered the withdrawal. Up front, Radyshevtsev was leading his "tongue," a German officer named Karl Kurt.

A day later, at the base, the commissar read to us Karl Kurt's unfinished letter. He persistently asked his relatives to insure his property against fire and, speaking with unhappy irony, was distressed that he could not be protected against Russian scouts. "And it would be nice to be insured against this terrible cold. I am afraid, Mama, that one day my intestines will freeze in my body. When Hans finishes military school, don't let him even think about asking for the North, for the Lapland Army. Show him this letter."

The younger Kurt didn't have the opportunity to read the letter. Young Kurt obtained for himself assignment to the Lapland Army. And we were made certain of this three months later, thanks to the same Radyshevtsev.

A blustery wind was blowing in our faces. The boat

turned its bow into the wave and for a long time moved toward the shore. The journey to the same enemy strongpoint was more difficult than the first time because the strong March ground wind of the night before had stripped the ice off the hills, making it impossible to ski.

During the night the enemy had strengthened his security, and we had to fight even before we reached his huts. We had wounded. Just the same, we set fire to his supplies and captured several dugouts. The Germans fell back into the main position, which they had carved beneath a cliff. It was difficult to approach the position. We tried to attack it frontally and again took casualties. Then Radyshevtsev and Sherstobitov went around the cliff and penetrated into the position by climbing. Coming out above, they jumped down onto the roof of the bunker. After the explosion of the grenade, only one jaeger managed to get out of the dugout. He tried to run.

"You fool, you can't escape!" cried Radyshevtsev, and ran after him.

The lightly dressed German kept running, so the senior petty officer picked up a rifle and fired. The jaeger immediately fell from view, and Radyshevstev moved carefully forward.

The jaeger's body was lying between the rocks. Radyshevtsev unbuttoned the dead lieutenant's tunic, took his documents from an inside pocket, and ran back to us.

One extract from the diary of Hans Kurt reads: "The notification arrived that Karl was missing in action. How could this be? I firmly decided to ask for assignment to the North, to Karl's unit, in order to replace him. My duty to my Führer requires me to do it!"

"What a fool! Then why did he run away?" interrupted Radyshevtsev. "He could have met his brother Karl in captivity, and another 'tongue' could be added to my score. But instead this—a debt to the Führer!"

Pavel Baryshev talked about Radyshevtsev. Radyshevtsev told about Major Dobrotin using the telephone to talk with the commandant of the German garrison at Titovka. Many others also told stories. Naturally, the more the newcomers listened to us, the more it seemed that the most interesting missions had already been accomplished.

"When will we go on a real reconnaissance?" Babikov asked me.

"Don't ask. We'll go, that's for sure."

Who could know that the next raid would be the most difficult, that the advance guard group of the detachment would be considered dead for several days, that only eight scouts from this group would return to their base, among them the newcomer, little Petty Officer First Class Makar Babikov.

5

In a Double Ring
of Encirclement

WE WERE IN OUR NEW temporary base at Ozerko.[1]

On clear days we could see the opposite shore of Motovskiy Bay with the two capes so dear to us. One cape—Pikshuev—was well-known to the scouts. It spread out in all directions. But now we were interested in the other cape, beyond which began the broad mouth of the Titovka River. Whenever our cutter appeared in the bay or an airplane flew over Rybachiy Peninsula, German observers from the second cape immediately spotted them, and an enemy battery opened fire.

"It's a hostile cape!" said one of the scouts, referring to the German strongpoint, which had been established overlooked the sea. This cape had a sorrowful name, Mogilnyy.[2]

Our new commander, Senior Lieutenant Frolov, led the difficult and complex raid on Cape Mogilnyy; Captain Inzartsev had recently left us for a training assignment.[3] Only after Inzartsev's departure did we realize how much we missed him, how much he was needed, how valuable and irreplaceable he was. Inzartsev knew the strengths and weaknesses of each scout and sensibly evaluated the capabilities of each group and the detachment as a whole. Our faith in the commander was limitless, as was our love for him—the reserved soldierly love that is a natural result of soldierly comradeship forged in battle. But, jumping ahead in the story, I will only say that the battle on Mogilnyy would have turned out differently if Nikolay Arkadevich Inzartsev had still commanded the detachment.

Autumn had arrived, and the days were noticeably shortening. The new commander of the detachment, Senior Lieutenant Frolov, reported our readiness for the mission to the fleet staff.[4] The onset of autumn did not sadden us. In the upcoming raid the long autumn night would be a faithful ally. It would permit the composite force—our scout detachment and a naval infantry unit[5]—to be landed west of Cape Pikshuev, execute a march, and before dawn be concentrated for the attack in the rear of the enemy garrison on Cape Mogilnyy.

This was the first phase of the upcoming operation. Inzartsev frequently reminded us that the first stage was no less important than the second, that is, the battle itself, and in many ways predetermined the success of each raid.

My group landed near Cape Pikshuev. The sea was to our right. To our left came the groups of Kashutin and Junior Lieutenant Shelavin. They selected Agafonov to be the point man, and I cautioned Semyon: "Step it out! There's not much time before dawn."

But word came up from the rear of the file that they were slowing down the movement, and then they stopped altogether. Even young scout Babikov understood that this presented problems to us. We could be deprived of our basic superiority—the surprise of a night attack. I ran back to find out what the problem was.

"They have fallen behind!" the detachment commander said with unconcealed anger. "The naval infantrymen are not keeping up with us."

"But is there time?"

"We'll make it!"

It is fine when such confidence is based on careful calculation, but time inexorably moves at its own pace, and it seemed to us that the commander was trying to stifle discussion. Everyone understood that the naval infantrymen had to fight their way ashore, and then they needed time to rest and gather their strength. But gradually the commander grew concerned.

"Damn, we're like the unlucky magpie—tail pulled out, claws tied up."[6]

Having finally received a report on the location of the infantrymen, the commander decided to execute a forced march toward the strongpoint on Mogilnyy with three advance guard groups—mine, Kashutin's, and Shelavin's. There we would engage the enemy and in so doing facilitate the approach of the infantrymen to the cape. But we soon learned that the possibility for a surprise attack was already gone.

Dawn was breaking when we approached the flat valley, beyond which began the steep approach to the two strongpoints on the crest of the saddled cape. The Germans had already noticed the column of naval infantrymen and opened fire on them from the batteries on Mogilnyy. At the same time the firing positions on the approaches to Titovka also opened up. That meant that the German garrison at Titovka knew about the landing and would rush reinforcements to Mogilnyy.

What should we do? What decision will the commander make? These thoughts troubled those of us with the forward groups. We were paying a high price for the previous delay and couldn't lie pressed against the cold rocks, awaiting orders. We were suffering losses, and our duty to render assistance prompted us to make the naturally correct decision. The enemy had superior numbers and firepower and was defending from steep heights. We had to attack him very aggressively; our rush would have to be unstoppable. With cries of "Forward! For the Motherland!" we stormed across the flat ground and began the climb up to the first height.

Mortar rounds were exploding behind us, and ahead of us grenades were going off. In the constant noise we heard neither the whistle of bullets nor the cries of the wounded.

We were already twenty meters from the first German forces and thirty meters from the first bunker.

A grenade exploded under the feet of Junior Lieutenant Shelavin. He went down, fell backward, and as he came even with us, cried, "Forward, sailors! Forward!"

Zinoviy Ryzhechkin passed me. Next to him ran that young, quick, agile—yes, it was our newcomer! "Forrwar-rd!" Makar Babikov yelled enthusiastically.

Our attack stunned the Germans. They withdrew to the end of the cape, to their second strongpoint.

Fired up by the battle and intoxicated by the first victory, we dug in on the height, looked around, and only then realized the situation we were in. Inspired by our first rush, we had not looked behind and had not noted that the column approaching the valley had been forced to the ground by massed enemy fires. Then fresh German forces—from Titovka—had attacked it and had begun to press the naval infantrymen toward the shore, toward the landing site.

Later we found out that the commander of the naval infantry reconnaissance detachment had been turned over to a military tribunal for criminal negligence and delay[7] and Senior Lieutenant Frolov had tried unsuccessfully to communicate with us. He led two groups of scouts to the cape but was wounded and evacuated from the battlefield. Also wounded were Dubrovskiy, the detachment's commissar, Petty Officer Tarashin, secretary of the party bureau, and many others. The scouts from Motovilin's group fought toward us furiously but were encircled. Breaking through the ring, they made it to the sea. The two friends—machine gunners Semyon Florinskiy and Boris Abramov—covered their withdrawal until they ran out of ammunition, then ran at the enemy with grenades in their hands. Mowed down by a machine-gun burst, they fell, faces toward the cape.

I still didn't know that Kashutin had died or that Shelavin, his feet smashed, had bitten his mouth and hands until they bled so that he would not cry out, had hidden himself from the Germans dashing around him, and was steadily crawling to the top of Mogilnyy. And even nearby

Barinov and Sherstobitov didn't tell anyone that they were wounded.

One thing was perfectly clear: we were cut off from the main force, surrounded by jaegers on their own strongpoint. But before we could take any action, we had to restore some sort of combat organization to the group. I counted our forces. On a small spit of rocky land, on the nose of Mogilnyy, were fifteen scouts.

The sea washed Cape Mogilnyy on three sides.

There were jaegers in front of us and behind us. They were firing at our position, and if we had not taken cover in the rocks, the shrapnel of enemy mortar rounds and shells would have gotten us all.

"Comrade Petty Officer! Let me do it! Comrade Petty Officer!"

Someone was tugging at my sleeve. I turned around—it was Makar Babikov! His gray narrow eyes gleamed with worry. A wet lock of hair hung out from under his woolen pile cap, and on his white face stood drops of sweat.

Makar looked at the slope of the mountain. "He's over there. He fell behind those rocks. He may be wounded."

"Who? Who are you talking about?"

"Kashutin."

"Vasya Kashutin!"

I prepared to break away from my position and run forward, but Makar held on to the sleeve of my fatigue shirt and pressed me to the ground.

Our glances met, and I saw decisiveness and pleading in the eyes of the newcomer. "I'm small and can crawl unnoticed."

It was difficult to conceal oneself on the open, almost naked slope. We couldn't risk the life of a sailor who had almost never been fired at in battle. "Don't get excited," I said to Makar, calming myself at the same time. "Don't get excited! Why did you jump ahead during the attack? Did you want to show that the sea is up to your knees?"

"I jerked with fear—I was afraid to get separated from you."

I liked Babikov's honest acknowledgment, but only if he was not deceiving me.

"And now suddenly you're not afraid?"

Babikov was quiet for a moment, then quickly, still without permission, he flashed among the rocks like a small fish and disappeared.

We had already beaten off three attacks when quiet unexpectedly descended on us. The Germans were planning something. I ordered my men to stay alert and to conserve ammunition.

Makar did not return, and below us they were firing an occasional shot at something. Perhaps the jaegers had spotted him.

"Air attack!"

With a heartrending howl three Messerschmitts passed overhead. Soaring upward, they began to dive on our position and to hurl bombs. The enemy battery struck again and the jaegers attacked right behind the barrage. They came so close that we heard them call, "Russians! Give up! You Russians are finished!"

Our position was quiet. We were waiting for the Germans to come within grenade distance.

Someone off to the jaegers' flank gave a sharp whistle, and from there we heard Babikov yell, "Tally ho, here they come!" Then he hurled a grenade, which exploded in the attackers' ranks. We threw several more lemons right behind it.[8]

With terrible cries of pain and anger, the jaegers withdrew.

"I made it in time!" I heard a familiar voice nearby.

Babikov had crawled back unnoticed. He was pale, disturbed about something. His eyes looked guiltily to the side.

"It's a good thing that you returned," I said sternly. "It was difficult to crawl to Kashutin, why risk it for nothing? Right now every sailor is worth a platoon."

And then Babikov pulled a dagger with a bone handle out of his boot top. This was that same dagger in a black sheath on which I had carved the initials "V. L.—V. K." for "Viktor Leonov—Vasiliy Kashutin." In training exercises and missions, Vasya was never without my gift.

"Kashutin is dead," Babikov said quietly. "I crawled to him. I was going to carry him back, but a jaeger spotted me and opened fire. I lay in a hollow behind his back. Though dead, he saved me. Then the attack began and I dashed back to you."

"Thank you, Makar! Call Ulenkov."

The favorite of the detachment, harmonica player and comedian Evgeniy Ulenkov, was with Zinoviy Ryzhechkin on the left flank of the position, covering the low ground to prevent the jaegers from infiltrating. Even on Mogilnyy, Ulenkov didn't lose his happy disposition. Coming over as ordered, he squatted down, saluted, and smartly reported, paraphrasing the words of a song, "Our proud assault force will not give in to the enemy!"

"Don't give up, Ulenkov, happy sailor soul! And Shelavin, even though wounded, will not give up. Where is he? You have to find him."

Ulenkov left, and after two or three minutes the Germans, who understood our predicament better than we did, again attacked. Apparently, they had decided to finish us off before nightfall. And, of course, we fully realized that we had to hold on until darkness and, to do so, hoard each bullet, each grenade.

The broadest part of Cape Mogilnyy did not exceed one hundred meters. The jaegers determined the exact location of our group, and when, after Ulenkov departed, the fire on the left flank weakened, they took advantage of this and began to infiltrate into the low ground.

Mortar rounds exploded only on the left flank, where Ryzhechkin was continuing to fire. Ryzhechkin's friend Yuriy Mikheev assured me that these short submachine-gun bursts were of an unknown origin. It was as if it was not Ryzhechkin firing but someone else.

"Perhaps Ryzhechkin's submachine gun is jammed? He is there alone."

Kurnosenko and Baryshev ran to help Ryzhechkin.

When this attack was also beaten off, Kurnosenko remained on the left flank, and Baryshev carried the mortally wounded Zinoviy Ryzhechkin in his arms. A shell splinter had mutilated Zinoviy's face. Earlier he had been wounded in the shoulder, then in the head. Placing the submachine gun on a rock, Ryzhechkin had been firing with one hand and had lost consciousness several times. Barely alive, the sailor had been firing the short bursts.

Yuriy Mikheev unbuttoned Ryzhechkin's jacket and angrily tapped his empty canteen. Nobody had any water. Zinoviy opened his eyes, recognized Mikheev, and, as if nothing was amiss, with a simplicity that tugged at all of us, said, "My water's gone. Yura, I wanted to quench my thirst, and get washed before I died."

"What are you saying! Ryzhik"—Mikheev waved his hand at him—"Don't talk like that!" His voice broke.

"All of you, brothers! You'll live, you'll fight until victory itself. But I'd just like a little drink."

"Right away, right away, Ryzhik!"

Yuri ran over to the cliff, where a little stream of water trickled from under a rock. The cliff was visible to the enemy. Hiding behind a rock, Yuriy extended his arm out with an empty ration can, which the tiny stream of water began to fill. A single shot of a German sniper rang out. Yuriy dropped the can and pulled his arm back. But he did not crawl away. He again stretched out his arm, this time his right, and propped the can against the rock. But when he returned with the water, Ryzhechkin was dead. Mikheev washed him, and we carried Ryzhik to a rock crevice, buried him, and closed up the entrance with large stones.

Behind us someone groaned, and we saw Ulenkov, carrying the wounded Shelavin on his back. While the scouts were bandaging Shelavin, Ulenkov whispered, "The jaegers have two machine guns in the depression. They have surrounded us. Two rings."

"Ulenkov, only two people know about this—you and I. Try to make your way to shore. It'll be easier for one man to sneak across the low ground. If you make it back to base, tell them about us. Got that? Move out."

A red rocket cut across the sky, then enemy artillery struck again. We carried Shelavin to a sheltered spot and took up out positions. This time the barrage was especially long. Large rocks split apart with a crack and crumbled. Four shells exploded next to Babikov and blanketed the small scout with smoke.

"Are you alive?" Agafonov cried out to him.

"Sort of," Babikov answered, swearing.

"Look, comrade! We're not far from base, but we've fallen into the kind of slaughterhouse you wouldn't drive cattle into, Makar."

Junior Lieutenant Shelavin called to me. Overcoming his pain, the officer tried to speak with authority. "Listen, Petty Officer! With the wounded, there are eleven of you. Don't count me. Look, do you think you can make it across that depression we crossed this morning? Well? Do you know what I'm talking about?"

I was silent.

"Begin to descend—the jaegers are closing in on you. Leave me here and I will cover your withdrawal. I'm already—"

I couldn't bear it. "Junior Lieutenant Shelavin, I am ashamed that you could think this way about us. Of course, I'll say nothing to them. But I am in command, now, and—"

"Forgive me, Viktor." Shelavin's weakening voice interrupted me. "You have to find a way out!"

"There is no way out; the jaegers have set up two machine guns in the low ground. No, we have to hold on until nightfall."

Our coastal artillery struck at the jaegers' second strongpoint along the end of the cape. If only we could get the fire from the battery on Rybachiy to come over our heads to the narrow neck of the cape! But how could we adjust that battery's fire without radio communications? Signal rockets? We and the Germans both used them a lot. It was difficult for the artillerymen on Rybachiy to determine which signal was whose. The explosions of the shells grew nearer and then blanketed our position.

Taking cover behind a boulder, someone shouted, "It's our own!"

Fortunately, the barrage lifted, but soon the German batteries opened up.

"The jaegers are coming from our rear!" Babikov reported as he looked out over the narrow neck of land.

I turned and saw a frenzied attack by a platoon of drunk jaegers that had arrived from Titovka. They did not sober up quickly, and when the attack was finally broken off, our ammunition was almost gone.

Half a day passed.

We sat behind the rocks and waited for darkness to fall. It would be easier at night. There were several of us, but if we climbed down the hill, it would be difficult to pick us out among the chaotic masses of boulders. At night it would be easier to exfiltrate into the low ground, to be concealed against pursuit, and to carry the seriously wounded Shelavin to the shore. The troops understood this and did not lose their spirit. Agafonov even tried to joke. Only the youngest among us, Nikolay Zhdanov, a slender, good-looking sailor, who until now had held on magnificently, suddenly grew morose and hung his head down.

"Hey, pretty boy! Act like a man!" Semyon Agafonov clapped him on the shoulder.

Zhdanov winced, then angrily replied, "It's over! Our gooses are cooked. There's no way we can get out of here."

"You fool, you're soft in the head!" Agafonov retorted.

Zhdanov flared up, grew pale, then answered sharply, "Nikolay Zhdanov will not fall into the enemy's hands alive! Is that clear?" And he walked off.

The sun was already half-hidden behind the mountain. The long, aimless shadows of the rocks disappeared as dusk closed in. We began to prepare for the breakout. I selected five scouts who were to punch a hole in the jaegers' defense and three to cover the withdrawal, and I ordered two lightly wounded men to place Shelavin on a poncho.

Just then Aleksey Kashtanov came up to me and whispered: "The jaegers are close by."

"How can you tell?"

"I was with Kurnosenko on the left flank. We heard their officer shout in German, 'I will shoot anyone who turns back! We must destroy the Russians before nightfall!' "

What happened next confirmed Kashtanov's observations. With furious shouts, clutching at the rocks, the jaegers doggedly crawled upward. Now our sparse fire could not stop them.

"I'm out of ammunition!" Babikov shouted.

"Mine is gone, too!" Baryshev echoed worriedly, crawling back.

The jaegers were dragging a machine gun to the crest of the hill. Shelavin raised himself up to a knee and with trembling hand lifted his pistol.

The critical moment of the battle was upon us. "Everyone follow me!" I commanded.

At that moment Nikolay Zhdanov screamed hysterically, "Brothers, this is the end!" Then he pulled the pin from a grenade, pressed it to his chest, and lay face down on the ground.[9]

"Ignore him, comrades!"

Then sailor Kiselev, who had run over to Zhdanov, jerked at the ring of the lemon clutched in his own fist and slowly kneeled.

"Get up, Kiselev!" I brought up my submachine gun. Anger, hurt, and shame for Kiselev took my breath away. With difficulty I blurted out, "Coward! I'll shoot you! Throw the grenade!"

Kiselev hurled the lemon in the direction of the jaegers, and immediately everyone breathed easier.

We couldn't delay any longer. "Agafonov—you and I

will destroy the machine guns! Kurnosenko, Babikov—cover the withdrawal. The rest of you—carry Shelavin."

Only a few rounds remained in the drum of my PPSh, but we still might drive a wedge into the enemy's position for a hand-to-hand fight; we still might be able to break out! Standing up straight, I saw the heads of the two German machine gunners and pressed the trigger. The machine gunners dove behind a rock, and Semyon Agafonov immediately hurled a grenade into their position and rushed in right behind it. "Over here, Petty Officer!" Agafonov shouted as he turned the captured machine gun around. Unfortunately, it had been damaged.

I ran up to him.

Babikov, Mikheev, and Kashtanov cleared the way for themselves with grenades. Behind them Barinov and Baryshev carried the wounded junior lieutenant on a poncho.

We had broken through the inner ring of the encirclement; the cape was behind us now. But there was still the single outer ring, and our path lay across the flat ground covered by the jaegers' fire. By this time, Agafonov, Baryshev, and Kashtanov were lightly wounded.

A constantly barking machine gun firing from a bunker blocked the path to the flat ground. The jaegers were firing illumination rockets. They had to be stopped.

Yuriy Mikheev stepped forward, saying, "Comrade Petty Officer, let's prepare a bundle of grenades. My left hand is wounded, but my right . . ."

He raised his clenched right fist, waiting for my answer. I was thinking that everyone should give up his last grenade for this bundle.

"I want to do it for Ryzhik!" Mikheev said, convinced that he would not be refused. "I won't miss!"

There was no other way out. Our best grenade thrower was the first to declare his right to go out and destroy the enemy bunker, his right to avenge the death of his best friend.[10]

Yuriy Mikheev crawled forward with the bundle of grenades. Crawling on his belly in the rocks, he approached the bunker meter by meter. A rocket burst into the sky. Mikheev froze until the light went out, then crawled again. Nevertheless, the Germans saw him and opened fire. By the way Yuriy was pulling himself, we could tell that he was wounded. I worried about what would happen if they killed him or if an enemy bullet found its way into our last bundle of grenades.

The clap of the signal pistol was heard, and a glimmering blue light illuminated the depression—and the figure of the scout, pressed against a rock. Suddenly Yuriy jumped to his feet. Dragging his leg, he ran forward, then fell down on his right side, brandishing and then hurling the bundle of grenades. It was still in the air when he was hit in the side, cut down by a machine-gun burst.

The explosion in the bunker reverberated in the mountains with many short echoes. Thus the last of the scouts who perished on Mogilnyy saluted us, the living.

We crossed the flat ground and moved to the shore. There were eight of us left, two healthy and six wounded.

An ominous silence fell over Cape Mogilnyy. We continued to move away from it, but the Germans doggedly pursued us. We could hear their chilling shouts and curses. Then we slipped into a ravine. The jaegers decided not to follow us. Skirting the ravine, they ran toward the sea so they could spend the remainder of the night combing the shoreline. They realized that we were exhausted, practically unarmed, and could not get too far away.

I was in the lead. Behind me, Babikov was carrying the quietly groaning Shelavin on his shoulders. He was heavy, so I slowed the pace. Shelavin had finally stopped asking to be left behind. Barinov, Kashtanov, Kurnosenko, and Baryshev were walking right behind Babikov, ready to replace him when he became tired. Only Semyon Agafonov, who was lightly wounded in the left arm, fell behind; he was bringing up the group's rear. Semyon stuck an unsheathed dagger in his belt and was holding a cocked pistol in his right hand. Its magazine held our entire ammunition supply, three rounds.

The jaegers were scouring the area. The night sky over our heads was constantly illuminated by the flicker of their flares.

Snow began to fall. That was good. It would conceal our tracks on the tundra and rocks as we hurried toward the shore.

We came out of the ravine, climbed down the steep slope, and crawled into some shoreline bushes. It was midnight. The snow covered the bushes with a white cap, concealing two clumps of live bodies. We lay immobile, keeping each other warm. Only then did we realize what the effort of the just completed battle had cost us. We grew cold, but no one moved a muscle. The first hour passed, then a second. Oh, how long those autumn polar nights were!

"What should we do now? What should we do?" Pavel Baryshev whispered, but he knew that no one would answer him. Everyone understood that we had to wait for a cutter.

Toward morning it became even colder, and Baryshev developed a cramp. He was lying still with doubled-up arms and legs and, almost joking, compared himself to the Hunchback of Notre Dame. Babikov began to massage and rub him. Baryshev was in great pain and bit his lips until they bled.

"Cry, but don't cry out," Makar cautioned him. "Just don't cry out. The Germans are nearby."

Pavel's pain eased somewhat. He could raise his hand to brush away a tear. "I didn't want to become a cripple," he explained.

Several times the file of jaegers passed near our bushes, and we lay perfectly still, clenching the handles of our knives, ready to battle to the death.

If thirst and hunger were tormenting Babikov and me, then what must it have been like for the wounded! One hope, which I couldn't stop remembering, kept us going.

"The night is long. The cutters are still coming. And if they don't come, Babikov and I will drag some logs over. I saw three logs not far from here." I invented that, but at the same time I believed that I could find those three logs. "We'll tie them together and swim to our side of the bay."

Finally, dawn began to break. Someone was mumbling incoherently. Kashtanov was probably delirious.

"Cutter! There's a cutter in the bay—a cutter is coming."

It wasn't delirium. Not only Kashtanov and I but everyone could now make out the contour of a small subchaser in the white fog.

I signaled with a flashlight. The cutter came closer.

"There he is!" Baryshev cried out, losing his self-control and forgetting about the jaegers.

Unexpectedly, the cutter turned about and went out to sea. We froze with fear.

"They probably decided that it was jaegers signaling. And they think we're dead," Kashtanov interrupted.

"How could the jaegers know our signals?" Baryshev responded.

"Ask *them*!" Kashtanov angrily replied, casting an unhappy glance at the departing cutter. "Now they won't pick us up."

Only Makar Babikov said anything encouraging. "They'll pick us up! Count on it; we'll soon be back at the base. They went after a second cutter. They'll be back again by evening."

Hope of rescue was reignited, and I was extremely grateful to Makar.

It later became clear that two other scouts, Warrant Officer Nikandrov and Seaman Panov, had been hiding on the shore not far from us. Cut off from the main group, they had been unable to reach us on the cape. At night, like us, Nikandrov and Panov had moved toward the bay and hidden themselves in bushes to wait for the cutters. But Nikandrov didn't have a flashlight. When he saw the cutter, he emptied the powder from several cartridges and set it afire. Our signals had been received and understood, but when the commander of the cutter saw the unusual flames, he feared a trap and returned to base for a second cutter.

It was almost dark when two cutters entered the bay. One laid a smoke screen, and the other, commanded by our old acquaintance Boris Lyakh, today a Hero of the Soviet Union, turned and began to move toward the shore.[11]

To dispel any doubts among the crew of the cutter, I shined the flashlight on my comrades.

On board the cutter they didn't even wait for the gangplank to be lowered. Someone jumped into the water, and we heard the familiar deep voice of our commissar, Dubrovskiy. "Brothers! Agafonov! Baryshev! Leonov! And who is this? Ah, the rookie."

Up to their waists in water, the cutter crewmen carried us in their arms, then handed us over to their comrades. At that moment I remembered the face of Pavel Baryshev—covered with grime, with dirt stains, which he smeared all the more when he wiped his tears. "They're ours! They're ours!" Pavel sobbed.

Later, warmed by ample portions of alcohol, we slept the sleep of the dead. I dreamed about Yuriy Mikheev. He was holding a large bundle of grenades above his bare, curly-haired head and singing a song, transposed to a new tune by Ulenkov, about a proud assault group that did not surrender to the enemy and did not ask for mercy.

With characteristic attention to detail, Commissar Dubrovskiy dissected the lessons of the battle just completed at the debriefing. After the critique, I went to Dubrovskiy and mentioned that the scouts were condemning Zhdanov though they understood what drove him to commit suicide. "As far as Kiselev goes, that was unfortunate," I acknowledged. "Kiselev later fought bravely and died during the hand-to-hand combat. I had called him a coward, in anger, of course! But, believe me, at the time I couldn't do anything else. And now I'm somewhat ashamed."

I wanted Dubrovskiy to understand that it was necessary

at that dangerous moment to prevent any possibility of panic among the men. But, perhaps, the survivors—who had still not completely comprehended the events on Mogilnyy—worried me. It was difficult for me to explain and justify my behavior. I especially did not want the commissar to think that I was vindicating myself. If I was guilty of something, let him tell me. Let him hold me accountable! One way or another, that would end the doubts that were troubling me.

Vasiliy Mikhaylovich Dubrovskiy understood my condition. "Besides," he said, "when the rear admiral delivered a speech about the battle on Mogilnyy, he reminded all of us officers about the sense of responsibility a commander has for his subordinates. The rear admiral didn't use your name, but believe it, Viktor"—for the first time the commissar called me by my first name—"he had you in mind. In a similar sense. In the final calculation."

Then Vasiliy Mikhaylovich sat down beside me and talked with me in a confiding tone. "What, in the end, is the main thing in the combat life of an officer? It is that he answers with his head for the fate of the people entrusted to him. This is an honored trust, a very large responsibility. It is especially important to you now, Viktor, to remember this. Why? Soon you will find out. In war there are deaths. The officer who thinks only about how to preserve the lives of his soldiers or sailors is not a good officer. We don't need guardians for our fighting men. But the senseless, meaningless death of a soldier always remains on the conscience of a commander."

I was all ears. The commissar looked intently at me, to be sure that I was understanding him, and then continued. "Take Makar Babikov. A young scout, a rookie. But what a soldier! No, you say to me, why did Babikov crawl to Kashutin, voluntarily risking his life? He wanted to distinguish himself? He is not a stupid lad, he understands that this is not the way to distinguish oneself. Makar was aware of your friendship with the senior petty officer and was afraid that in the heat of the moment you would rush to

Kashutin yourself. Babikov was protecting your life. And he overcame his fear and crawled to Kashutin himself. That is the sacred sense of comradeship! But Zhdanov, and then Kiselev, fought differently. At that most frightening moment they became frightened for themselves. Only for themselves! They were thinking about what would happen if they had fallen into the hands of the jaegers. And you are the commander! You are responsible for everyone, for the entire battle. While a soldier lives, he fights. And when he fights, then, perhaps, he will be victorious! By this standard we commanders and, yes, all scouts, evaluate our conduct."

That evening the scouts gathered in the mess hall, where behind a table covered with a red tablecloth sat the senior officers of the fleet. The command "Stand up! Attention!" rang out, and in solemn silence we heard the order bestowing posthumous awards on our comrade scouts.

Then they began to call up to the table those present.

"Petty Officer Second Class Agafonov, Semyon Mikhaylovich!"

"Petty Officer First Class Babikov, Makar Andreevich!"

Makar approached the member of the Military Council, received a decoration from him, and wanted to say something. But, perhaps overwhelmed by a combination of joy and embarrassment, Makar was silent. For some reason I recalled my first battle. Babikov's first battle was a more serious test.

"Petty Officer Second Class Baryshev, Pavel Sergeevich!"

Perhaps Baryshev would give a speech? He never wanted for words. Baryshev held the Order of the Red Banner[12] in his hands for a long time, waiting for something, then resolutely turned toward the rear admiral and declared: "I serve the Soviet Union."

Barinov, Kashtanov, and Kurnosenko received decorations. They called me up last. Dubrovskiy accompanied me to the table with a significant glance. Even the rear admiral, shaking my hand, quietly said: "Say something, Leonov, it's needed now."

I looked at my friends, and I saw among them those with whom I had shared the grief and the joy of the recent events. What should I say to them?

"We won a tough battle. We destroyed a strongpoint on Mogilnyy and killed many of the enemy. They are congratulating us here now as though it was our birthday. But we left our comrades there, on Mogilnyy. And there were among them the bravest men in the detachment."

I named Florinskiy and Abramov. I wanted to talk about Kashutin, my best friend, and about Mikheev's feat, and about Ryzhechkin.

"Well, here is how it turned out, comrades! There was among us a scout nicknamed Ryzhik, small, ordinary looking. And who would have thought that he would be so steady in an unequal fight with the jaegers? But Ryzhechkin alone covered our flank and fought until his heart stopped. While his finger was pulling the trigger! Hitler paid for the death of Ryzhechkin, for our little Ryzhik, with the bodies of many of his jaegers. We buried him there, on Mogilnyy, and continued to fight."

Now it was appropriate to talk about Mikheev, but it suddenly became difficult, almost impossible to speak. But I couldn't cut short my remarks. I tried to think about someone else, and in my mind I saw Ryzhechkin, just the way he appeared to us in the last minute of his life. He was very calm when he bequeathed to us the duty to fight on to the final victory. He had also asked to be washed before his death, perhaps so that we could understand that there was nothing terrible in his death there, on Mogilnyy. "Here I am, senior sailor scout Ryzhechkin. I did my duty, fulfilled my sailor's debt to the degree that I was able. And you, brothers, good-bye, and fight on to the final victory."

"Comrades!" My voice grew firm; I had found a way to conclude the speech. "We will remember, comrades, the words from that song which Lenin loved to sing. We were still children, some of us were not yet born, but Lenin already was saying these words. And let them now sound out for us, as an order of our dead friends, as a response to our party, our Motherland: 'Do not cry over the bodies of fallen warriors—carry their banner forward!' "

An outstanding peculiarity of every scout was his ability to maintain his composure in any situation. But, I must confess, I lost it that evening when the rear admiral, in the presence of the senior intelligence officers, said, "They have petitioned me about promoting you to the rank of junior lieutenant. After a number of battles, and especially after the raid on Mogilnyy, I am convinced that you can serve at this rank. Comrade Leonov, you are now an officer!"[13]

The member of the Military Council looked at me, the officers of the intelligence section looked at me, ready to accept me into their family. Would I be able to justify their belief in me?

For a Soviet soldier there is an answer that contains the whole essence of his existence. And I said the same thing that an hour ago had come up out of the depths of the soul of Pavel Baryshev.

"I serve the Soviet Union!"

6

Black Devils

REAR ADMIRAL NIKOLAEV said to us officers of the intelligence section, "A great ship is made for a great voyage, and experienced scouts should be used for long-range reconnaissance." After a short pause, he added, "It's not so far off, but we must check out the coast of the Norwegian Varanger Peninsula."

Dubrovskiy was assigned to another unit, and in my new position as *zampolit* of the detachment, I had to get to know the young scouts who had recently arrived.[1]

First, I remember, arrived the electrician's mate from the base, slender gray-eyed Petty Officer Second Class Pavel Kolosov. Pavel was twenty-one years old. He received his tenth-grade education in Leningrad. His father died there in the difficult days of the blockade. Pavel's brother and other close relatives died fighting at the front in the Leningrad area, and neighbors had evacuated his sick mother to Siberia.

I looked at this young sailor and thought about how he would have a better chance of seeing his mother if he remained at the base as an electrician's mate. Then another thought came to my mind. There had been a whole family of Kolosovs, a large working family of Leningraders. And now, in the third year of the war, this widow and mother had remaining of her sons only this bright-eyed, stately lad. He had voluntarily chosen the path of a scout, full of danger and deprivation. Perhaps the romantic stories of our adventures had attracted him? Perhaps he saw only the heroic side of the life of a scout? *Krasnoflotets* and other front newspapers wrote about them.

"Have you heard anything about the battles on Mogilnyy, Kolosov?" I asked, then regretted it. Why ask a rookie such a question? But Pavel Kolosov, perhaps suspecting what I was thinking, spoke quickly and convincingly.

"Even before your raid on Mogilnyy I had submitted several requests to the rear admiral for assignment to reconnaissance. I wrote another one after Mogilnyy. I have my second-class sports rating. My father and my brother are dead, and I very much want to be a scout. You watch—I'll be a good scout!"

I was looking for the words to encourage Kolosov to think seriously about his decision but could not find them.

"We assign rookies to Petty Officer Manin's squad. Remember, Kolosov, Manin has a seventh-grade education, and that's stretching it. On the other hand, he is a great master in certain aspects of reconnaissance. He is strict and demanding, and if you break the rules, we will kick you out of the detachment. A detachment reject can envy someone who was simply drafted for shore duty. I know of a few men in this situation. If we (I sharply emphasized the word 'we') throw someone out of the detachment, it means that he is an idiot, a liar, or a coward!"

It was ironic. The more sternly I spoke, the brighter his face became. Happiness filled the eyes of this young sailor when he learned that his fate had been decided—he had been accepted into the detachment.

Mikhail Kalaganskiy, a pal of Kolosov, dropped by the office. Pavel was slow to leave and looked at me with the cryptic smile of someone who wants to say something but can't get it out. But the fixed glance that Pavel gave me, clearer than any words, said, "This is Kalaganskiy, Misha Kalaganskiy himself!"

Dear Pasha, you worried for nothing! We know your friend, he is a fully suitable comrade for us. And not, as you may think, Pasha, because Kalaganskiy went up against our detachment athlete Ivan Lysenko on the wrestling mat in the officers' club. Not because Kalaganskiy, while still at the institute, left the first-year course, where he was considered a championship wrestler, and went voluntarily to the front. The base command had recommended Komsomolist Kalaganskiy. His references indicated that his knowledge of all weapons and, especially important for us, of radio communications, was outstanding. We needed radio operatiors like Kalaganskiy.

Finally, Pavel left. I remained with the broad-shouldered, slightly stooping senior sailor. Smooth black hair framed a face with a large forehead and long, eaglelike nose. His answers to questions were short, precise, and completely clear. Kalaganskiy was said to be a good poet, and he played the accordion. He appeared sullen and reserved. A bit of time would pass, and the achievements and deficiencies of this rookie would be known in the friendly family of sailor-scouts. In the meantime, we placed him in the care of our experienced radio operator—scout Petty Officer First Class Dmitriy Kazhaev.

Andrey Pshenichnykh arrived in the detachment from an air defense unit. I knew Pshenichnykh as an experienced skier but I never imagined that he would request assignment to reconnaissance. Andrey had been demobilized into the reserves a short time before the war, had settled down in Murmansk, married, and had four children. When I was at the detachment ski base, Pshenichnykh often dropped in and helped me train the scouts.[2] Pshenichnykh's family had been evacuated to their relatives in Voronezh oblast, an area that was now occupied by the enemy.[3] The newspapers wrote about the brutality of the Germans, and Andrey was worried about the fate of his family.

"Here I am, I finally got into reconnaissance," he said, intently looking at me with his black, somewhat slanting eyes. "Now I can fight!"

Later, two gunners arrived in the detachment from one of the coastal artillery batteries: two Viktors—Sobolev and

Karpov. With them was a young, handsome sailor, Volodya Fatkin. All were athletes with a middle education and a burning desire to serve in our detachment.

We placed great emphasis on the physical training of future scouts. Among us were fleet skiing champion Tikhonov, wrestling champion Lysenko, and swimming champion Maksimov, "our Max," as the scouts called him.

One of the newcomers who arrived in the detachment said, "I was confused when I got here. Are the naval scouts based here? I thought that I had come upon some kind of sports school."

During the hours of physical training our detachment area indeed reminded one of a sports school.[4] In one corner they were melting ski wax, in another they were demonstrating how to disarm an armed opponent, and in a third they were busy with *sambo* or boxing.[5] The scouts loved to watch Semyon Agafonov and Pavel Baryshev step into an improvised ring. They were almost the same height and of equal weight. Slender, adroit, and quick, Baryshev had earlier studied in the Leningrad *tekhnikum* of physical training, and at one time was flyweight champion among the youth.[6] And here, pulling on the gloves, coming to meet him, was former cook Semyon Agafonov. Semyon was sluggish but stubborn and almost impervious to the opponent's blows.

Semyon used to tease Pavel with lines like, "Hey, flyweight, watch out! I'm going to make a fly out of you."

Baryshev would get angry but give no sign of it. He'd land a whole combination of rapid punches on Agafonov and then slip away from Semyon's frontal attacks. Baryshev would really begin to light up when the onlookers shouted, "You're strong, Pashka! Thrash this bear from Onega![7] Sting, fly!"

Everyone cheered for Baryshev, fearing that he would miss and fall under the heavy, hammerlike fists of Semyon Agafonov.

It was especially noisy and animated around the heaving gangplank, which we nicknamed the naval scout's ladder.[8]

The rookie was supposed to run from one end of the bucking ladder to the other in full combat gear. "Hold on to the air or you'll drown!" the onlookers would shout to the newcomer, who was desperately balancing on the gangway. When he fell off, to everyone's delight, he stood in a formation of the "wet." We competed by squads. The squad with the fewest "wet" was the winner.

The newcomers were told, "Naval scouts fight tough battles. Polar cold, storms, Arctic snowstorms and blizzards, steep cliffs—nothing can stop them! If you want to be in the detachment, harden yourself, become strong and clever."[9]

When the program for individual training was finished, group exercises in tactics and other disciplines began. We rejoiced in the outstanding successes of the young scouts, and I listened as Agafonov said something to Manin, the commander of the newcomers: "I don't know, Sasha, how these youngsters will show themselves in battle, but right now it would be hard for me to compete with them in theory. Sketching and topography, photography and astronomy—they know it all, down to the last detail! They can handle the Dippers, Big and Little, without any trouble.[10] Professors! Wherever you want to go, Vologda or Onega! No, Sasha, I'm not joking when I ask you, how do you command them?"

"By regulation!" Manin answered quietly and convincingly.

A new era soon began in our combat life—sorties to the Norwegian peninsula.

The detachment's veterans were glad. They had become bored with plowing the nearby waters, or, as they say, "messing around in Motovskiy Bay." Passing on their experience to the young, the veterans understood that even for them, experienced, combat-tested pathfinders, old lessons and habits were not enough for the accomplishment of new missions. They had to train also.

Yes, we knew how to operate in the enemy's rear area;

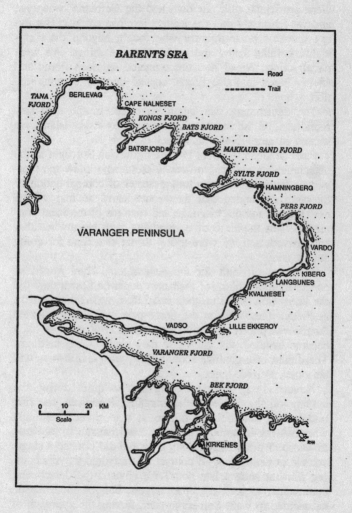

BARENTS SEA

——— Road
------- Trail

TANA FJORD

BERLEVAG

CAPE NALNESET

KONOS FJORD

BATS FJORD

BATSFJORD

MAKKAUR SAND FJORD

SYLTE FJORD

HAMNINGBERG

PERS FJORD

VARDO

VARANGER PENINSULA

KIBERG

LANGBUNES

KVALNESET

VADSO

LILLE EKKEROY

VARANGER FJORD

BEK FJORD

0 10 20 KM
Scale

KIRKENES

RHH

we had mastered the enemy's strong and weak points; we were proficient with our own and the Germans' weapons; and we fearlessly met the jaegers in close combat. But every scout of polar infantry who fought beyond the sixty-eighth parallel knew and could do these things. We were naval scouts! Naval horizons attracted us, deep fjords and enemy bases in those fjords, coastal lines of communication.

The detachment was again relocated. In the new surroundings, on the shores of a bay on Solovetskiy Island, we trained in amphibious landings.[11]

Fleet headquarters sent Pavel Grigorevich Sutyagin to the detachment, a cultured officer, a scout who knew the Norwegian language and the future theater of combat actions.[12] Sutyagin demanded that the scouts learn the map of the new theater and the language and customs of the local population. But the time of dark nights with stormy weather had arrived, and we were trying to use that time for going out to sea.

It was difficult for the newcomers. They rowed so poorly that the splash of their oars could be heard; they did not know how to tie up their boat; they rattled the oarlocks as though they were at the home port dock; they oriented themselves poorly on unfamiliar terrain. But most of all, I became irritated with the noise they made during landings. The dream of a genuine scout always was, and always will be, quiet. Perfect quiet.

Nevertheless, despite having perfect quiet during the landing on the shore of the Varanger Peninsula, the first raid turned out to be a failure. It was already midnight when we lay in ambush near the road that ran from Vardø to Vadsø. We lay there a long time and did not see a single vehicle or pedestrian. Of course, where would they be coming from at such a late hour? We advised the detachment commander to look for other targets, but for some reason he decided to wait. Sometime later, fearing the approach of dawn, he ordered us back to the cutters.

It was embarrassing to look the cutter crews in the eye,

these men who with such difficulty had delivered us to the shore. They were expecting us to come back to the boat with booty.

On the return voyage the sea ran high, drenching those who stood on the deck. A cold, gusty wind covered our clothing with an icy crust. But the men didn't notice this in their distress and confusion over the failure.

They greeted us at the base with more than a little unhappiness. The chief of the intelligence section of fleet staff, Captain Second Rank Vizgin, called in the detachment commander, me, and Sutyagin. We were hardly gallant in our appearance. But the bottom really fell out when Vizgin rendered us "honors." Barely concealing his irritation, he read us some lines from the monologue of Tsar Saltan, which we knew so well from our childhood:[13] "Oh, gentlemen guests, did you travel far? Where did you go? In harmony with the sea, or in discord?"

The "gentlemen guests" were silent.

"Badly!" Vizgin angrily interjected, then he ordered Sutyagin and me to leave.

I don't know what Vizgin said to the detachment commander, but he soon received another assignment, and we parted company with him without regrets. The veterans in the detachment fondly remembered the names of the officers who brought them up well, trained and hardened them. We often recounted to the younger scouts the names of Dobrotin, Lebedev, and Inzartsev. Their deeds served as an example for us.

They summoned me to the headquarters and said: "Do it again! Admiral of the Fleet Golovko has ordered it. You have been given command of the operation. Your mission is the same. You have three days to prepare. Go over all the details with Sutyagin and report."

I was already preparing to leave, but a question delayed me: "Leonov, do you think that our scouts have forgotten how to take a tongue?"

* * *

What would you do in my place, Dobrotin, Lebedev, or Inzartsev? They were nowhere around, but I mentally put the question to them. They were my best advisers in those crucial hours as I worked out the new and—for me first—independent operation.

Stun the enemy with surprise and daring! Plunge him into panic! Operate like Suvorov, like Ushakov![14] Do that which the enemy considers to be impossible! This was what Major Dobrotin—who could combine prudence with a clever imagination—would say to me.

"You don't have to fear the jaegers, let them fear us!" Lebedev said to us in the first, most difficult days of the war. Let those sons of bitches worry about their own skins, even in the far rear.

"Don't hurry!" Inzartsev warned. "You're not catching fleas, you're hunting for tongues. The main thing is to reach the objective. That is already half the battle."

Sutyagin and I crouched over the map, where the line that traced the path of the cutters on the first unsuccessful raid on Varanger showed a sharp curve. Why did the cutters take such a roundabout path? Could it have been because of the lighthouse?

Sutyagin described the situation. "Yes, there is a lighthouse here on the island Lille Ekkeroy. It's right next to the coast. We lost a great deal of time avoiding it. The lighthouse is small. But why does it interest you, Viktor?"

"A direct path—"

"In war the straightest is not always the shortest. Remember your geometry, my friend."

"Listen, Pavel Grigorevich, what if we first called on the lighthouse operator?"

"I understand!" A spark glimmered in Sutyagin's eyes. "The tongue in the lighthouse could help us capture other tongues. And what if . . ."

And so we discussed it. Sometimes we got carried away and then, when we stopped to consider various aspects, slowed down to think about each separate detail. Then we discussed the plan of the operation again, to which the fleet commander finally gave his short but welcome approval.[15]

On the first night I landed with six scouts on the shore of the island Lille Ekkeroy. We captured the lighthouse operator and delivered him to the shore, where the cutter was waiting. On the way back to base, Sutyagin interrogated him and, turning to the map, said, "The garrison is quartered on Cape Langbunes. The highway from Vardø to Vadsø runs here, not far from the cape. The lighthouse operator says that traffic on the road is halted at eleven o'clock at night. So it was clear why we lay in ambush the entire night and didn't see a single vehicle or pedestrian!"

Two days later, three groups of scouts—approximately half of the detachment—set out to sea in time to reach the Varanger Peninsula by the onset of darkness.

Aleksandr Osipovich Shabalin, eventually Twice Hero of the Soviet Union, commanded the cutter.[16] He had deposited us on enemy-occupied shores many times and returned to pick us up. He was not very tall, surprisingly cool-headed, and unusually intelligent. A glance from him served to calm us in the most crucial moments of a landing. His presence on the cutter invigorated the scouts. And now, having learned of my plan, Shabalin talked as if it would be a routine run. "Good! I know this coastline. Cliffs. We won't tie up. Order your men to inflate their boats, and I will wait for you near the shore."

We prepared for the landing and lowered our boats to the water. The waves swept over them, but with enormous efforts the drenched oarsmen maintained their balance.

When we came up on shore, I checked the men and was going to give instructions to each group. But Agafonov ran up to me, yelling, "Vehicles are approaching! They can be seen above."

We climbed the hill and saw a column of vehicles. The dotted line of lights was getting nearer. The vehicles were still far off, but I knew that the road passed our location at a point about two kilometers away.

"Move out! We'll intercept the vehicles!"

The deep snow pulled at our feet, and we had to run through drifts and over hills. Along the way I gave orders for setting up the ambush. I warned everyone that scout Barinov would be the first to open fire.

The vehicles were still coming toward us when we positioned ourselves along the sides of the road. All around us it was so quiet that we could hear the rhythmic pulsing of the truck motors. One covered truck passed by, then another, and a third. How many had passed Nikandrov's group? Perhaps the lead vehicle had not yet reached Barinov's position.

Babikov whispered, "Why is Barinov quiet? Perhaps we should initiate the ambush?"

I shook my head disapprovingly. "No, Makar, let's not hurry it! The column is still moving, the road goes up a hill. Hold steady! Barinov will do his job."

A powerful explosion convincingly established that Barinov's group was on the alert. Immediately after the first, still more explosions rocked the road at regular intervals and submachine guns cut loose. And then we began to witness a totally unexpected scene. The entire column stopped, all the lights were turned out, and the jaegers jumped down out of their cabs and from their cars and began to look up in the sky. They were convinced that they were under air attack.

We captured two dumbfounded Germans without firing a single shot, and I ordered them taken to the cutter.

A runner from Barinov reported that his group had blown up the first two vehicles and captured a prisoner. At this time Nikandrov's group was engaged in a fierce exchange of fire with the tail of the column, and we hurried to help him. The jaegers were lying under their vehicles and firing, but several grenades quieted them.

Having taken the documents from the staff car (the convoy, it later became clear, belonged to an antiaircraft regiment and was en route to an airfield), we departed to the cutters to get away from the Varanger Peninsula before the enemy could determine what had happened.

The cutter crewmen greeted us excitedly. Only Aleksandr Osipovich was his usual quiet self and, suggesting that I check my watch, said: "Exactly two hours from the moment of landing. Never have we so quickly returned from an operation. This is a happy war!"

On the way back to base, when the danger was left behind, laughter, joking, and a lively exchange of impressions were heard everywhere.

The lighthouse on the island Lille Ekkeroy sent out its signal as before and finally disappeared.[17]

It was a great stroke of luck for the detachment, but we needed a boost that would inspire us to believe in the success of these deep raids.

In the winter of 1943–44 we conducted several voyages to the northern shores of Norway, of which two were the most notable—to Cape Kalnes and into Batsfjord.

In December 1943 (by then I had been confirmed as detachment commander), Shabalin delivered us to the area of a new objective—Cape Kalnes. The cutter passed close to the shore, and we saw the water splashing at the base of the ice-covered cliff. It would be difficult to land there, but also comparatively safe because there were no guardposts.

I coordinated with Shabalin on the signals and about the planned pickup point after the mission and then jumped straight from the deck of the cutter to the first carved-out foothold.

Above me, cutting footholds in the ice, the scouts slowly climbed the mountain. We assaulted this cliff for more than an hour, and when we reached the top, we were confronted with a gaping ravine, which we would lose precious time in bypassing. Volodya Fatkin tied a rope around himself, gave the other end to Lysenko, and went over the edge.

"There is a lot of snow. Dive in!" Fatkin yelled up to us.

The ravine was six meters deep. We jumped and were buried up to our heads in fluffy snow. Then we crawled up again, once more climbed a steep hill, and rolled head over heels down its icy slope. Finally, we saw a road, near which stood a hut guarded by two men. Not far from the house six pairs of skis were standing in the snow.

Barinov and Manin quietly took out the German guards, and I established a listening post and said to Agafonov, "Today is Christmas. Semyon, you love to drop in on people. Wouldn't they be happy to have guests like us in this Norwegian home? Let's find out."

"It's possible." Agafonov moved toward the house, with us close behind.

Opening the first, outside door, Semyon knocked with his fist on the other, felt-covered door, which led into the room. No one answered.

We listened. On the other side of the door we could hear a discordant choir of voices, and someone was hysterically shouting or singing.

"Aha?!" Agafonov squatted in surprise. "They are inviting us in. On my word of honor, they are inviting us in! They are angry that we are late for Christmas supper."

"Do it, Semyon!"

Agafonov flew at the door with his shoulder, and it fell in with a groan.

Cloaked in a cloud of steam, we stumbled into the house. It was bright, cozy, and warm in the large, well-furnished room. At the serving table, waving bottles, bawled a contingent of drunk jaegers. In the corner stood a well-decorated Christmas tree, shimmering with colored lights. Next to it stood a tall, weary old Norwegian, perhaps the master of the house.

We were dressed in white camouflage smocks and covered from head to toe with snow. We did not in the least resemble those whom the master of the house had in mind. Then he cried: *"Syrtye d'yavolye!"*

What the hell! These words stunned the guests like a hammer blow. Three dropped their bottles and raised their hands. Three others began to cower, perhaps intending to jump under the table, but pointed submachine guns brought them to their senses.

"Hands up! Hands up! Come on, jaegers, lie down on

the floor one at a time!" Agafonov commanded. "Tie them up, Fatkin."

We disarmed the Germans and tied their hands with a single rope. The master of the house, who up to this time had not displayed any timidity, invited us to the table.

But what about the magical two words the old man had uttered upon our appearance? Why did the cry of the master of the house cause the jaegers to raise their hands even before our command?

Syrtye d'yavolye means "black devils" in Norwegian. It seems that the inhabitants of Varanger Peninsula first learned about the black devil sailors after the battle on Mogilnyy. One of the wounded jaegers, recovering in a hospital on the Varanger Peninsula, told a nurse about the group of Soviet sailors that had infiltrated Cape Mogilnyy and was encircled there in a double ring. The jaegers were convinced that they would kill the sailors or take them captive. But the enemy fought for an entire day and, when night came, disappeared. They dissolved into the darkness without a trace.

Sometime later the column on the Vardø-Vadsø road was destroyed, and the Germans couldn't figure out who had done it. The Norwegians themselves began to spread the rumor that the group of Russian *syrtye d'yavolye* who had disappeared from Cape Mogilnyy had done it. These rumors frightened and irritated the jaegers.

We couldn't stay here long, but the master of the house decided to refute the opinion that northern Norwegians were quiet, reserved people and began to talk about things that were very interesting to the scouts.

Had we heard about the legendary Larsen, the uncatchable Larsen, leader of a detachment of the Norwegian resistance movement? How could it be that on our side of the front we did not know about the famous Larsen from Varanger Peninsula? No, the old man himself, of course, did not know Larsen—he had not yet had the privilege. But any Norwegian could tell us how even on a stormy night Larsen would set sail in his boat and go to sea. He was armed only with a submachine gun, a pistol, and grenades. The Germans were unable to catch him and did not know where the men of his detachment were located. Larsen knew every path in the mountains and every brook that flowed down to the fjords. The Germans said that he was acting in concert with the Russians, and therefore they called him too a black devil. Thus, the Russians should not be offended by these words. Wherever there was a fisherman's house—and on the Varanger coast everyone was a fisherman—they would find friends of Larsen, friends of this *syrtye d'yavolye*.

"Then, perhaps, a friend of Larsen would help a *syrtye d'yavolye* make it to the sea, to a nearby pier?"

The old man looked intently at me, paused for a bit, and shouted loudly in Norwegian. From the next room came a middle-aged man, just as tall and long-faced as the old man.

"This is my son and my guest. He has been hiding in the cellar. He will guide you."

We noted the hatred with which the prisoners looked at the master of the house and especially his guest. The old man glanced at his son with alarm, but the son said absolutely nothing.

"Don't worry!" I said to the old man. "If anything should happen to us on the way down to the sea, these tongues"—I pointed at the prisoners—"will never say a word."

"I believe you. Drop my son off at the bend of Cape Kalnes. His friend lives there."

We offered the old man chocolate, canned rations, and biscuits, but he flatly refused to take anything. On the way toward the pier he said, "When I return home, I will turn my house upside down. I will spare nothing, even if it was gained through long, hard effort. I will tell the Germans that black devils appeared unexpectedly at my house in the night and destroyed my house. I wish you good luck!"

* * *

Shabalin's cutter was plying the waters near Cape Kalnes and immediately noticed our signal. Aleksandr Osipovich confessed that finally he had become worried over our long absence. The greater was the joy of our meeting.

The six German Air Force officers who, it turned out, had been in Kirkenes that very evening, walked that night to Kalnes, sobered up in the hold of our cutter, and in the morning were greeted at our base. We soon learned that we had delivered very valuable, genuine transpolar tongues to headquarters. They gave exhaustive information about the enemy dispositions and, incidentally, told us about a battle one of our submarines had participated in, in the throat of Batsfjord.

But the information of the tongues had to be checked and verified. And we began to prepare for a new, even more crucial mission.

In the northern part of Varanger Peninsula there is a small fjord, Makkaur-sand [bank or shoal].

If we could manage to sneak into that fjord, land on the shore, and go straight north, to the end of the cape, then we would come out in the rear of the enemy battery guarding the entrance to the large bay of Batsfjord.

What was in Batsfjord?

Up to this time no one knew. There was some reason to think that enemy torpedo cutters were based there. The throat of Batsfjord resembled the jaws of a beast. The eyes of the beast were its lighthouses, its teeth were the guns on the cape. That is why, just then, only the small bay of Makkaur-sand attracted us.

We departed on 22 February [1944], Sunday night. The next day our army, air force, and navy would celebrate the twenty-sixth anniversary of the Soviet Armed Forces. Shabalin and I, the cutter crewmen and the scouts, wanted to make the Motherland happy for a while with combat successes on the eve of the holiday.

But we didn't succeed in approaching Makkaur-sand fjord. The lights of the observation posts, from which they challenged us with light signals, began to blink, and

Shabalin put the cutter on a course to the northeast. We moved more to sea, changed direction, and, slicing through the waves, the cutter came to a totally unfamiliar Norwegian shore.

The scouts were resting in the cabin. Shabalin and I were up in the wheelhouse, intently peering into the darkness of the polar night. Finally, an icy crust frozen along the shore loomed dimly white, the features of an ice-covered granite cliff could be distinguished, and suddenly two lights flashed—the cape light markers.

We were approaching the throat of Batsfjord.

Shabalin gave the command to muffle the motor, ordered "ahead slow," and looked toward me.

I nodded. We understood each other without a word.

The cutter slipped noiselessly into the fjord.

Immediately the boat's rolling and pitching stopped, and the wind calmed. It was quiet all around us, and in this watchful silence the shore observation posts challenged us with light signals two times.

We didn't answer.

But the batteries on the capes of Batsfjord remained quiet behind us.

Did the scouts resting down in the crew's quarters know where we were? Perhaps, by the movement of the cutter, they had guessed that we had penetrated into the jaws of the beast, and some were worried about the outcome of this raid.

"Everything is in order," Shabalin said calmly. "The shore observation posts have determined that this is one of their cutters returning from a mission. It passed through without noticing their signals. How could it be any different? Would a Soviet cutter dare to enter into Batsfjord, to certain death? They have reasoned it this way, and this, Viktor, is our advantage. Now we will take care of your business. Work quietly, and we will leave quietly. And if a commotion with firing begins, you must realize that the jaws will close."

I shook Shabalin's hand and quickly went down into the cabin.

We were landed on a deserted shore.

Ivan Lysenko and two other sailors went out on reconnaissance, while the remaining scouts moved into the rocks and camouflaged themselves. We were worried about the cutter crewmen—it was more difficult for them to camouflage.

A short time passed, and Lysenko came back leading a Norwegian fisherman from the nearest village. He confirmed that the village Batsfjord was a kilometer away and that two German sailors from a cutter crew were staying in a house on the outskirts, the approach to which Lysenko had already managed to inspect. The fisherman had seen the sailors that evening when they were returning from a mission.

I divided the detachment into two groups: a capture force and a covering force. My assistant, Lieutenant Kokorin, remained with the second group.

The scouts of Warrant Officer Nikandrov went on ahead toward the village.

"Don't make any noise!" I warned them. "Use your weapons only in the most extreme situation."

We contacted Shabalin. He approved our plan and quietly moved toward the settlement, holding the cutter almost up against the rocky shore of the fjord.

Although there was some noise, none of it could be blamed on the scouts. Nikandrov's group dragged the tongues out of the house with their hands tied. They stumbled around and dug their feet into the dirt, but they couldn't cry out because of gags in their mouths. When they saw the rest of us, the tongues grew quiet, stopped resisting, and moved out.

We were climbing down toward the shore between two cliffs when we suddenly heard someone singing below. There was no other way down, and it was senseless to climb back up. All we could do was wait for the approach of the singers.

We froze in place, pressed up against the cliffs, prepared to open fire at the first alarm. The choirlike song was drawn out and grew louder. It was being sung by young voices. Finally, we saw some Norwegians, young men and a girl, perhaps returning from a party.

The Norwegians saw us when they got right up to us. They stopped, raggedly broke off their singing, and then were silent. Slowing their steps, they passed by, looking at each of us. We were dressed in white camouflage smocks. Our submachine guns were hung around our necks with cheesecloth, grenades concealed in white pouches. There were only two among us dressed in black—the captive German sailors.

This eerie scene lasted two or three minutes.

I waited for the Norwegians to move off before we continued our movement. But the last person in the group, a tall young man, stopped not far from us, turned around, raised a clenched fist, and said something loudly. From his tone we understood that he was greeting us. And then, as if in answer to him, the song sprang up again, but this time not stately as before, but boldly, like a march.

It was a song of the resistance movement.

We heard this song more than once some eight months later, when the liberation campaign began in Norway. They sang it at meetings and assemblies. I remember only the last lines of the refrain:

> Free thoughts
> Quisling does not trace.
> We are going down to the blue fjords.

Blue fjords! In the light of the polar sun the Norwegians, perhaps, saw them as blue, deep, and soft. But to us on night reconnaissance they were as black as could be.

The song died away in the mountains.

We climbed down to the shore, and soon the cutter cast off to the north, slicing through the black surface of Batsfjord. The shore posts signaled us again. Again we didn't answer. Instead, we burst out into the open sea at full speed.

Behind us in Batsfjord, the battle alarm might already have been sounding. But even if the observation posts on the capes had opened fire, we would not have heard it in the furious whistling of the wind that engulfed the cutter as soon as it cleared the fjord. The sea crashed over us and soon the sides and deck were iced over, and we had to break off the ice because it was slowing us down.

It took a long time to reach our base, and just before dawn we continued with all hands on deck.

That's the way we greeted the twenty-sixth anniversary of the Soviet Army.

After delivering our tongues, we got some well-deserved time off. But no one wanted to leave the barracks. Shabalin and I went to the officers' holiday banquet. The master of ceremonies at the head table, the toastmaster, raised the first toast for us scouts and our combat companions, the cutter crewmen. "When the submarine crews sink an enemy ship, we present them with a roasted pig. This has become a tradition. It would be appropriate to feast the naval scouts with roasted tongue. But the *syrtye d'yavolye* have dragged in so many tongues that the quartermasters are complaining—'We can't handle it! Exchange tongues for another dish!' "

The *syrtye d'yavolye* conducted raids on the shores of Norway until the onset of spring 1944.

We did not have any losses on these Norwegian voyages, which spoke for the growing proficiency of the naval scouts. After each raid, the cutters returned to the base with more passengers than were on board when they departed. The admiral of the fleet congratulated us on our combat achievements, emphasizing three factors that ensured the successes: secrecy, surprise, and daring.

The detachment received a short rest, immediately following which it was to begin intensive preparation for new, even more serious operations.

The summer of 1944 came. Far to the south our ground forces were clearing the Ukraine and Belorussia of the enemy and crossed into Romania and Poland. We knew that the smashing blow against the northern group of German forces would soon follow. The inhabitants of northern Norway greeted the first Soviet naval scouts as heralds of their impending liberation from Nazi tyranny.

There remained considerable time before the end of the period of twenty-four hours of daylight, so they granted me leave for a trip to Zaraysk, to my home and relatives, whom I had not seen for more than five years.

At my departure I handed command over to Lieutenant Kokorin. They told me at the political section that soon they would assign a new deputy commander for political affairs to the detachment.

[Leonov's subsequent writings tell a somewhat different story of the 1944 raids into the Varanger Peninsula. There were, in fact, personnel losses. On the late February mission described above, one of Leonov's squad leaders was left behind enemy lines.[18] When the torpedo boats reached the landing site, Leonov and his men moved from the first boat to the shore in small boats without difficulty. The support group and communications cell on the other torpedo boat, however, did not organize themselves properly for a rapid landing. As a result, one of the assault team leaders was left on the shoreline with the radio operators while the main force was executing the raid on the nearby small German garrison. The stranded team leader moved forward alone, seeking to rejoin his unit. The main force completed the mission, called the boats forward to pick them up, and the entire force departed the area. The team leader was lost, not only because he had sought to catch up to his men but also because his absence was not reported before departure from the area.

Occasionally, a raiding force was not able to reach the objective area because of action at sea en route. In one such occurrence, when Shabalin—with two patrol torpedo boats—was delivering Leonov's detachment to the Varanger Peninsula, they came upon a well-escorted German convoy.[19] In the ensuing sea battle, one of Leonov's men was killed. Although the Germans lost two ships to Soviet torpedoes, the reconnaissance mission was scrubbed and Shabalin returned Leonov's men to the forward base at Pummanki in Sredniy Peninsula.

In another similar incident, the detachment was returning from a successful raid on the Varanger Peninsula when it encountered a German convoy.[20] The smoke-generating apparatus on the deck of one of the patrol torpedo boats was struck by a shell, setting it afire and threatening the safety of the boat. Two nearby scouts, risking their lives, were able to tear the apparatus away from its mountings and push it overboard. One of the men later died as a result of burns, and the other had to be transferred to the Black Sea Fleet, away from the cold northern climate. These few examples, the first two from Leonov's second book and the third from Babikov, paint a somewhat less glowing portrait of the Varanger Peninsula sorties.]

7

Before the Decisive Blow

IVAN GUZNENKOV, tall and lean, in a knee-length, gray infantryman's coat, with a soldier's rucksack on his back, walked toward the detachment headquarters and in the doorway was confronted by Petty Officer First Class Ivan Polyakov. It would have been better if Polyakov had not been on duty on that day.

"Where do you think you're going, soldier?" The petty officer blocked Guznenkov's way. "Were you thrown off course? Can't you see who is stationed here?"

"Get out of the way!" Guznenkov commanded sharply and clicked his heels slightly. "What is your last name?"

Polyakov gave the lanky infantryman a puzzled look, but he could not determine if he was dealing with an officer or a private. The shoulder boards on the stranger's short coat were covered by the broad straps of the rucksack.

"My last name?" Polyakov expectantly asked just in case. "And why, soldier, do you [tebye] need to know my last name?"[1]

"Don't use the familiar form with me, Petty Officer. Report in accordance with regulations!"

"Really? No, this is even very interesting."

Ivan Polyakov was already concerned that he might get into trouble with the strange infantryman. But Polyakov was pulling unscheduled duty and was ready to vent his anger on anyone. He was bored, so, disregarding common sense, he continued to posture.[2] In mock salute, he deliberately and carelessly touched two fingers to the sailor's hat sitting flat on his head, but at the same time with his thumb adroitly moved the hat to his right ear, in the process raising his forelock. Rocking on his heels, Polyakov began defiantly to move his broad shoulders, obviously trying to draw the stranger's attention to his faded, pale blue collar, in the opening of which could barely be seen the blue and white stripes of his undershirt.[3]

Polyakov never surmised that the infantryman standing before him in low-topped canvas boots, with a rucksack on his back, had served in the fleet as long as any scout in the detachment. Polyakov's worn sailor's collar reminded Guznenkov of the pranks and naive tricks of those years when he himself was a *salazhonka*, as experienced sailors used to call a youngster in the navy.[4]

But Polyakov continued to show off. Placing his hands behind his back, he threw out his chest, where a polished combat decoration brilliantly glittered,[5] and through his teeth said, "What exactly is your business?"

But Guznenkov was not listening.

"Report to your commander that the detachment's *zampolit* has arrived! As you were!" he commanded the instantly transformed Polyakov, who was preparing to dart away to carry out the command. "You haven't given your name. You did not repeat the order."

The dumbstruck Polyakov only then remembered that a new *zampolit* was supposed to report. He stood before Guznenkov at attention and for a long time blinked his eyes until the gift of speech returned.

"I—Comrade, I did not know your rank. Our commander is not here, he is on leave. Lieutenant Kokorin is standing in for him. Petty Officer First Class Polyakov reports," he finished very smartly.

"First class? M-m-mm."

Guznenkov went in, and Polyakov followed behind him,

anxiously shaking his head and straightening his belt and cap on the way.

In the orderly room, yet another petty officer first class hunched over a typewriter at the desk. He was small, with light, reddish hair. An Order of the Red Star was pinned to his fatigue shirt.[6]

"Babikov, attention!" Polyakov barked from the doorway. Crossing the threshold right behind Guznenkov, Polyakov, now closely following regulation, turned toward Guznenkov. "Comrade *zampolit*, permit me to call Lieutenant Kokorin!"

Guznenkov looked searchingly at Polyakov to see if he was still showing off or if he was trying to atone for his negligence. "Go."

Guznenkov pulled the rucksack from his shoulders, looked around the orderly room, then moved toward Babikov, who was still standing quietly at attention, and extended his hand. "Let's get acquainted. Lieutenant Guznenkov. Please, sit down, go back to your work."

"I've finished it."

"Then let's talk," Guznenkov said, sitting. Babikov also sat down. "Did you receive the Order of the Red Star for Mogilnyy?"

"Yes, sir!" Babikov jumped to his feet again.

"Sit down, please." Guznenkov smiled softly. He liked Babikov's conduct. "I heard about the battles on Mogilnyy, and I know you demonstrated exemplary courage. By the way, was *partorg* Tarashnin wounded there?"[7]

"During the attack. Tarashnin was not on the cape itself. Commissar Dubrovskiy was with us. Lightly wounded himself, he dragged our *partorg* out from under the jaegers' fires and carried him in his arms to the sea."

"Is that so?" answered Guznenkov, noting to himself that Babikov apparently incidentally recalled the former detachment commissar, fleet officer Dubrovskiy. "Tell me, Babikov, what do they write from Ust-Tsylma? Didn't you work as a schoolteacher there before you were drafted?"

"Yes, sir!" Babikov was so surprised that his whitish

eyebrows arched upward. "I was a teacher. But permit me to ask, Comrade Lieutenant, how did you know that?"

Guznenkov smiled. "Petty Officer, I am supposed to know a lot of things. It's my job."

The depth of the new *zampolit*'s knowledge of the detachment's affairs astonished not only them but also my stand-in, Lieutenant Kokorin, the detachment's senior petty officer Chekmachev, the *partorg*, and the *komsorg*.[8] Before he was ordered to report to the detachment, Guznenkov became acquainted with the personnel and the combat records of the scouts and with the history of the detachment. In the intelligence and political sections of the Northern Fleet staff, he received exhaustive information about the good and the bad in the detachment and to what aspects of our life he should give his attention. The member of the fleet Military Council talked at length with Guznenkov.[9]

"You are in for some interesting but far from easy work," the rear admiral warned Guznenkov. "You will meet people in the detachment whose heads are spinning because of their awards and the enthusiastic praise they have received. And some scouts love to emphasize their exclusivity, their special position in the fleet. And though it is indeed special, does that exempt them from the discipline required of everyone else? The fleet commander was complaining to me, 'The scouts are spoiled. It's a well-known fact that some of them are cutthroats!' This cannot be permitted to dilute the detachment's good reputation. The scouts are not cutthroats. Do I make myself clear?"

"The mission is clear, Comrade Rear Admiral!"

"The mission is clear, but you have to accomplish it with brains. Whatever else we may say, the people there are a little different. And combat life does leave a definite imprint on people. I confess that even I have a weakness for the scouts. These famous combat veterans! But old fame loves new. Now, as never before, the combat readiness of the naval scouts of the Northern Fleet must be strengthened. Important missions await them."

Saying farewell, the rear admiral said to Guznenkov,

"Your authority will determine the success of your work. You must win your authority from the scouts, not only by word, and not so much by word as with deeds! Always keep this in mind. Begin with the usual shared experiences. Tell them where you have served and fought, in what raids in the enemy rear you have participated yourself. Scouts are a shrewd people. They will understand why headquarters sent naval infantry officer Guznenkov to them. Comrade Lieutenant, I wish you success!"

After the brief skirmish with Polyakov, Lieutenant Guznenkov recalled his conversation with the rear admiral and these parting words.

Even before the mission to Cape Mogilnyy, experienced pathfinders like Motovilin, Losev, and Kharabrin left the detachment, and immediately after the raid on Mogilnyy, Radyshevtsev went. Kharabrin went to an officers' course and never returned. Motovilin was sent to another unit. Losev took advantage of the continuing recruitment of cutter crewmen in the North for combat duty in the South and submitted a request for transfer to one of the crews.

All the veteran scouts assembled for Losev's farewell. For such an occasion the petty officer had a fit of generosity and advanced the necessary norm of wine for the farewell from his emergency supply.

As always during such partings, the celebration got noisy. Interrupting each other with stories, the men recalled battles and raids they had endured and scouts, living and dead. Looking around at the departees, I also recalled how the three Nikolays and Aleksey had come into the workshop where Sasha Senchuk and I were working in the first days of the war. I remembered how Motovilin taught us—scouts still unchristened by fire—the ABCs of military affairs.

"Up to this day I have not been able to forget Sasha Senchuk," I said to Radyshevtsev.

"And Ryabov and Damanov?" Radyshevtsev turned and shouted to Losev. "Losev! Koyla Losev! Do you remember your namesakes?"

Losev hung his head, then shook it, as if he were trying to drive out some unhappy thought. He came out from behind the table, took the guitar down off the wall, and raised his hand, demanding everyone's attention.

"Do I remember my namesakes?" he asked Radyshevtsev. "Well, listen, Aleksey! Everyone listen."

Slowly strumming the strings, Losev played a familiar tune. But he suddenly began singing a song that we had never heard before about himself and about his friends.

> There once lived and served three friends,
>   Sing the song, sing!
> Ryabov, Damanov, and Losev,
>   They are as thick as thieves.

The singer was clearly at odds with the rhyme and rhythm. But he wasn't embarrassed. He told an unsophisticated and true story.

> They called them all Nikolays
>   Sing the song, sing!
> The first died in the first battle,
>   And a year later—the other.

Nikolay Losev's face showed his pain. It was as if only now did he sense the grief of old losses and the impending farewell of his comrades. Everyone wanted him to stop, but no one tried to interrupt him.

> The third is saying farewell to you, friends.

"Stop, Kolya!" Stepan Motovilin cried, and then grabbed the guitar from Losev's hands. "The guys will go into battle soon. They are seeing you off to bigger and better things, and you—?"

"I just don't want anyone to forget our friendship, Stepan. Am I right?"

"You're right!" Radyshevtsev replied.

The merriment continued.

They accompanied Losev down to the dock. After taking him aboard, the motor launch left for Murmansk. Suddenly subdued, we returned to our barracks, where Radyshevtsev said, "Soon you'll be saying good-bye to me too. I'm a torpedoman and haven't forgotten my specialty."

"Alyosha, this came up suddenly. What's gotten into you?"

But Radyshevtsev didn't want to dwell on this theme. "I've lost my heart for it. And without the desire, how can I serve in reconnaissance?"

Several days later we accompanied Radyshevtsev to the dock, and soon yet another incident alarmed the scouts: Chernyaev, a sharp, clever sailor, was caught selling watches from the detachment's trophy property at the secondhand market.[10]

I learned about Chernyaev's crime before the first mission to the Varanger Peninsula. Although Cherenyaev was already prepared to go out, I reluctantly punished him with something much more onerous than extra duty or the taking away of a pass into the city. The scouts considered it equivalent to transfer to shore duty.

"Senior Sailor Chernyaev!" I called in front of the formation when the group of scouts was prepared to go down to the piers, where the cutter awaited us.

Chernyaev stepped forward.

"For misappropriation of trophy property, I deprive you of the right to participate in the operation. Give the chief petty officer your rucksack, weapon, and ammunition."

We went on the operation, and Chernyaev, knowing that his crime would not go without further punishment, began to complain to the scouts remaining behind about his fate, saying that they were picking on their "brother" over nothing. He got some sympathy from scouts such as Polyakov and Byzov.

"Well, I sold the watches; the hell with them!" Chernyaev grumbled. "Well, I was a little drunk! Don't we risk our lives, brothers? We walk within a hair's breadth of death. Can't we live it up a little when we're in base?"

"The charge is stupid, of course!" Byzov agreed with him. "What kind of life do we have? Like in that aria: 'Today you, and tomorrow I.' "

That dashing lad Polyakov slapped Chernyaev on the shoulder. "Don't cry, Chernyavka! You look like an eagle! And what are we, scouts-eagles? A day of work, two days off! That's the way it is, that's the way it will always be!"

Many considered this conversation to be idle chatter and didn't rebuke the "eagles." Soon we would pay a great price for this.

On pass in the city, Byzov, Polyakov, and Chernyaev drank something to get their courage up, and not far from the officers' club they started a fight with some civilians. Someone called the military police. At that time another group of scouts was approaching the officers' club. Seeing the tall Lysenko among them, Byzov broke away from the grasp of the patrol and shouted, "Vanya, come help!"

Without understanding what was going on, Lysenko rushed to the aid of Byzov and also ended up being detained by the military police.

No one felt sorry for the carousing *troika*—they had sufficiently compromised themselves.[11] But we were upset for Lysenko, who had accidentally become involved in the incident. The scouts even intended to plead collectively for him before the command, but after some argument, Lysenko persuaded them he could speak for himself.

I called in the guilty scouts. The three "friends" confessed with one voice, alluded to their past combat achievements, and promised to reform. Lysenko did not repent. Looking me straight in the eye, he said, "In a fit of anger I did not stop to figure out what was going on. If I had known that our well-known trio had stirred up trouble, then it would be another matter. But I'm a sailor and should help out another sailor whenever I can. But they, the drunk devils. . . . I realized this by the time we got to the military police station. After a beating with fists they did not give up. This is all I am guilty of."

I listened to Lysenko's somewhat incoherent speech and understood his situation.

"You have nothing more to say? About yourself? About your comrades?"

"It's all been said. And several comrades think that I should leave the detachment. That's wrong."

Like everybody else, I very much wanted Lysenko to remain in the detachment. I thought about how the rear admiral would assess the scouts' misconduct. I was supposed to give him a report that evening.

"You have a heavy hand, Lysenko!" I looked at the scout's enormous fists and tried to sound stern. "You're supposed to hammer on German skulls with those fists, but you . . . lost control of your temper, you say? A scout is not supposed to lose control. Get out!"

Two days later an order of the member of the Military Council arrived concerning the expulsion of undisciplined scouts from the detachment. Lysenko was not on the list, but he did receive a stern punishment.

Having become acquainted with the personnel of the detachment, Guznenkov reminded Lysenko of his recent misconduct, and the scout was surprised by this.

"Besides, Lysenko, keep in mind that your experienced *zampolit*—now the detachment commander—interceded for you."

"I will never forget, Comrade Lieutenant!" Lysenko answered.

Guznenkov's authority grew remarkably after the scouts learned that he had been among the heroic defenders of Hanko and was with the last naval infantry detachment to leave that peninsula.[12] And once, when there was talk about battles in the enemy rear area, Guznenkov named one point on the peak Musta-Tunturi,[13] and it was clear that he had climbed the peak, had captured some tongues there, was

Viktor Leonov, twice Hero of the Soviet Union.

Viktor Leonov in 1940.

Major L. V. Dobrotin, Northern Fleet headquarters intelligence staff, ground reconnaissance chief.

Senior Lieutenant Georgiy Lebedev, killed by a sniper's bullet in the fall of 1941.

Stepan Motovilin, Northern Fleet detachment, along with Vasiliy Kashutin an early mentor of Viktor Leonov.

Vasiliy Kashutin, Northern Fleet detachment, killed on Cape Mogilnyy in September 1942.

Anatoliy Barinov, Northern Fleet detachment, killed at Cape Krestovyy in October 1944.

Ivan Guznenkov, Leonov's deputy commander for political affairs in the Northern Fleet and Pacific Fleet detachments.

Ivan Lysenko, Northern Fleet wrestling champion, killed at Cape Krestovyy in October 1944.

May 1942. Not waiting for a second gangplank to be put out, the scouts jump into the water.

August 1945. Seisin port. After the battle. V. Leonov is sitting in the foreground (arm on knee), and seated to his right is Colonel Denisin.

Hero of the Soviet Union Semyon Agafonov, former cook on a submarine, scout in the Northern Fleet detachment and assistant platoon leader in the Pacific Fleet detachment.

Warrant Officer Aleksandr Nikandrov, platoon leader in the Pacific Fleet detachment who was awarded Hero of the Soviet Union for the Seisin operation.

Makar Babikov, awarded Hero of the Soviet Union for his actions as platoon leader during the Seisin operation.

P. Kolosov, veteran of both Northern Fleet and Pacific Fleet detachments.

Colonel A. Denisin (l.), of the intelligence section of Pacific Fleet headquarters, and Senior Lieutenant Viktor Leonov (r.), in the summer of 1945.

V. Sobolev, I. Reznik, N. Mal'tsev (l. to r.). Sobolev came to the Northern Fleet detachment from a coast artillery battery. Mal'tsev was wounded at Cape Krestovyy in October 1944, and when the detachment went to the Pacific Fleet he became the boot repairman in the headquarters section.

Twice Hero of the Soviet Union, Aleksandr Shabalin was a patrol torpedo boat commander in the Northern Fleet who frequently inserted or extracted Leonov's men during raids on the Varanger Peninsula.

Detachment Petty Officer Grigoriy Chekmachev (both Northern and Pacific fleets), shown here in a postwar photograph.

V. Maksimov, who led the squad of photographers. He was seriously wounded in the Seisin landing.

K. Ermakov, a member of Makar Babikov's platoon, was wounded at Seisin. Here he carries a *PPSh* 7.62-mm. submachine gun.

V. Bratukhin, V. Korotkikh, and A. Zalevskiy (l. to r.), who went to the Amur River Flotilla reconnaissance detachment from the Northern Fleet in the spring of 1945.

Viktor Leonov, photographed in 1960.

subsequently a junior *politruk*, and then the *politruk* of a separate scout platoon in the naval infantry brigade.[14] The detachment's scouts were convinced that they had been sent a seasoned officer who had been in numerous scrapes.

Training exercises began anew. The new *zampolit* completed the marches with full kit just like one of the junior scouts. Everyone else rested on the breaks, but Guznenkov stayed on his feet and passed among the scouts, engaging in conversation and helping distribute the combat newspaper. Even Semyon Agafonov, a tireless marcher, was surprised. "We White Sea coast hunters are used to roaming about in tundra and rocks, but we can't keep up with the lieutenant. Is he from the White Sea area?" But it turned out that Guznenkov was born and grew up around Smolensk, in Belorussia, far to the south.

The detachment began tactical exercises, topography, and mine and demolitions training. Here the new *zampolit* showed himself to be an experienced commander. The men also began to compete in rock climbing and *sambo* fighting, areas in which the *zampolit* was knowledgeable. He was a crack shot and one time was called upon to direct the photography club. We also studied photography in our spare time.[15]

Some people in the detachment were unhappy with the new *zampolit*. Actually, not with him so much as with the standard operating procedures he began to impose. He became more strict about issuing passes to the city. The detachment's senior petty officer had to account for each ration issued, and he became accustomed to living with a reserve, just in case any dignitaries or guests showed up to visit the hospital scouts. Now every scout knew that any poorly made bunk or cigarette butts on the barracks floor could bring unpleasantness down upon him—the new *zampolit* would be sure of that.

I learned about these happenings from a letter the detachment sent me in Zaraysk. I approved of the new *zampolit*'s actions but at the same time was troubled by a groundless worry. Later I came to understand the feeling as something like jealousy toward someone who had come in and taken over in a detachment that had confidence in me and who was gaining respect and admiration from people who were dear to me. I scolded myself for this petty and mean feeling. Nevertheless, in spite of my good intentions, I greeted Guznenkov coldly and officially at the base dock, where he came to meet me upon my return.

Guznenkov obviously perceived the meeting quite differently. He asked me when I could receive him in my office and left.

We met again that same day in the detachment orderly room. I thought the conversation would begin with an accounting by Guznenkov of the detachment's activities for the month and what he, the new *zampolit*, had succeeded in accomplishing. Then, perhaps, I would have the chance to express my approval or disapproval of each item.

But as soon as Guznenko closed the door behind himself and our eyes met, he smiled like an old friend, sat opposite me, and by his countenance showed how happy he was that we were in this together.

"You've just arrived! And here I am," he forlornly threw up his hands, "running to and fro, inspecting and fussing over things. I haven't gotten down to business yet. I have some thoughts and ideas, but haven't yet put together a work plan."

"Why not?" I asked with some severity, naively thinking that his delay merited some reproach. Perhaps he had been meddling in unimportant areas, disregarding his immediate political tasks.

"I can work up a plan quickly. But of what value would it be?" Guznenko asked in reply. "We have a gallery of heroes in the Lenin Room. I need to know what the young scout should know about each of the detachment's heroes. And as to the discussions with the veterans—with whom and about what? We need your guidance and counsel. The communists and I decided to conduct an open party meeting on the theme 'The honor of the detachment is my honor.' Babikov suggested it, and the others supported it.

Several of the scouts had forgotten about the detachment's traditions. But shouldn't the discussion at the meeting cover other things as well? Am I right?"

I agreed with Guznenkov.

"Look, I put off the meeting until your arrival. It would have been easy for me to write in the plan: 'indoctrination in combat traditions.' I could have given a speech about this. In general and on the whole." He threw up his hands again. "But who needs this? The plan should support the upcoming combat mission. The plan should be based on people, on the key members. And what's more, I've gathered the general information. Now I am waiting for my commander to express himself."

And so it happened that instead of getting an official introduction and an accounting, between us there unfolded free and open conversation during which Guznenkov untied my tongue. I told him about the scouts who had died and who were the outstanding among them. Then we talked about future missions.

We parted after midnight. Lying down to sleep, I thought about how our digressions into the past had turned out to be useful to me. And Ivan Ivanovich—as I came to call Guznenkov at the end of our talks—would be a good comrade and combat companion in the heated engagements that would very soon begin on our sector of the front.

Everyone felt that the decisive battle was coming.

We scouts knew what was going on in the enemy camp. The jaegers were becoming nervous in expectation of our offensive. Special engineer units arrived in the North, in the sector of the German 20th Lapland Army. They busied themselves with improving the already formidable defenses. The Lapland Army's newspaper, *Wart im Norden* [*The Lookout in the North*], demanded that commanders of mountain units suppress any rumors about the Russian scouts, who allegedly, whenever they felt like it, could penetrate the front line. "Our lines are impenetrable," boasted *Wart im Norden*. "Nothing can slip through our lines alive!"

The enemy began more skillfully and cleverly to mine sectors of the coastline where a landing could be made—the mountain passes, depressions, and gullies. The jaegers now began to use signal flares on the approaches to their strongpoints. A scout had only to brush up against a camouflaged wire with a careless movement and the polar night was ablaze with many flares, which, even after they had fallen into the ground, emitted a red smoke. The mountain divisions' sappers constructed winter shelters in the granite cliffs of the shoreline. Strongpoints were now a multilayered system of permanent firing points, covered with steel-reinforced roofs and joined together by trenches.

But no fortifications could raise the fighting morale of the "heroes of Crete and Narvik."[16] They awaited the approaching fourth winter of the war with alarm, never contemplating that in the polar region the offensive would begin even before the freeze-up. Warning about a possible Soviet winter offensive and encouraging the jaegers, the command of one of the mountain divisions wrote in his order: "We will permit the Russians to hurl themselves against our fortified positions. When the enemy has spent his blood after unsuccessful attacks on our strongpoints, we will destroy him with a counterattack."[17]

The Lapland Army placed great faith in its strongpoints, among which the powerful position on Cape Krestovyy particularly stood out, which was armed with artillery pieces.

At this time we were relocated to Rybachiy Peninsula and had already selected a hill that in its contours resembled the strongpoint on Cape Krestovyy.[18] For about two weeks we "attacked" this hill at night, divided into three mutually coordinated groups commanded by me, Lieutenant Zmeev, and Lieutenant Guznenkov. In conditions that were as close as possible to combat, we taught the scouts *camouflage, observation, and reporting.* We trained the men *in hand-to-hand combat, in rock climbing, and in navigation by azimuth.* All exercises were conducted at night and included unannounced ambushes and checking each scout on patrol.

A short day, if one discounts the breaks, was spent in party political and mass cultural work, which, with the arrival of Guznenkov, had become specific and meaningful. Discussions were frequently held in the Lenin Room.[19] The veterans talked about past battles to enlighten the young. We brought in infantrymen, artillerymen, cutter crewmen, and pilots as guests for evening parties of combat friendship. Our dancers, singers, and musicians performed at these occasions. We also had a few dignitaries—a delegation of workers from Novosibirsk.[20]

On the eve of an open party meeting, at which the topic "The honor of the detachment is my honor" was finally discussed, we were ordered to prepare for a combat mission. After a brief report the experienced scouts talked about their faithfulness to traditions and the young about their burning desire to be deserving repositories and passers on of these traditions. I well remember the speech of Vladimir Fatkin. Turning to a letter he had received from home, Fatkin said, "We took an oath to the Motherland to fulfill our military duty. This is our sacred promise. Now listen to what my mother writes me from Spassk, Ryazan oblast."[21]

Dear Volodya, I give a great motherly greeting to your combat comrades, about whom you have told me much in your letters. Not long ago I received a photograph from the fleet command of a group of scouts who had displayed exemplary conduct in battle. I was very happy to see your face in this photograph. So, Volodya, you serve in reconnaissance? And you hid this from your mother! I will not hide it, my son, I am very worried for you and for your friends. You are all so young, so handsome, and happy! My little boys! There in the far North, let your heart not falter nor your hand weaken in those difficult moments. And dear son. . . .

"Well, the rest is personal. Thus, comrades, how could I not value the honor and combat reputation of our detachment after receiving such a letter!" Fatkin exclaimed.

Tarashnin informed us that sailors Smirnov and Ryabchinskiy had stated their desire to be accepted to membership in the party. Manin read the last names of some young scouts whom the Komsomol organization was recommending for acceptance into the party.

Ivan Lysenko, who never before had spoken at a party gathering, asked to be allowed to say a few words. He moved with his unsteady gait to the table of the presidium, turned his face toward the gathering, and appeared to be uncomfortable and embarrassed.

"I am a sailor who does not belong to the party," Lysenko began. "Not that I'm afraid to join the party—not out of shyness. But I have thought about it and still feel that I haven't prepared myself for such a big step. Once our commander and the detachment's communists stood up for me, and now here I am, among my friends—naval scouts. For this, comrade communists, I give great thanks. As for your confidence in me, perhaps the time will come when I'll ask our commanders, comrades Leonov and Guznenkov, for their recommendation to the party. And they will not refuse me."

At that point, an orderly arrived from headquarters. They were summoning me for a meeting with Major General Dubovtsev.[22]

I knew why they were calling me. Not long ago Admiral Golovko had assigned the detachment a mission for which we had been preparing ever since. The admiral had notified me that the detachment of naval scouts with eighty men and a detachment of naval infantrymen would be subordinated to Major General Dubovtsev.

"Be prepared to deploy tonight," the general ordered. "I hope that soon we will meet here." The general pointed at a port in the enemy rear outlined in red pencil on the map. It was actually quite near, a bit more than ten kilometers from Pechenga. "We will meet, Leonov, if the detachment accomplishes the mission." The general pointed with his pencil at two lines, which marked the location of the jaegers' batteries on Cape Krestovyy. "These batteries are the most dangerous for our assault cutters. And they must be silenced so that they cannot interfere with the delivery of the amphibious assault to its target." The point of the general's pencil again was directed at the enemy port. "Here is the key to Pechenga! The cutter of your friend Shabalin will approach the port first. How many times has he landed you in the enemy rear and recovered you from hostile shores? Now you have to help him. Briefly and clearly explain the mission to your scouts. Tell them that they know about this assault in Moscow. Is your mission clear?"

"It is clear, Comrade General!"

"Good luck."

We knew about the various operations of many assault detachments of Soviet forces. Capturing enemy bases, continuously reconnoitering the enemy's deep defenses, destroying his communications and troops, Soviet raiders accomplished their difficult and dangerous work with honor. It must be noted in all of this that, when Hitler's army was conducting its offensive, the flanks of our ground fronts were not exposed to attacks from the sea. In the Far North, as is well-known, the front line had remained almost stationary.

By the fall of 1944, our detachment had accumulated much experience in combat operations on the shores of the Barents Sea. A basic core of scouts in the detachment had garnered and continuously improved upon this experience. The fleet headquarters knew of the detachment's capability to accomplish the most responsible tasks. And at the same time, everyone—from the commander to the seaman scout—considered that the assault on Cape Krestovyy many times exceeded all our previous raids in its complexity and difficulty.

The second week of October began. The forces of the Karelian *Front* went over to the offensive against the enemy's reinforced positions in the area of Lake Chapr.[23] Having broken through the enemy defense in the mountain passes of Great and Little Karikvayvish, having forced the Titovka River, and having seized Luostari, our forces reached the road to Pechenga and to the sea. By this time the first naval assaults had already been landed on the shore of Motovskiy Bay, and battles were raging on the northernmost sector of the ground front.

During the night of 9–10 October the naval infantry began the assault on Musta-Tunturi Mountain.

On that same night we were prepared for the raid in the enemy's deep rear, toward Cape Krestovyy, to the gateway of the port Liinakhamari.

Liinakhamari was the outpost of Pechenga, the Germans' main military base. Here there were large warehouses with armaments and provisions. And nickel was delivered there for transshipment to Germany. From there began the highways to the Norwegian port of Kirkenes and to the central region of Finland.

Liinakhamari port is located in the depth of Devkin drainage, on its right shore. To penetrate into the drainage, one must first cross part of Petsamo Bay. Petsamo-vuono is three to four miles long and was covered by shore batteries from the capes of the bay. The cutter crews nicknamed it the corridor of death.

The most powerful strongpoint, a jaeger bastion that guarded the far approaches to Liinakhamari, was located on rocky Cape Krestovyy. There, encased in permanent fortifications, bristled the barrels of two four-gun batteries—an 88-mm. antiaircraft and antiship battery and a 155-mm. heavy coastal battery.

It was decided to attack the batteries on Cape Krestovyy from the rear. To accomplish this, we had to cross thirty kilometers of enemy territory from the landing site. It lay across marshy swamp and tundra, across hills and almost vertical cliffs. We were ordered to traverse this route, take the jaegers' strongpoint on Cape Krestovyy by storm, capture the batteries, and destroy the enemy garrison if it refused to surrender.

Major General Dubovtsev introduced me to Captain Barchenko, the commander of the naval infantry detachment.[24] We received all our instructions, and when I returned to the detachment I found many of the scouts still in the Lenin Room. In anticipation of my return, they had not dismissed the meeting.

Everything had been prepared for the mission, and the meeting was brief. We argued with the senior petty officer concerning the rations. "Two cans of meat? Still another package of hardtack? No, Chief! It would be better if I took an extra drum for my submachine gun and an extra grenade than dehydrated milk."

In jackets and swamp boots, some men in special coveralls tucked into woolen stockings and in boots, heads covered with the waterproof cutter crewman's cap, the scouts formed up on the pier. Then the member of the Military Council arrived to see us off. I reported our readiness for embarkation to the rear admiral. He slowly walked around the scouts' formation, trying in the darkness to look at each one and shake each one's hand. His voice was solemn in the night stillness.

"I wish you a good journey, naval scouts! When you find yourself there on that shore," he turned his head toward the sea, "then you will hear the rumble of the cannonade. It has begun, friends! A great offensive is under way. And you know what business lies ahead. The Military Council hopes that you will raise even higher the combat reputation of the men of the Northern Fleet. I wish you a wind always at your back, dear comrades!"

We began to board the cutter commanded by Boris Lyakh, who had pulled us off of Cape Mogilnyy.

Barinov, Agafonov, Baryshev, and Babikov, scouts well-known to the cutter commander, filed past him.

"Oh, it will be a hot night for the jaegers on Krestovyy!" Lyakh said to me, rubbing his hands together.

The cutter pulled away from the pier, and the shore quickly disappeared in the darkness of the autumn night.

8

Face to Face

A NORTHWEST WIND drove powerful waves to meet the cutter. Storm clouds were gathering overhead. They covered the whole sky, further thickening the gloom of the polar night.

Far ahead the beams of searchlights appeared and disappeared, marking land, but we could not see the shore. Slicing through the waves, the cutter headed toward the darting searchlight beams and away from the barely audible cannonade.

A battle was being fought on land. The naval infantry were storming Musta-Tunturi, a mountain that should be far behind us by morning.

I tried to think about the upcoming march and battle and, considering the circumstances, the thoughts persistently creeping into my head were trivial. For some reason I was recalling the telegram Makar Babikov had sent his fiancée, Lyuba, that evening. The young girl worked in one of the fleet's rear area units. She met Makar by chance at the communications center—both of them had gone there on the way to the docks. The next two weeks none of the scouts received a pass, and when we returned from Rybachiy Peninsula, we immediately began to prepare for the raid. Makar, of course, missed his Lyubushka. At the telegraph window Makar showed me the accurately com-

pleted form with a single line—the prearranged code of
people who are in love: Wait for me!

"Wait for me." Two years ago we were the first readers
of the famous poem by that title, at the time still unpub-
lished. The poet Konstantin Simonov went with us on a
mission to Cape Pikshuev.[1] That time we avoided contact
with the jaegers, but we discovered a hidden cache of ammunition, destroyed it, and returned to the sea, to our cutter.
But several scouts well-known to the poet did not return to
the base from the following raid. We were troubled over
their fate, but believed they would come back, and so we
waited. Perhaps still under the impressions of the sortie to
Pikshuev, the poet also wrote the lines that became so pop-
ular among soldiers at the fronts. A piece of paper containing the lines was given to Major Dobrotin and then passed
from hand to hand. We recopied and memorized this poem
and sent it to our loved ones.

"Wait For Me"

Wait for me, and I'll return.
But you must really wait.
Wait, when the autumn rains bring melancholy.
Wait, when the snows blow,
Wait, when it is hot,
Wait, when others do not wait,
    having forgotten yesterday.
Wait, when from far-off places
    letters do not come.
Wait, when everyone else has grown tired
    of waiting with you.

Wait for me, and I'll return.
Do not wish those well
Who are convinced that it is time to forget.
Let my son and mother believe that
I no longer exist,
Let friends become tired of waiting.

They will sit by the fire
   and drink bitter wine
In memory of my soul ...
Wait. Do not hurry
   to drink with them.
Wait for me, and I'll return
   to spite death.
Let those who did not wait for me say:
"He was lucky."
They will not understand how
   amid the fire
You saved me by your waiting.
How I survived, only you and I will know,
—Simply you knew how to wait
   As no one else.

1941[2]

The wind grew stronger, savagely lashed our faces with sleet and salty spray, and howled threateningly. Gigantic daggers of light from the searchlights crisscrossed and impotently ripped at the curtain of the sky. The storm clouds came lower and lower and hung over our heads.

The rumble of battle was growing clearer.

Sailors ran along the cutter's deck. They picked up the gangplank. This meant that we soon would be leaving the deck. The cutter would depart. Lyakh's boat would not come for us because this time the assault force of naval scouts would walk from one seashore to another, from the bay to the cape, and not to return to base. After we seized Krestovyy, we would join in the general flow of the offensive. There would be new raids, terrible new battles. But through it all, as the poet wrote, wait for me! I will return, in spite of everyone else's death!

No, I had to think about something else! In the first place, about communications between the three groups, about observation and reporting. Did I act correctly, dividing the detachment into three groups? Guznenkov was a good comrade, but what would he be like leading a group in battle?

"We're coming to the shore," Lyakh said to me.

The shore was not visible in the pitch darkness. The cutter slowed, then stopped.

One after another, the scouts came up out of the cabin onto the deck. They looked suspiciously toward the shore and waited for the sailors to throw off long gangplanks made especially for the landing. We listened as the gangplank slapped the water. The cutter crewmen jumped down and picked up the end of it. Standing up to their waists in the freezing water, they provided us a dry path to the shore.

"Your men are good to us!" I said to Lyakh. "Thank them."

Lyakh held my hand in his longer than usual. The cutter commander knew where and why we were going. The day before he'd joked, "And why, Viktor, do they give you such happy march routes: Mogilnyy? Krestovyy?"

"Because from Lyakh's cutter you can take the devil by the horns!" I said.[3]

Now Boris Lyakh was silent; his long and firm handshake replaced the words that he wanted to say.

"Say hello to Shabalin for me," I said to Lyakh on parting. "Tell him that we'll meet him there."

"Of course, you'll meet him! I'm worried for you. Do you know what the words Viktor and Viktoriya stand for?"[4]

"No! You can tell me later. When we meet."

Satisfied with such an innocent lie and naive symbol (if there are grounds for a meeting, then a meeting *will* take place), I ran along the gangplank and jumped onto the slippery rocks of the shore.

The motor of the withdrawing cutter started up. I didn't turn around but hurried toward the scouts. They were setting up a defense just in case.

Judging by the time, Barchenko's detachment already had begun to negotiate the hills and rocks.

Our path to Cape Krestovyy was shorter and more difficult.[5]

At midnight we were scaling a steep hill.

Standing on Semyon Agafonov's shoulders and leaning against the cliff, the detachment *partorg*, Arkadiy Tarashnin, was cutting steps in the almost vertical granite wall. Others followed his example. With the aid of these steps and rope we made it to the top of the hill and saw new,

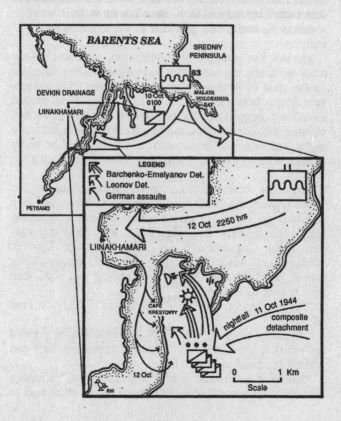

BARENTS SEA

SREDNIY PENINSULA

DEVKIN DRAINAGE

LIINAKHAMARI

10 Oct 0100

MALAYA VOLOKAVAYA BAY

PETSAMO

LEGEND
Barchenko-Emelyanov Det.
Leonov Det.
German assaults

12 Oct 2250 hrs

LIINAKHAMARI

CAPE KRESTOVYY

nightfall 11 Oct 1944

composite detachment

12 Oct

RHI

0 1 Km
Scale

even steeper mountains ahead. It was a difficult path to the "key to Liinakhamari!"[6]

The wind had subsided a bit, but sleet was falling.

We came into a valley, which led to the next checkpoint of the march route. Covered with a flat layer of snow, the valley was very dangerous. It might seem to the newcomers that it would be easier here. But Fatkin, the point man, raised his arm, and the file of scouts froze. Fatkin tied one end of the rope around himself, gave the other end to Andrey Pshenichnykh, then lay in the snow and crawled. He crawled slowly, feeling out each meter with his hands to detect any crevasses hidden under the snow.

Fatkin cleared a safe path for us on this mountain plateau.

The sky was getting a bit lighter when we scaled yet another peak, and the battle that had erupted during the night on the crest of Musta-Tunturi seemed closer.[7] The searchlight beams from the direction of Liiankhamari still probed the cliffs. I stopped and let the file of scouts move past me, walking with long strides, moving their legs with difficulty in the darkness. The men needed a rest. It would be better to sleep a bit so that we could move more safely during the day.

The snow continued to fall, covering our tracks.

We organized a break under a rock overhang, and in a half hour the figures of curled-up scouts were transformed into white mounds. Everyone fell asleep. Only my runner, Boris Guguev, and my radio operator, Dmitriy Kazhaev, kept watch. I closed my eyes and, already falling asleep, heard Kazhaev repeat headquarters call sign, then switch over to receive.

"Jupiter, Jupiter, how do you hear me? I hear you loud and clear."

I instantly tuned in. The radio operator, having pressed his palms to the headset, gave me an expressive look and nodded his head in affirmation.

"Jupiter, I understood you! I understood you," Kazhaev distinctly repeated. "Earth is nearby. Earth is right next to

me. Everything will be passed to him immediately. How do
you read me? Over."

The fleet commander was informing us that Mount
Musta-Tunturi was cleared of the enemy and that units of
the Karelian *Front* had reached the road to Petsamo from
the south. He ordered us to speed up our movement.

I ordered the men to get up. The snow mounds began to
move as they came to life. Guznenkov, Tarashnin, and
Manin, the group agitators, informed the scouts about the
successes of the attacking forces and about the upcoming
day's march. They encouraged the tired scouts.[8]

Once again, we were on the way.

It was getting dark when we saw the outline of Cape
Krestovyy ahead of us, a rocky, black cape hanging over
the sea. The jaegers had positioned their guns in a high location. From there they could see the bay of Petsamo-
vuono and the sea, and, if the weather was clear, our
Rybachiy Peninsula, on which they trained the barrels of
their guns. Tomorrow at this time our assault cutters would
begin their raid past Cape Krestovyy into Liinakhamari. But
there was still a night ahead of us, a long autumn polar
night.

When they saw the cape, the scouts picked up their pace.

We scaled down the last and steepest rocky face into the
rear of the firing positions of Cape Krestovyy.[9]

Night was falling, and we crawled closer but did not
climb up onto the rock-strewn plateau of the gun positions.
We divided into three groups to form a semicircle around
the first battery.[10] The second battery was below, at the very
edge of the water.

It was quiet all around. At times it seemed that there was
no one on Krestovyy, and if there were any batteries there,
the artillerymen, feeling safe in their rear, slept soundly.

We crawled noiselessly between large and small boulders, approaching closer and closer to the center of the
cape. Boris Guguev, crawling ahead, was wriggling across
the ground like a lizard.

Then suddenly, having touched a barbed wire point with

his hand, Guguev jerked back. But it was too late. One small bell jingled, and from various places others responded. The sound traveled around, and a series of colored flares arched up into the sky. Their blinding light pressed us to the ground. Straight ahead of us was a barbed-wire fence. On the other side of the wire a barrack, half-buried in the earth, could be seen. The figure of a sentry, who was guarding the entrance to the earthen barrack, loomed above the roof. We also spotted two guns with elevated barrels, which now were slowly being lowered in our direction, and a guard running from the barbed wire toward the barrack. All of this was twenty to forty meters from us.

The guard didn't make it to the guns—Guguev cut him down with a burst from his submachine gun. But the second guard managed to scamper into the revetment.

"Move out!" I commanded.

"Forward, Northern Fleet sailors!" Ivan Guznenkov echoed my call.

Barinov's platoon was the closest to the obstacle. Taking off his quilted jacket, Pavel Baryshev threw it onto the barbed wire and then crossed over it. Tall Guznenkov vaulted across the wire on the run, fell, crawled forward, and then opened fire on the barrack doors.

The scouts began to pull their jackets and ponchos off as they approached the wire. But Ivan Lysenko ran up to the iron stanchions on which the wire was hung, bent down, and with a powerful jerk hoisted the stanchion to his shoulders. He slowly raised himself up to his full height and, spreading his legs wide apart, shouted frantically: "Forward, brothers! Dive under!"

"Atta-boy, Lysenko!"

I charged through the breach that had been created in the fence.

Rushing past me, the scouts ran toward the barrack and cannons, toward the shelters and positions.

Semyon Agafonov climbed onto the roof of a dugout, near a cannon. Why did he do that? I pondered. Two officers rushed out from the dugout. Agafonov shot the first (later it was discovered that he was the battery commander) and knocked out the second with a buttstroke of his submachine gun. Jumping down, Agafonov caught up with Andrey Pshenichnykh, and they began to clear the path to the guns with grenades.

Agafonov and Pshenichnykh were still fighting in hand-to-hand combat with the gun crew, while Guznenkov and two scouts, Kolosov and Ryabchinskiy, were turning a cannon in the direction of Liinakhamari.

Jaegers were streaming out of the barrack to meet the scouts who were running toward them. They opened fire on our men from the run.

Wounded in the chest, Ivan Lysenko fell on his side but did not drop the stanchion. Scouts were still crawling under the wire, which Lysenko held up. When no one remained behind Lysenko, he began to sway and, breathing heavily, fell face forward on the ground, dropping the stanchion.

"Cover Guznenkov! Cut the jaegers' path from the barrack to the guns!" I ordered Barinov. I led a group of scouts to suppress two bunkers, from which machine guns were banging away. We blinded the machine gunners with aimed fire at the embrasures from submachine guns and rifles and closed in with short rushes to throw grenades.

Scouts from Barinov's squad were in heavy fighting with the jaegers, who were desperately seeking to reach their firing positions. Badly wounded, sailor Smirnov fell at the very door of the barrack. The detachment doctor, Lieutenant Luppov, crawled over to Smirnov and lifted him to his shoulder. A machine gun fired from the barrack window, and our doctor fell motionless with the dead sailor on his back.[11]

Fatkin and Sobolev, Kolosov and Kalaganskiy ran toward the barrack window and hurled grenades into the room. The machine gun fell silent amid the dying jaegers' cries and groans.

"Don't slow down!" Anatoliy Barinov shouted. He was getting up to lead the scouts in the seizure of the third cannon. But at that moment he saw a large group of jaegers, reinforcements from the gun crews of the second battery, going around toward our rear.[12]

"Watch out!" Volodya Fatkin shouted behind us.

I turned and saw Barinov's scouts dashing into the attack.

The Germans wavered and went to ground, but did not fall back, and opened heavy fire.

A runner came over from Babikov, who had replaced the wounded Barinov, and informed me that the jaegers were pressing in. I hurried over to help.

The Germans withdrew toward their battery, but platoon commander Barinov and Volodya Fatkin, the youngest scout in the detachment, were already dead. They died heroes' deaths. Kolosov and Kalaganskiy were wounded.

Having lost control of the battle, the enemy artillerymen were rushing from dugout to dugout, from shelter to shelter. There were many of them. Although the jaegers had suffered enormous losses, centers of resistance sprang up first in one place and then another.

"We've captured the second gun!" Zmeev's runner reported to me. "But the lieutenant is wounded. And Tarashnin is wounded in the hand. And also . . ."

"Well, speak!"

"Sasha Manin is dead. Our *komsorg*."

The firing died down. By dawn the last center of resistance was suppressed. The first battery on the crest of the hill was in our hands.

But difficult trials still lay ahead of us.

Guns and mortars were firing at us from the opposite shore—long-range artillery fired from Liinakhamari. We lay pressed to the ground, and fragments of rock and shells flew above us in a cloud of snow spray.

I ordered the men to remove the breech blocks from the cannons and crawl toward the nearest ridge, from which we could overwatch the destroyed battery.[13]

When the artillery barrage lifted and the air cleared over

from which the jaegers were already firing, trying to get a toehold on the hill. Bent over, hiding behind rocks, we crawled closer to the Germans. Still unable to see each other in the tight labyrinth of rocks and boulders, we clashed, face to face.[14]

An unusual battle flared up, rare for its intensity and suddenness. There were warlike cries and desperate howls, the chatter of submachine gun bursts, and the metallic clash of barrels. Scouts and jaegers darted between the rocks. There were buttstrokes and short-dagger thrusts. It was the kind of struggle in which fists, cold steel, and a rock picked up off the ground went into motion, as well as violent thrusts and grappling, kicks in the stomachs, and trips.

A few short meters separated the Germans from the edge of the steep hill they had climbed. We knew that other jaegers were climbing this same incline, step by step, foothold by foothold. Those who had made it to the top were awaiting help. They had nowhere to retreat to, and they fought with the savage fury of men who had only one chance—to hold on in the rocks at the edge of the hill.

But we pushed forward to the edge with even greater determination. Behind us were our wounded comrades. Still farther behind us, Babikov's group was fighting along the shoreline. Everyone would perish—the entire operation would collapse—if we did not throw the first group of jaegers that had clambered up the cliff into the abyss.

Andrey Pshenichnykh cleared himself a path quicker than the others. Thin, wiry, strong, and agile, he lunged, fell, disappeared, and then reappeared in another place. I saw Andrey quite near, hiding behind a large rock. On the other side of the rock two jaegers waited for him to appear. A short thrust forward, then a feinting movement, and one German collapsed, knocked down with a buttstroke. But in falling, he hacked at Andrey, who then sprawled on the slippery rock. Another jaeger immediately hurried toward him. I raised my submachine gun but fired the burst into the air because I saw Tarashnin and Guguev behind the German. With his uninjured right hand, Tarashnin swung his submachine gun. Grenades flew toward him. Tarashnin and Guguev dropped flat.

"Hold on, Andrey!" I shouted, rushing to help Pshenichnykh.

Two bayonets blocked my path. I dove to the side, and one bayonet, slicing toward my head, damaged my helmet.[15]

"Andrey, watch out! Hey—"

A tall jaeger was holding a rifle over the scout sprawled on the ground. I did not see how Andrey got out of harm's way, but I heard the clatter of the buttstock on the rock. Then the rifle was falling out of the German's hands, and he was bending over to pick it up. At that instant I jumped over the rock and knocked him out with a buttstroke of my submachine gun.

"Hey, behind you!" Pshenichnykh shouted.

I turned around and fired a burst from my submachine gun. The jaeger who had followed me did not get off a shot.

"How are the other men doing?" Andrey asked, getting up, and calmly glanced around.

We surged far forward.

"I'm here! Here I am!" little Pavel Baryshev cried, as he made his way toward us. But we couldn't see him behind the large rocks. Then Tarashnin and Guguev ran up, and Nikandrov showed up with his group.

We closed in on the enemy. With the edge of the cliff yawning behind them, they hurled themselves forward in a last counterattack. We beat it back. One more decisive rush forward and the surviving jaegers fell below with desperate cries.

Everyone was in awe of Andrey Pshenichnykh and was congratulating him. They were comparing Andrey with the best master of hand-to-hand combat, Semyon Agafonov, who was then in Babikov's group. But when nothing any longer threatened him, the hero of the battle trembled, looked at me with frightened eyes, and smiled guiltily. "How could I stumble like that? Ooh, they were evil! Death looked me in the eye, but the commander saved me. Honestly speaking, brother!"

"It's all right, Pshenichnykh, calm down! You fought remarkably well. It's easy to slip here."

We got ourselves back in order. Our losses were four lightly and two seriously wounded. We left guards at the edge of the cliff and hurried toward Guznenkov and Babikov. But even on the way toward them we heard increasing fire to the left and right of the hill that our scouts were defending.

While we were fighting near the edge of the cliff, the jaegers had managed to land two more small assault groups near the hill and were closing in on Babikov. They also forced us to go to ground and then to pull back.

Once again there were wounded behind us, and still farther. If the enemy held on to the shore and brought in reinforcements, then the same fate awaited us as those whom we not long ago had thrown into the abyss.

We pinned the landing force to the ground with dense fire and at the same time fired on the cutter that was approaching the shore. But several launches came out into the bay.

The situation worsened.

I thought about our ammunition supply with alarm. Not much remained. In the din of the battle I forgot about the radio message. But the howl of the red-starred *shturmoviks* over the cape reminded me of it.[16]

"They're ours!" Guguev cried, and he shook his uninjured arm. "Give us a hand, flyboys!"

Three Ilyushins made the first pass and began to dive on the cutter and the launches, which now were quickly leaving the bay. The pilots radioed us for orientation. We marked our positions with flares, then directed the aircraft onto the enemy positions. They dropped us ammunition and provisions by parachute. The first three aircraft circled over the cape, continuously raking the jaegers with fire, and prevented them from renewing the attack until another flight of *shturmoviks* arrived.

The pilots helped us hold on until darkness.

The enemy brought reinforcements in by boat at night. We beat off several attacks but nonetheless were forced to withdraw to a hill occupied by the naval infantrymen from Barchenko's detachment.[17] With an advance group, Barchenko himself had penetrated along the shore toward the second battery and pinned it down. We maintained communications with his group.

"Comrade Lieutenant, they are leaving!" I heard the voice of runner Kashtanov, who had clambered up the hill. "The Germans are dragging some kind of cargo along the shore toward the dock."

I led the detachment toward the sea. We caught up to the withdrawing jaegers and from the march fell upon the column, which was moving along the shore and was already close to the dock. The column was broken up, leaving boxes with cargo on the shore. Here too the jaegers counterattacked us. Short, savage fights again flared up. New groups of Germans hurried from the dock to the aid of the beleaguered column. Returning fire, we began to withdraw to our hill. But the jaegers were all around, stubbornly crawling upward, in spite of their losses. It seemed they had decided to finish us off.

I shouted that we had the strength: "Help will come soon! Hold on!"

"Hold on! Hold on! Hold on!" The words resounded along the crest of the hill.

Then searchlights came on in Liinakhamari and on the heights of the opposite shore of the bay. We saw jaegers quite near to us and threw our last grenades on the move. Illuminated by their own searchlights, the enemy pulled back. But the beams of the searchlights, picking the folds of the cliffs and the ridges of the mountains out of the darkness, concentrated toward the bay. I will never forget that moment—in the light beam was a stretch of bay along which small ships were moving quickly.

They were our assault cutters. One, a second, a third.[18]

They moved, maneuvering and firing from cannons and machine guns along the right shoreline of Devkin drainage.

Now they were approaching Cape Krestovyy. The cape was silent. Guns from Liinakhamari were firing randomly. There was a duel between the cannons on the right shoreline and the guns of the cutters. Cape Krestovyy was silent! The breechblocks of the first battery's guns were in our hands, and the gun crews of the second battery were defending themselves against the infantrymen of Captain Barchenko's detachment, which was besieging them.

"Ura!" Guznenkov stood up to his full height and greeted the cutters coming into the bay.

"U-rra-a!" The shouts rolled along the crest of the hill.

Not waiting for a command, the scouts dashed into battle. Even the wounded who could still walk and fire joined us.

Their morale broken, overcome by panic and fear, the jaegers wavered and, not able to withstand our charge, ran toward the sea. But they couldn't run far. By morning the battle was being fought along a narrow strip of shoreline. Only the most desperate Germans from the Krestovyy garrison were resisting. They did not surrender, even after they had exhausted their ammunition. At one point, Semyon Agafonov fought with two Germans. Having cut one down, he threw the other one into the water and shouted, "Give up, you son of a bitch! I'll kill you! Hands up! Well?"

The German threw his rifle down, raised his left hand, and squatted down. With his right hand he picked up a rock, waved it threateningly, and then fell, cut down by a short submarine-gun burst.

Agafonov went to the shore of the bay, squatted down, and rinsed his hands. "Well, it's done! It seems, everyone."

Guznenkov was now back at the first battery with his group. The scouts replaced the breech blocks in the weapons, loaded the guns, and fired a salvo into Liinakhamari port. We were not great marksmen, but we had plenty of shells, and we finally managed to set fire to a gasoline tank and a wooden warehouse near the dock.

Fires burned in Liinakhamari, where naval infantrymen landed from the cutters were moving into the town. Fighting was also going on along the eastern shore of the bay, from which the bypass of the port had begun. Only on Cape Krestovyy was it quiet. Then the second battery capitulated, and the prisoners were gathered in one place. Seventy defeated and disarmed jaegers sat, guarded by a single, lightly wounded scout.

Soon Shabalin's torpedo cutter came over to Cape Krestovyy.

"So here we meet," Aleksandr Osipovich said to me calmly. Only the gleam in his eyes betrayed his joy. "Thank you, brother! I was pressed close to the left shore, I put my trust in you. If the guns on Krestovyy had spoken, we'd have been fish food by now. But there's no time to think about that now." Shabalin relayed Major General Dubovtsev's order that we come to the aid of the naval infantrymen who were storming Liinakhamari.

Admiral Golovko was already in Liinakhamari. On his order, we established security patrols and posts for guarding the most important facilities. I asked permission from the admiral to return to Krestovyy for the burial of the dead scouts.

"The detachment fought heroically!" the admiral said. "Put everyone in for an award. Don't be bashful! We are recommending you for the award Hero."

"I thank you, Comrade Admiral! Only, how about Agafonov and Pshenichnykh? They broke into the battery first and captured it. And how they fought later! All the detachment's scouts consider them to be heroes."

"Well, if everyone feels that way"—the admiral smiled a bit—"then there will be no mistakes. Write the reports."[19]

I returned to Krestovyy toward the end of the day and recounted my conversation with the admiral. It turned out that the admiral had already met with the wounded scouts and asked them about the battles on Krestovyy.

"After the conversation with the admiral," Guznenkov

said to me, "Kolosov and Kalaganskiy immediately asked him for a favor."

That worried me, but Guznenkov calmed me down. "They said to the fleet commander, 'We are lightly wounded. Therefore, Comrade Admiral, order them not to send us far into the rear. We'll quickly heal in the base, by the sea, near the detachment.' And the admiral promised to intercede for them."

New combat missions awaited us.

On Krestovyy there remained only two items of business: to evacuate the prisoners, who had already buried all the dead jaegers—more than a hundred of them—and to bury our own comrades.

Guznenkov led me to the valley where all the scouts were formed up to pay a last tribute to their comrades who had fallen in battle on Cape Krestovyy. There our friends lay in a single row near a large, freshly dug grave. Their dead faces were turned toward the northwest, where the gloomy cliff of Krestovyy towered.

First was Ivan Lysenko. A light brown forelock peeked out from under his helmet. His large hands were crossed on his broad chest. This chest had received a lot of lead, perhaps until his indomitable and tenacious sailor's heart stopped beating. His mouth was firmly closed. Lysenko was waiting for that approaching hour, when with a clean conscience he could ask Guznenkov and me for a recommendation to the party. He would not have to wait. But he died like a communist! Ivan Lysenko earned this rank, just as he earned the highest award of the Motherland. When he picked up the stanchion with the barbed wire under the enemy's fire, he knew the mortal risk he was taking to save many other lives.

Next to Lysenko lay a veteran of the detachment, our oldest—Chief Petty Officer Anatoliy Barinov. Barinov's wife and two children waited for the return of their husband and father at the base. Barinov's little boy, also named Tolya, often came to visit us at the detachment. The scouts called him the son of the detachment. Pshenichnykh used to say to Barinov, "Nothing bad can happen to us because our family awaits us at home." Now Andrey Pshenichnykh stood in formation and looked directly at Anatoliy Barinov. Andrey's worn, pock-marked face darkened as if in pain. His eyes were red and inflamed and, it seemed, if a tear had appeared, it would have boiled and then disappeared. I now understood where Andrey Pshenichnykh got such savage fury in hand-to-hand combat with the jaegers.

As they had died together, so also lay side by side the detachment doctor, Lieutenant of Medical Service Aleksey Ilich Luppov, and Senior Sailor Pavel Smirnov. And on the other side of them was Vladimir Fatkin. Oh, Volodya, how handsome you are in death! Your mother's most recent letter, which you read to us at the meeting, is preserved in your sailor's locker box. It would be easier to fight another heavy battle than to answer Volodya Fatkin's mother.

Last in the row lay the detachment *komsorg*, Petty Officer Second Class Manin. Before the raid on Krestovyy the command awarded Manin a combat decoration for the first sortie to Varanger Fjord. "Manin, Aleksandr Vasilevich" was printed in the order for the award. Warrant Officer Nikandrov good-naturedly teased Manin: "Well, which Aleksandr Vasilevich are you? You are Sashka! Sashka Manin, our *komsorg*! Perhaps it was a misprint in the newspaper."

"With me, Warrant Officer, misprints do not happen in life," Manin steadily retorted. "Sometimes it's Sashka, and sometimes it's Aleksandr Vasilevich!"

Five, then ten minutes passed, and we all were still standing over the freshly dug grave. I did not have the strength to give the order to bury them. But the rumble of the faraway battle beckoned us onward. If the dead could speak, they would have hurried us along.

Ivan Ivanovich Guznenkov and I exchanged glances. He understood my condition and gave a short speech himself.

"Load!"

Raising their submachine gun and rifle barrels upward,

the men aimed at the top of Cape Krestovyy, where, buried beneath the barrels of their cannons, lay the destroyed battery.

German prisoners passed nearby. The enemy saw ten dead Soviet scouts, and they remembered how many of their own they had buried.[20]

The jaegers removed their peaked caps from their heads, pressed their hands to their sides, and filed past the grave.

"Fire!"

The salute rang out.

The sky was lit with flare bursts, and the reflections of their light settled on the faces of the dead for the last time.

The living took cold, damp earth in their burning cupped palms.

"This is ours!" the choked voice of Ivan Guznenko said. "This is Russian, Pechenga soil."[21]

Attack followed attack, from land, from the sea, from the air. All the enemy's defenses in the Far North were crushed.

Having captured Pechenga, Soviet troops pressed toward the Norwegian port of Kirkenes. They had already forced Bek Fjord, the last water barrier in front of Kirkenes. From everywhere reports came in about the Germans' excesses in northern Norway. Embittered by their inability to stop the Soviet offensive, the Germans blew up bridges, burned villages, drove the civilian population toward the west, and removed confiscated wealth to Germany.[22]

The fleet commander ordered our detachment to land on the shore of Varanger Fjord, move to the enemy's main line of communication, and take all necessary measures for the iprotection of Norwegian property.

[Leonov wrote the following in a compendium about the Petsamo-Kirkenes operation in 1969:[23] The fleet command decided to land a large amphibious assault in the enemy rear. Our reconnaissance detachment was to seize a good beachhead for the landing in the area of Vadsø.

This was the plan. Ten men led by Captain Third Rank

Lobanov would first be parachuted into the Varanger Peninsula. They would select a good landing site for the reconnaissance detachment along the coast. The detachment would move to the Vadsø area and support the landing there of the main assault force.

But from the very beginning this plan went awry.

The parachutists, who had been dropped over Varanger during the night of 27 October, radioed that the wind had widely scattered the group. After this message the radio went silent.

This was more than strange. The chief of the fleet parachute assault service, Colonel Orlov, had supervised the insertion.[24] We considered him to be a very experienced parachutist and a good organizer. Upon his return from the mission, Orlov reported that Captain Third Rank Lobanov's group had landed normally.

We could not reestablish communications with the parachutists. And time was passing.

Then the order came down to relocate our detachment from Polyarnyy to Rybachiy Peninsula and hold it there in preparation for the landing. Captain First Rank Bekrenev with a communications group also arrived there. They repeated the radio messages from fleet headquarters for Lobanov and monitored the radio continuously. The hours of waiting dragged by slowly.

On the morning of 29 October, Bekrenev received a report from Kirkenes that scouts Agafonov and Pshenichnykh, who had jumped with Lobanov, had arrived in a Norwegian motorboat. But earlier another Norwegian boat had arrived at Pummanki from Vadsø with still another parachutist of the same group—sailor Mikhalenko. He said that after landing he was unable to find anyone around him. There also was no one at the rally point. After waiting three hours, Mikhalenko began to make his way to the coastline. He came out in the Vadsø area. Seeing that there were no Germans nearby, he made contact with Norwegians. They agreed to take the scout across Varanger Fjord to Pummanki.

The sailor said that they had jumped in a very strong wind. Therefore, many had perhaps received serious injuries during their landing. Mikhalenko himself had fallen heavily in the rocks and walked with difficulty.

The Norwegians added that the Nazis intended to withdraw from Vadsø and were preparing the demolition of the residential areas. They intended to evacuate the populace to the west. On behalf of the population of Vadsø, the Norwegians asked us to prevent the Germans from accomplishing that.

During the night of 30 October our detachment was landed at Cape Langbunes. After a march, Captain Lieutenant Sutyagin (who during this sortie acted as detachment chief of staff) and I took with us three sailors and began to climb a hill, from which we had a good view of the surrounding terrain. Along the way we smelled smoke, and, looking around, we saw a cabin. In it, it turned out, were the missing scouts from Lobanov's group. Only Lobanov himself was absent. Their radio was destroyed; the radio operator had only by a miracle managed to transmit the fragment of a radio message that we had received.

We found Nikolay Lobanov only around noon on 31 October. He was dead—smashed on the rocks.]

Once again we were on Varanger Peninsula, in familiar surroundings where we had come the previous autumn and where they knew us as *syrtye d'yavolye*.

We hurried toward the port, the enemy's base. In wayside villages the Norwegians met us cordially and accompanied us. Ahead were fifty kilometers along a mountain road. We force-marched, but happy rumors spread along the entire Varanger Fjord coastline faster than we: "The Russians are coming!" Good rumors fly on fast wings. Coming to meet us and following behind us were Norwegians who had hidden from the Germans. They walked toward their homes with knapsacks and bundles of household goods. A countless multitude of people were moving along the road, and in Kiberg, which we were approaching, rumors abounded of a column of thousands of Soviet soldiers. Eyes were great with fear, and jaegers hurriedly abandoned Kiberg.

"*Ruserne kom khit*!—The Russians are coming!"—cried little boys running to meet us on the outskirts of Kiberg. "The Russians are coming!" the fishermen shouted as they greeted us, removing their wide-brimmed hats. "Russians!" astonished and happy women called. They smiled at us and called us to their homes, to share with us the little bit that they had in their run-down houses.

The populace of Kiberg, a small fishing settlement, lived half-starving.[25] There were flour, meat, grain, and canned fish in the warehouses, a half hour before guarded by Germans. But the Norwegians could not decide if they should enter because the Germans could have booby-trapped or poisoned the food. Besides that, the warehouses were military storage facilities, which meant they were booty for the victors. "The Russians themselves will decide how to deal with the warehouses," the oldest and most respected fisherman among them said to the people of Kiberg.

We opened the warehouses. Doctors—ours and a Norwegian—confirmed the safe condition of the food items. Pavel Sutyagin was with us on that mission, and he suggested that the people of Kiberg take everything that they needed.[26] When he relayed this to the fisherman, the old man, timid and confused, repeated Sutyagin's suggestion to confirm it. Did he understand the Russian officer correctly? Yes, he heard him right. The Russians requested only that everything be done in an orderly and fair manner.

Then the old man turned to the assembled people of Kiberg. "Look and listen! The Germans stole from us. The Russians are returning our property to us. They ask only that it all be distributed fairly, that each family receive the agreed-upon share."

The people answered him with a roar of approval and shouts of greeting.

We took a short break in Kiberg. The Norwegians were coming up to us with the same phrase, over and over: "*Vi onsker elpye Dem.*"

"What does this mean?" we asked Sutyagin.

"They're saying, 'We want to help you.' The young people are asking if we need guides in the mountains; they know every path. The fishermen are offering their boats if we will be going by sea. Where are the boats? The fishermen hid them from the Nazis in small inlets and concealed them under rocks. But all we have to do is ask for them. Viktor, these are good people! They adore their village. You know what they've nicknamed it? Little Moscow—Lille Moskva."

To guard our rear, we decided to leave a small group of scouts in Kiberg, with Makar Babikov in charge, and to move the remainder by Norwegian boats farther on, to our objective. The fishermen went off to prepare their boats for sea. But the old fisherman remained with us and whispered something secretly to Sutyagin. Pavel Grigorevich nodded his head approvingly, then turned to me and told me the old man's secret. "He says that their harbor pilots know the German mine fields. He advises us to take them along."

Such advise was tempting to me, but I was awaiting the return of the scouts I had sent ahead. Soon they came back and informed us that the enemy had abandoned the port and was retreating to the west.[27]

We set off on our journey.

In a new, fairly large town we helped the Norwegians create armed volunteer detachments for maintaining order in the waterfront area and for guarding the property of those inhabitants who had fled into the mountains.[28] Almost all of those who had fled the Germans returned to the town the next day. They thanked us, told us about their experiences, and asked us about Moscow and the Soviet Union.

Makar Babikov's group arrived from Kiberg.

Together with the Norwegians we celebrated the twenty-seventh anniversary of the great October socialist revolution. On the eve of the holiday we received news by radio concerning the awarding to me, Semyon Agafonov, and Andrey Pshenichnykh the rank of Hero of the Soviet

Union. All the scouts who had participated in the battles on Krestovyy were awarded decorations.

A month had passed, the most memorable month of our existence in the North. We had begun it with ferocious battles face-to-face with a hated enemy. We concluded it in friendly meetings and conversations face-to-face with our Norwegian fisherman friends, port workers, and their families.

The entire population of the village and the base was gathered on the docks for the detachment's farewell. A meeting sprang up spontaneously. We again heard the song of the Norwegian resistance fighters which we had first heard a year earlier in the mountains of Batsfjord:

> Free thoughts
> Quisling does not trace.

The Norwegians ardently congratulated us for the victory in the Far North and wished us a pleasant return to the Motherland.

"Give our thanks to your government, to your command, to all the valorous Soviet soldiers."

"We wish you a quick and final victory over the enemy!"

Pavel Grigorevich [Sutyagin] barely managed to interpret our wishes for the Norwegians. "Live happily, as Norwegians should live on their native soil. Don't forget the black days of the occupation. Remember our meeting. Fight for peace and happiness in the whole world."

"We won't forget you!" shouted the Norwegians who had memorized these four Russian words. "We will not forget!" chanted young men and women.

The Norwegian national flag waved over the pier.

We watched as people waved their arms and their hats and for a long time stood on the shore, until they disappeared in the sea's haze.

Picking up speed, our cutter took a course toward our native shores.

* * *

The battles in the north died away.

We felt strange; the war wasn't over, yet there was no enemy before us.

Bigger battles were unfolding in East Prussia. The front was approaching Budapest and Berlin, then Vienna and Prague. The radio brought the news of the meeting of Soviet and Allied forces on the Elbe. This meant that there was no longer a front there either.

We were still stationed at Polyarnyy, the base where the war had found us almost four years ago.[29]

The fates of front-line soldiers took shape in different ways, and in various regions and countries they greeted the May day of the great victory.

Some Siberians, who had traveled to the field of conflict for a week by train, perhaps remembered on this day the difficult front-line path from Moscow to Stalingrad and from Stalingrad to Berlin. How many natives of the North, who had become soldiers, spent the last year of the war in the warm regions of the Balkans? Behind them remained the battle-trod Ukraine and Moldavia, Romania and Bulgaria, the cities and villages of Yugoslavia. Only we Northern Fleet sailors never once changed our base, which lay in the enemy's path toward Murmansk.

May 1945 arrived, and above us was the same sky in which we first saw enemy aircraft, not knowing that their bellies carried a deadly cargo. We assembled for a meeting on 9 May, Victory Day,[30] admiring the clear May sky. The same sea lapped against our native shores, and the earth under us was the same—the bleak and beautiful, cold polar soil, rich with inexhaustible energy. The feet of the jaegers from the celebrated Edelweis division never touched it. The heroes of Narvik and Crete did not defile it, though from Polyarnyy to the old border, where the powerful offensive fist of Hitler's 20th Lapland Army was concentrated, was only a few score kilometers. We could be proud of that!

"I am proud that I commanded you brave Northern Fleet sailors during the war! The youngest fleet of our

Motherland—the Northern—fulfilled its debt to the Motherland with honor and glory."

Thus Admiral Golovko spoke at the meeting.

Makar Babikov spoke at the meeting on behalf of the naval scouts. He was nervous when he began his speech. And all of us became uneasy when he dedicated his first words to the eternal memory of our comrades who had fallen in battle, to the memory of those who had given their lives for the triumph of our great and just cause.

A month passed after the victory holiday.

Several scouts were discharged into the reserves. We sadly parted with Zmeev, Tarashnin, and our other comrades. We took a vow of friendship and fidelity to our sailor brotherhood, born in battles.

Then began a period of peacetime training. Those who remained in the unit wondered about the detachment's future. Created in the first month of the war, and only for war, the detachment could be disbanded, of course. But since there were so few of us left, the command also had the option of holding us in reserve. Then one day we received an order to prepare for a long—very long—journey.

At our departure the admiral said to me, "Soon they will call you not Northern Fleet men, but Pacific Fleet men. They'll greet you like heroes. They'll give you the welcome you deserve! But wherever you are, uphold the combat reputation of Northern Fleet men. Hold it high, so that if we should hear about you—and I know we will—we'll be able to say with pride that these were *our* eagles! Those men from Rybachiy! Heroes of Pikshuev and Mogilnyy, Krestovyy and Norwegian shores!"

"Comrade Admiral! How could we do anything else?" I hesitated, overwhelmed with emotion. "We'll always fight like Northern Fleet men."

"I understand, Leonov!" The admiral smiled. "Such things are not forgotten! A combat reputation gained at a high price cannot be ignored. Have a pleasant trip, friends, and I wish you new fame!"

The scouts knew where and why they were going. We were going to reinforce the Pacific Fleet. There weren't many of us, but each scout who had volunteered to remain in the detachment was experienced, proven, and hardened in combat. Warrant Officer Aleksandr Nikandrov, a detachment veteran, was going with us. He and I began our service as scouts in the summer of 1941. Heroes of the Soviet Union Andrey Pshenichnykh and Semyon Agafonov were going along. With us also was Senior Lieutenant Guznenkov. We had both been promoted to that rank after Krestovyy. Among the volunteers were Boris Guguev, Pavel Baryshev, Makar Babikov, and some rookies who had distinguished themselves on Krestovyy: Pavel Kolosov, Mikhail Kalaganskiy, Viktor Karpov, Sergey Byvalov, and other scouts who had returned to the detachment from the hospital. These were the pick of the Northern Fleet detachment.[31]

At noon on a summerlike June day we left the North.

We would travel through Moscow, where we would stop over for several days. Along the way we would meet relatives and acquaintances. Everyone was in a holiday mood. Combat decorations and awards brightly adorned the tunics and flannels of the newcomers.

When we were sitting in the train coach, the normally happy lad Boris Guguev said, "Good-bye, North!" with a sadness unusual for him. He turned sharply toward Kalaganskiy. "Misha—get out your accordion!"

Kalaganskiy took his time in putting the accordion, our trophy from the battle on Krestovyy, on his knee. Dancing and singing would now begin! But Misha Kalaganskiy suddenly lowered his head. Finally, Misha got up and with the accordion in his hands, slowly went over toward the window. The locomotive gave a long whistle, and to us it seemed that this whistle was answered by a farewell echo in the mountains and on the far-off capes.

The train quietly pulled out, and we heard the tune of a favorite song—ours, Northern Fleet men. One couldn't dance to it, but it had a tenor solo. Boris Guguev also moved to the window and lifted up his voice:

> Good-bye, rocky mountains,
>> Our native land calls us to a heroic deed.

Peace reigned across Europe, but our Motherland was calling us to new battles, to new exploits.

The song resurrected in my memory the voyages and raids deep in the enemy's rear areas. A vision appeared, the outlines of native shores and a boiling sea and fog—everything that we might be leaving behind forever.

> *But the waves groan, and cry,*
>> *And splash over the side of the ship . . .*
> *Rybachiy has faded away in the distant fog.*
>> *Our dear land.*

9

Final Missions

THE DAYS OF OUR STOPOVER in Moscow flew by quickly, and on 31 May 1945 we were once again on the road. We were going to Vladivostok on the longest railroad line on the planet earth.[1]

Russian Island.[2] There was much sun and green here. We northerners missed these things! There were hills here also, not bald and rocky as in the Far North, but covered with dense forest. Misha Kalaganskiy maintained that pomegranate trees grew in these areas, as well as Chinese camellias and Japanese magnolias, and that tigers and snow leopards roamed in the thick taiga. The scouts did not believe Kalaganskiy, though he claimed to cite such an authoritative source as geography.

"Misha, don't confuse me! And don't frighten the rookies! True, there *were* tigers here, but they ran away when they found out that Misha Kalaganskiy, the noted scout from the Far North, was coming to Russian Island," Pavel Baryshev teased. Baryshev delighted in arguing or joking around. This time, at least, he had a basis for a discussion. In fact, what did geography have to do with it, Baryshev reasoned—he'd already surveyed the terrain and hadn't seen any camellias. And, thank God, he didn't meet with any snow leopards either.

"But there is something here, brothers!" Baryshev temptingly smacked his lips and gave us a mischievous wink.

"Grapes! Wild grapes! And walnuts galore, the size of one's fist. I've tasted them myself."

"Oh, come on, Pashka, you're lying!" Semyon Agafonov, a native of Onega Bay who had never seen a grape on the vine or a walnut, shook his head.

The rest of us guessed that Pavel had greatly exaggerated the size of the walnuts but did not doubt that he had found a nut grove. But then, after four years of war in the North, everything here was a wonder to us.

The men of the Pacific Fleet knew about the combat escapades of the Northern Fleet scout detachment and often invited us as guests. Almost every day there was a request for a "meeting with the heroes." But at these gatherings it became clear that several courageous pathfinders and valiant tongue stalkers were too shy to be good storytellers. Semyon Agafonov, for example, demanded that he be exempt from public appearances. "Let Baryshev give speeches for everyone. Pasha loves it. He can tell stories!"

"But the sailors want to hear from you," we reasoned with Semyon.

"So what am I, some kind of actor? It's easier for me to capture a tongue than to speak to a crowd."

At this time we had formed the detachment into two platoons.[3] Warrant Officer Aleksandr Nikandrov commanded the first and Senior Petty Officer Makar Babikov the second, which had many new men. Semyon Agafonov was Babikov's deputy, and he worked tirelessly with the young scouts. Agafonov taught by example. Any rookie to whom a Hero of the Soviet Union like Semyon Agafonov said, "Do as I do!" was firmly convinced that he should crawl, camouflage, or do whatever else just like the deputy platoon commander. And in general, our newcomers tried to imitate the experienced scouts.

[In early August] the platoons were training for assault landings when we got the news about the initiation of combat activities against the Japanese aggressors.[4] We immediately returned to base and read the radio message from the minister of foreign affairs. The government's objective was clear: to hasten the coming of peace and liberate people from further death and suffering.

Soviet ground forces had already broken through the Japanese defenses and were conducting an offensive into Manchuria.[5] Many ships had gone out on combat sorties, but we were still waiting, so impatience grew. The scouts were convinced that the *zampolit* and I were keeping something from them, but we didn't know anything yet either. Guznenkov remained conspicuously silent in response to the scouts' questions. In discussions with me, he compared the detachment with a bowstring. The tighter the string, the stronger and faster would be the flight of the arrow.

On the morning of 11 August we received orders,[6] and the detachment—having loaded up on two assault cutters— took a course toward the northern coast of Korea, toward Yuki, a port on the Sea of Japan.[7]

Distance and a morning fog hid the mountainous coast of northern Korea from our view, but smoke showed on the horizon, and behind it Yuki was aflame. Abandoning the port, the Japanese had set fire to the warehouses and homes near the docks.[8]

We landed on the shore.[9] The streets of Yuki were empty.

"Arasa! Arasa!" We initially heard shouts of greeting, and only then did we see Koreans, who were running from their homes to meet us. Our interpreter explained to us that *"Arasa"* meant "Russian." I recalled the joyous cries of the Norwegians when they saw us for the first time on their shore.

The enemy had so hurriedly left the city that they forgot to evacuate their wounded and sick from the hospital. I asked the Koreans to look after the wounded until the arrival of our units. Dropping his head to his chest, an old Korean, to whom the interpreter had given my request, said, "You have arrived in an empty city, because the Japanese have driven away the population. These fires are also their work. The Russian officer asks that we take care of the wounded Japanese soldiers—for us this is an order. But

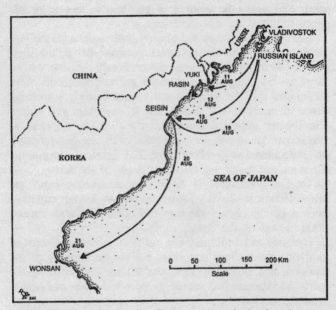

let the Russians know that Japanese remain in the city, not in uniform. They conceal pistols and grenades under Korean peasants' shirts. They will shoot you in the back. There are few of you. Be careful."

Soon it was revealed that there were many of us. A column of Soviet motorized infantry came down from the mountains.[10] The lead vehicle stopped near the hospital, and a sergeant with a mustache shouted to the sailors, "Well, I'll be! So this is how it turns out! We were pushing hard along the rail route to be the first ones in Yuki, and you're already here!"

"Don't cry, soldier!" Pavel Baryshev called. "Stay in the sailors' wake, and you won't get lost!"

"You're pretty young to be teaching me, sailor!" The mustachioed infantryman took offense. "From Stalingrad to Berlin, from the German Spree to the Sea of Japan, I've never gone off course. Besides that, I did it without a compass! And you talk about a wake. You've got a lot of nerve!"

"Excuse me, old man," Pavel said deferentially.

The order came in by radio: the detachment had to go to the port of Rasin. But there were no Japanese there either.

[Rasin was not so devoid of Japanese troops as Leonov states. Once again, Babikov has provided a detailed description of the detachment's actions ashore in Rasin.[11] Their mission was the same as in Yuki: land, reconnoiter the port, determine enemy strength and intentions, and seize a beachhead for the follow-on force. Their landing on 12 August was preceded by more than four hundred air bombardment sorties from fleet aviation.[12] On the way into the harbor, the detachment received ineffective small-arms fire from two small islands. The detachment went ashore at the docks and quickly moved into the city. One platoon secured the railroad station, military barracks, and industrial area of the port, while the other moved along the shore. The detachment met light resistance from Japanese rear guards. The interrogation of Korean civilians revealed the recent retreat of the Japanese garrison, which Leonov reported to fleet headquarters by radio. In reply, fleet headquarters ordered him to make contact with a company of naval infantry landed nearby, turn control of the port over to them, and return to base. Leonov made contact with both the naval infantry company to the south of the port and a forward detachment from the 393d Rifle Division that arrived from the north. The detachment arrived back at Russian Island on the evening of 12 August.]

"This is a strange war!" Semyon Agafonov exclaimed when we returned to Russian Island. "We've gone into two ports and haven't fired a shot at a Japanese yet. We fought with the jaegers in the open. Who are these 'sons of the sun?' How will the famous samurai fight? I'd really like to know."

"You'll find out!" Makar Babikov retorted. "The samurai will show you."

And on the following day erupted one of the most terrible battles in the history of the detachment—the battle for Seisin.

Seisin, a large northern Korean city with a population in excess of two hundred thousand people, was situated on the shore of a broad bay and bordered on three sides by the ridges of green hills.

Seisin occupied a special place in Japanese plans as a military base and bridgehead for an attack on the Soviet coastal region.[13] Through Seisin passed the supplies for the Kwangtung Army in Manchuria. The rail and road systems that passed through Seisin connected northern Korea with the central and southern regions of the country.

The Military Council of the Pacific Fleet ordered our detachment and a company of naval infantry submachine gunners, commanded by officer Ivan Yarotskiy,[14] to reconnoiter the bay and capture and hold the dock area by which units of the Kwangtung Army would retreat through Seisin. They gave us ten torpedo cutters. Five were used to move the assault force; the remaining five provided cover. Approximately two hundred naval scouts and naval infantrymen would execute the first assault. Behind us would come the forward detachment—a machine-gun company and Major Barabolko's naval infantry battalion.[15] We were to secure the unhindered entrance of the main forces into the bay.

A member of the Military Council of the Pacific Fleet warned us that the Seisin operation was complicated and crucial. The Japanese would resist fiercely, defending their lines of communication in Seisin. If we managed to capture a beachhead by surprise, the Japanese would expend every effort to liquidate us.

"Subunits of an imperial division are quartered near Seisin," the fleet commander said. "These crack samurai are guarding the ports, bridges, and railroad station. But we believe in the success of this operation, and we know that they will not be able to withstand the skill and tenacity, determination and courage of Soviet sailors. That is why we are sending you."

Yarotskiy, the commanders from the division of torpedo cutters, and I—participants in the first wave—thanked the fleet commander for his confidence and departed to our units.

It was already late. The scouts were sleeping, not knowing that they would be getting up long before dawn and that they would greet the morning in the midst of the sharp engagements of street battles.

After reveille, a short party meeting, then an equally brief gathering of the platoons before loading onto the cutters, we departed Russian Island.[16]

I went down into the cabin of the lead cutter. The scouts were keeping their spirits raised, singing their "Song of the North" at full voice. I heard Agafonov's bass voice: "We go out to meet the enemy with a heavy sailor's step." How many times have we gone? And what kind of man is he, our new enemy?

I had complete confidence in each scout assault troop [*razvedchik-desantnik*], even in the rookies, for whom this would be the first raid and the first battle. Senior Sailor Zubkov, a detachment veteran, surprised me. Zubkov asked me not to appoint him as a squad commander in Nikandrov's platoon, alluding to the quarrelsome character of the warrant officer. For me this was unexpected. In the North, Zubkov and Nikandrov had been on good terms. When Nikandrov found out about Zubkov's request, he shook his head but was silent. Only Babikov told me about a small argument that had arisen between the warrant officer and the senior sailor several days before the combat operation.[17]

Zubkov had mentioned that it would be an awful pity if they were killed or wounded on the eve of victory. "We've never been in such a mess!" he'd said to Nikandrov and Babikov. "Remember Pikshuev and Mogilnyy, the Norwegian voyages, and Krestovyy? They were all for nothing!

And suddenly, just before the final victory, some samurai scum sticks you with a bayonet or cripples you with a bullet? And you could even die."

The warrant officer did not like such discussions before a battle. "Go to the detachment commander and tell him about this," Nikandrov said to Zubkov. "Tell him honestly that you're scared. If you can't do that, I'll ask the senior lieutenant to leave you behind."

"What do you mean?" Zubkov was startled. "I was only kidding." Pretending to be offended, Zubkov walked away.

The incident with Zubkov upset us. In war they talk about life and death. One can understand from the human perspective the dream of a young soldier: "Hey, I'd like to live until I get married!" But if in anticipation of approaching victory, the same soldier thinks only about surviving unscathed, he shouldn't be entrusted with a crucial task.

In the end, I didn't name Zubkov a squad commander. But just the same, it was unfortunate that this happened.

[From Babikov, *Na vostochnom*: "At the end of the second hour at sea, the chief of the fleet intelligence section, Colonel A. Z. Denisin, summoned us. He had been named to command the composite detachment of scouts who were going in the first assault wave. Both our detachment and the company of submachine gunners, commanded by Senior Lieutenant Yarotskiy, were subordinated to him. Denisin's deputy, Captain Third Rank Khoder, was also involved in the operation. Denisin, covering the table with his map, explained to us the details of the detachment's combat mission. In three hours we were to land in the port of Seisin. We had been ordered to conduct reconnaissance by battle, determine the enemy's strength and intentions, capture a beachhead, and hold it until the arrival of the first echelon."][18]

It was getting light slowly. White-breasted gulls soared over the mirrorlike surface of the sea. They were flying far from shore, which meant that the day promised to be clear and the sea calm. The morning haze was breaking up, but ahead a milky shroud of fog hung over the bay which we were approaching. For a while only the green tops of hills could be seen, but then the break of the foamy surf along the shoreline could be made out. Finally, the moorages of the commercial port came into view.

The hard pounding of a Japanese machine gun broke the morning quiet. The gunners of the first cutter suppressed the firing point on the dock, but a Japanese cannon opened fire from the closest hill of Cape Kolokoltsev. One shot, a second, a third. Our cutters burst into the port at full speed and landed the amphibious force.[19]

The cannons on Cape Kolokoltsev were still firing at the cutters as they went back out to sea, and we were moving into the waterfront quarter in small groups.

So far there was no resistance.

From a small hillock Seisin could be seen. It was cut into sections by canals, with two main thoroughfares, a railroad right-of-way, and a highway. In spite of the early hour, the streets of Seisin were busy. Steam swirled up from a locomotive, invisible behind some houses, and automobiles rushed along the highway. The railroad cars and automobiles were all going in the same direction—to the south—where a large embankment rose up between the bridges across the canal. The shape of a steel mill could be seen behind the embankment.

"Bridges!" I heard Guznenkov's voice behind me.[20]

Yes, bridges. They would now become the objects of a battle. The embankment between them would be a good line for a defense. I coordinated with Yarotskiy so he would cover our rear and right flank.

"Do you see the bridges?" I turned toward Nikandrov and Babikov. "You, Warrant Officer Nikandrov, take the railroad bridge, and Senior Petty Officer Babikov the automobile bridge. If you can't capture the bridge, blow up the bed and the road. We've got to stop the cars and trains!"

Nikandrov's platoon took out the bridge security, then rushed toward the railroad embankment. Japanese soldiers were scattered among the corn patches along the railroad, and they opened fire with rifles.

It was difficult for the second platoon—Babikov's—which was moving toward the automobile highway. The Seisin garrison had been alerted, and Babikov's scouts were involved in a street battle, something unusual for them. Japanese snipers were firing from attic and house windows. Samurai from a suicide squad, dressed in civilian clothes (the scouts had taken them to be local inhabitants and therefore had not bothered with them), hit us in the rear.

Skirmishes, unexpected and brief, broke out in various places. It was difficult to deal with them.

Guznenkov's orderly (the *zampolit* was with Nikandrov's platoon) ran up and reported that armed Japanese had penetrated to the commercial port. The enemy obviously intended to cut us off from the shore, so Guznenkov had sent a group of scouts under the command of Chief Petty Officer Tyarosov to clear the dock area. The scouts had managed that task and were then guarding the port. Our wounded were there also.

We had just managed to eliminate one danger when another appeared. A large enemy column was moving from the direction of the steel mill toward the highway. Yarotskiy's submachine gunners were firing on the column, preventing the Japanese from approaching the embankment. But Babikov's scouts had still not captured the automobile bridge; they were fighting on the highway and threatening the vehicle column. From the direction of the bridge a platoon of Japanese counterattacked us fiercely, clearing their path to the roadway with grenades.

I hurried to the aid of Babikov, who was wounded. A grenade fragment had cut his brow. Babikov crawled toward me, raised his bandaged head, and reported that his scouts were lying along the embankment because to move farther was impossible. At this time the firing increased from the direction of the bridge. Yarotskiy's submachine gunners were holding off the Japanese, but with difficulty, anticipating our capture of the bridge.

"Chief Petty Officer Babikov, is your mission clear?" By the tone of my voice, Babikov understood that I was displeased with his platoon's actions.

"Perhaps we can go around the embankment?" he asked hesitantly, thinking only about helping Yarotskiy's submachine gunners and forgetting about the bridge.

I got angry. "I do not consider you to be wounded. Carry out your order!"

Makar turned pale. Barely audible, he said, "Yes, sir," unfastened an antitank grenade, and ran in the direction of the embankment.

Digging into the sand, Babikov and two other sailors crawled toward the bridge and then threw their antitank grenades. We surged forward, firing almost point-blank at the Japanese defending the bridge. Part of the scouts remaining near the bridge to meet a new Japanese vehicle column. I led the remainder to the aid of Yarotskiy's submachine gunners. The Japanese withdrew toward the steel mill.

Japanese lines of communication were now cut in Seisin so it was possible to go about the task of reconnoitering the central sections of the city.

The enemy's main force was located in the military port, but we had to be concerned about an attack from the rear, from the direction of the steel mill. It was noon, and the forward detachment—a machine-gun company and a naval infantry battalion—would not be landed until nightfall. We had many wounded and a limited supply of ammunition. After consulting with Yarotskiy, I decided to continue reconnaissance but to avoid major engagements.

The closer we got to the center of the city, the broader were the streets, and, finally, we came out on a square where a crowd of people was gathered near the theater building. A group of young people ran to meet us. A dark-complexioned, stocky Korean was holding an unfurled red banner. The young Koreans asked us if it was possible for them to hoist this banner over the theater. Of course, we gave them permission, and after several minutes the stocky

Korean with the banner was climbing the stairs to the spire of the theater's cupola. Meanwhile, the people shouted to him from below. "Moon! Hurry, Moon, so the Japanese don't shoot you!" Then firing broke out from somewhere near, and several rounds passed by the cupola of the theater. But Moon kept climbing until he reached his goal.

Soon our patrols had engaged Japanese approaching the squad, and the Koreans dispersed. Only Moon remained with us. With a proudly uplifted head he looked at the banner, then ran toward the detachment's interpreter and heatedly said something.

"What does he want?" I asked.

"Moon wants to be my assistant," the interpreter said. "Moon knows the city and can speak Japanese. It wouldn't hurt to have him nearby as an interpreter."

"He's your responsibility!" I said.

The red flag above the theater building infuriated the Japanese, who began an artillery barrage on the city center from Cape Kolokoltsev. When it lifted, the samurai went into the attack, and street fighting broke out once again.

A group of scouts from Nikandrov's platoon counterattacked the Japanese. Having taken out a guard near the gate of a home, Warrant Officer Nikandrov and Senior Sailor Olyashev ran through the door and were confronted by two Japanese officers. "*Ruki vverkh!* [Hands up!]" the warrant officer commanded. One of the Japanese officers turned crimson, pulled out his sword, and whirled at Nikandrov. It would have turned out badly for the warrant officer, but the blow of the sword was absorbed by the stock of the Russian submachine gun, and Vladimir Olyashev knocked the Japanese down with a blow of his buttstock. The other officer then raised his hands.

We were shielded from the Japanese who were attacking us from the direction of the military port by an irrigation canal that passed through the center of the city. The submachine gunners were defending the embankment behind us. But with daybreak, a battle unexpectedly broke out near the bay. I sent several scouts there with Agafonov in charge.

After an hour Semyon returned, and we learned that the coming day promised to bring us still more serious trials.

[From Babikov's *Na vostochnom* ("I" in the following passage is Makar Babikov, who was one of Leonov's platoon leaders):[21] Guznenkov came over to us. He sat down and listened to the men in conversation. I asked him what was new. Nothing, he said. There was still no comforting news. He suggested that we go around and inspect my platoon's positions.

Along the way I asked him where Denisin was because I hadn't seen him in a while. Ivan Ivanovich answered that the colonel had taken Agafonov and two additional submachine gunners with him and, under cover of darkness, went off somewhere in the port. Before his departure he had had a private conversation with Leonov. The colonel's departure interested and concerned me. I said this straight out to Guznenkov.

I have to say that the participation of the colonel in our small first-wave group concerned not only me. He occupied an important position—as chief of intelligence of the fleet he knew a great deal. God help us if something happened to him. Right now we had stirred up a hornets' nest. Therefore, we had to exercise great care in protecting the colonel. But he'd gone off somewhere. Who knew where and how to find him if he was urgently needed? I pressed Guznenkov to find out what else he knew.

Ivan Ivanovich suggested, "In the past, Denisin was a ground forces officer, and the command is counting on his knowledge during the shore operations.[22] Also," he added, "the colonel has served in the East a long time, and knows this theater best."

Guznenkov's arguments were not sufficiently persuasive to make me believe that they had to send a colonel, who possessed knowledge of the fleet's entire intelligence, on such a risky operation. These were very high stakes. Were they justified? Our experience was not so limited as to warrant a lack of confidence in our ability to accomplish the mission without a watchdog.

There was still another thought that would explain such a decision. Military events were unfolding at such a rapid tempo that they had outstripped plans developed beforehand. Why did the enemy retreat, abandoning two coastal cities without a battle? Where did the Japanese intend to stop and give us a fight? The command had to be concerned about all of this. Perhaps it had sent the colonel to view the situation through the eyes of an officer who had access to more comprehensive reports on the operational situation.

"I suspect that this has something in common with our evening stroll in Yuki," Guznenkov suggested.

The colonel's patrol returned after an hour and a half. I asked Agafonov where they had been. Semyon mumbled something indistinctly, not telling me anything. So we didn't get the truth then. And we didn't think about it any longer—that would get us nowhere. The colonel had returned, and the nearer he was to us, the less we worried about his fate. Later, other events shed light on Denisin's presence in the landing force. It turned out that in strict secrecy, agents [*razvedchiki*] prepared and dispatched by Denisin had settled into the enemy rear. To receive their reports firsthand, to provide him a perspective on the unfolding situation, and to point us in the right direction were the reasons why Colonel Denisin was moving in such dangerous company.]

The Seisin garrison had received reinforcement. The Japanese were stubbornly holding on to almost the entire shore of the bay, the military port, and the steel mill. Agafonov had seen two enemy cutters and several launches. They were crossing the bay and moving toward the commercial port, where Chief Petty Officer Tyarosov's small group and the wounded were located.[23] The road leading toward the commercial port had already been cut.

The situation was complicated by the fact that our

machine-gun company had not managed to accomplish its mission. The Japanese had detected the assault force and prevented the machine gunners from landing. We heard the battle of the Japanese with the assault force at dawn. But even before that, at midnight, Major Barabolko's naval infantrymen had landed not far from the military port and had occupied a defense on one of the hills.[24] A radio message from Barabolko encouraged us.

In such a situation, passivity, deliberation, and temporizing could lead to the death of our men and to the disruption of the entire operation. If the enemy had numerical superiority over us, then it was all the more important to hold on to the initiative. We penetrated toward the hill occupied by the naval infantrymen, and I asked Barabolko to strengthen our detachment with a company of submachine gunners. After receiving it, I led the assault force in clearing the area adjoining the shore. We made it to the embankment and, together with Yarotskiy's submachine gunners, vigorously counterattacked the enemy and captured the steel mill. Then the enemy threw in fresh forces from the nearby hills and surrounded the mill. Now the hill near the military port, which two of Barabolko's companies were defending, and the steel mill were surrounded by Japanese. We knew nothing about Tyarosov's group in the commercial port.

We received a radio message from Admiral Yumashev: "Barabolko's naval infantrymen are receiving the main attack and are beating off the Japanese who have besieged them from all sides. Move your detachment toward his position in the military port."

We still had no communication with Tyarosov's group. The shortest path to the military port lay through the waterfront. Ahead of us were street battles, and I was again concerned about our limited supply of ammunition. But an order was an order, and I gave the command to prepare for a breakout.

Yarotskiy was wounded. A Japanese bullet had struck a grenade that he was holding. Makar Babikov was noticeably weakening after his wounding. But the two men continued to command their subunits.[25] Senior Sailor Maksimov was seriously wounded, and Vladimir Olyashev was carrying him from position to position on his back. Kazhaev remained alone at the radio, Misha Kalaganskiy having taken up a submachine gun and gone into the line.

The sun was at its peak; sweltering heat tortured the sailors; the intensity of the battle did not subside. We were thankful to Moon, who looked after food and water. Risking their lives, citizens of Seisin and their guide, Moon, got us water in pails and rice porridge and even bowls of fruit. A Korean woman considerately bandaged our wounded comrades.

The counterattack did not ease our situation. There were many Japanese; their resistance strengthened, and we could not even get near the commercial port. We were engaged in heavy and unequal combat and didn't know that Semyon Agafonov, whom we had left in the tower of the steel mill, had seen two of our ships out at sea.

A frigate and a minesweeper entered Seisin Harbor.

Agafonov had two scraps of red material and used them to signal the ships: "We are surrounded by Japanese. We will move toward the military port along the shore. Support us with fire."

The first explosions of shells fired by our ships determined the line toward which we surged in the attack. We moved right behind the creeping barrage. The gunners from the frigate and minesweeper did their work well, clearing us a path. The ships alternately turned about, firing continuously first from one side and then the other. The gunners later told us that the gun barrels got so hot they had to wash them down with water from the fire hoses.

With grenades, we had to burn out the samurai who had settled into the cellars of the houses along the shoreline, while we moved continuously behind the rolling barrage of the frigate and the minesweeper. Guznenkov and Agafonov ran to find Tyarosov's group. They knew the house in the cellar of which Tyarosov's scouts and the wounded were located, but there was no one in the cellar. A slip of paper was pinned to the door: "Give to the political directorate of Pacific Fleet."

Guznenkov read the following words on the other side of the paper:

Dear comrades! We, sailors from Leonov's detachment, six healthy and eighteen wounded, are going into battle with the Japanese assault force that is approaching the commercial port. We will not permit them to reach the shore. While we are alive, not one samurai will set foot on the docks. We take a pledge on this!

By the hand of all the defenders of the commercial piers—Chief Petty Officer Tyarosov, sailors Ermakov, Kalchenko, Kedyarov, Baev, and Grishchenko.

Guznenkov and Agafonov moved toward the docks but found no one there. By the scraps of bandages and the pieces of spent cartridges it was possible to determine that something had happened there. But there were no signs of Tyarosov's group in the waterfront area.

Guznenkov and Agafonov worriedly looked around, not knowing what else to do. At this time they saw Tyarosov running toward them.

"What happened? Where are your men?" Guznenkov asked Tyarosov.

"Everything's okay. They've linked up with the detachment, and the commander sent me after you. Comrade Senior Lieutenant, were you in the cellar?"

"I was there. And I read your letter. Here it is."

"Do you see what happened?" Tyarosov blushed with embarrassment. "We decided not to leave the waterfront. We fought a battle to the death with the Japanese and drove them back. And when we heard fighting behind us, we went to find you and forgot about the note."

"I will preserve this document!" Guznenkov put the letter away.

Before dawn the Japanese attacked us with unusual ferocity and seized the ground overlooking the waterfront.

They charged forward screaming "banzai," intending to hurl us into the sea. The same cries that we had heard ten months earlier on Cape Krestovyy also arose along the scouts' skirmish line: "Hold on! Hold on!"

And we did hold on until we heard the salvos of the ships coming into Seisin port. Soon the landing of General Trushin's naval infantry brigade began.[26] The outcome of the Seisin operation had been decided.

Of course, none of us thought that the two-day battle in Seisin would close the annals of the detachment of naval scouts in the Second World War.

I sat on a box near the sea wall to have a smoke and dozed off. Through my sleep I heard someone arguing nearby and, opening my eyes, saw Mikhaylin, the frigate commander.

I got up, rubbed my eyes, ran my fingers through my tousled hair, and said, "Don't you recognize us, Captain-Lieutenant? There's only a few of us, it's true, and we're covered with dirt. Give me the packet."

While I read the order about our return to base, Mikhaylin looked at me the entire time, as if he doubted whether he had given the packet to the right person.

"What's the matter, Captain?"

"It's nothing! Now I recognize you. On the frigate we'll wash you up, feed you, and give you a place to sleep. Everyone on Russian Island already knows about your accomplishments."

An hour later we left Seisin.

Together with Guznenkov I went around the cabin where the scouts were in a deep sleep. Then I went up on the deck.

"Do you see it?" Guznenkov pointed at Seisin.

From the deck of the frigate the city was clearly visible. Above it stood out the cupola of the theater.

On the spire of the cupola fluttered the red flag raised by the Korean Moon.

Japan surrendered unconditionally.

This news reached us in the port Genzan [Wonsan],

where we took a large quantity of Japanese soldiers and officers captive.

[The reconnaissance detachment's actions in Wonsan merit close examination, even though little combat was involved. Leonov wrote about the Wonsan operation in much greater detail in his 1985 book, *Gotovs'ya k podvigu*, from which the following material is extracted and translated:[27]

Over the years the rumor has spread that "with ten scouts Leonov created the appearance of an encirclement of three-and-a-half thousand Japanese troops in the port Wonsan and took them all captive." When I first heard about this, I was embarrassed. How a specific combat episode can be blown out of proportion! No matter how hard they tried, ten men could not possibly create the impression of an encirclement of thirty-five hundred enemy troops and then take them into captivity.

Yes, it was a genuine psychological battle that determined the fate of the Japanese military unit.

I will talk about it in some detail because it is quite instructive.

At the moment of the landing of our assault force in the port of Wonsan (on the morning of 21 August, four days after Japanese forces in Manchuria and Korea had stopped fighting), the Japanese already knew that they had lost the war, and any desperate resistance on their part would unavoidably lead to the destruction of their army. They were trying to prevent this.

Close behind our detachment, literally a half hour behind, fifteen hundred naval infantrymen were to land in Wonsan.[28] But for several reasons they were delayed, and the actions of the detachment, which was left stranded, became extremely complicated. We did not let down our guard. We even managed to slip through to the police headquarters and meet there with the garrison commander.

The meeting took place in the street. They brought out an armchair for the colonel. He quietly sat with his hands cupped. I stood nearby, with my faithful battle companions—Petty Officer Second Class Pshenichnykh and Senior Lieutenant Ivan Guznenkov. We noted police standing at the ready with machine guns behind the latticed fence of the headquarters and tried to remain close to the colonel. We knew about the "samurai spirit" and were convinced that the machine gunners would not open fire—the colonel would not sacrifice himself to destroy us.

The conversation was slow and unfocused. The colonel smiled at our attempts to threaten his rash actions with dire consequences. He nodded his head to show that he understood all this, but he did not accord us the strength needed to give meaning to these stern warnings.

By that time the main assault of our naval infantry had landed but was isolated from the city. The Japanese for the moment did not open fire an did not attempt to destroy our amphibious force but prevented them from penetrating into the city where we were operating.

Our conversation with the colonel was at an impasse. To the question of when the garrison would begin to lay down its arms, the colonel simply did not answer. He sat, with closed eyes, either thinking about or waiting for something. When I reminded him that we had little time and were awaiting a reply, the colonel shouted, "You are interrupting my thinking; you broke my train of thought, and I must begin again."

We did not expect such a tactic. My deputy Ivan Ivanovich Guznenkov twice tried to reason with the colonel, but he sat there with closed eyes and remained quiet. He gave the appearance that he was immersed in deep contemplation. We were also thinking. We had to come up with something. The Japanese forces in the city were steadily increasing in number. They literally filled all the streets. Our headquarters had informed us earlier that the capitulation of Japan was a matter of several hours and, perhaps, the order had already been signed. For what was the colonel waiting? Or was he indeed prepared to display the samurai spirit, to take more Soviet soldiers with him into the next world?

From the reports that the colonel received and heard without opening his eyes, from the disposition of the troops being pulled into the city, the Japanese plan became clear to us. The colonel did not realize that among us was a person, and not just one, who knew Japanese.[29] It was becoming clear what he was thinking about and more obvious what he was anticipating. He knew about his country's impending capitulation, and he also had an order not to surrender his troops to the Russians but instead to bring them into the port and destroy our assault force. Then, if he could manage to seize them, he was to flee on his ships or ours to the American zone, located nearby (Wonsan is not far north of the thirty-eighth parallel, the demarcation line between Soviet and American zones of Korean occupation), and there lay down his troops' arms. Our detachment, along with the naval infantry amphibious force, was to prevent this at all costs.

Considering all this, and knowing that samurai feared accusations of cowardice, I stated, "Honorable Colonel, the time for reflection has passed. I am forced once again to interrupt your thoughts. But I am obliged to warn you: soon our ships will employ weapons that will leave not a single one of your men alive, and their deaths will be on your conscience."

The colonel winced and, getting up from the armchair, asked, "What kind of weapons?"

"If you are not a coward," I answered, "and do not wish to destroy your people, you can see for yourself."

"Let's go."

"I will remain here, and they will take you there. I will answer for your life."

The colonel left for our ship in the company of our comrades and one Korean, who had joined the detachment as an interpreter after the Seisin operation. This was already a victory! A small one, not decisive in the overall scheme of things, but a victory. We had managed to render the enemy forces leaderless at a critical moment. Somewhat the same thing happened also with the (Japanese) rear admiral, the commander of the naval base.[30]

For some time a calm settled over the city. The Japanese troops awaited the return of their leader, and when they suspected that their commander might not return, alarm began to spread among them. It was very dangerous for our reconnaissance detachment to remain in the city, so, quickly slipping through the city center, we moved to the outskirts, where we occupied a small but steep hill. On one side was an infantry school and on the other the jail. These were not very good neighbors, but in the event of danger, we would be covered by the walls of the jail and could hold on there until the arrival of our troops. Meanwhile, we rested on the hill.

For a while everything was quiet in the infantry school. Suddenly, horns sounded and the troops began to form up. "Training" began, and our hill was subjected to demonstrational attacks, which threatened at any moment to cross over into combat actions. We firmly warned the organizers that we would open fire if they did not settle down. It all became quiet as suddenly as it had begun.

Soon we received the order to return to the port.

The still unfinished discussions about capitulation had been moved to our ship. The Japanese were still refusing to lay down their weapons. Our command decided first to force the capitulation of the airfield garrison and then to form them up and march them through the city to the barracks of the infantry school. Let this confirm to everyone that the capitulation had begun! It had to be demonstrated that there was nowhere to go to avoid surrender, and the sooner the better. Our detachment was to convince the Japanese of this.

The airfield was located on a spit across the bay, and the best way to get there was by boat. A company of naval infantry had already tried to land, but the Japanese broke up the landing. How would they react to the detachment? This could be an extremely dangerous venture. But in war one does not vacillate—one obeys.

We set out to fulfill our mission in eight torpedo cutters under the command of Hero of the Soviet Union Captain Lieutenant Malik.[31] We moved slowly and quietly, with exhausts diverted under the water. The scouts were positioned on the decks in relaxed poses, as if on vacation. When about one-and-a-half miles remained to the spit, the cutters accelerated to full speed and raced toward the docks in a column, with exhausts above the water. The sixteen aircraft motors created such a noise that we had to cover our ears.[32] The Japanese had set up a reliable defense near the docks, a dense line of machine guns and guns stupidly pointed out at us. While the cutters were moving at slow speed, those on the spit conducted themselves calmly, observing us with a vigilant eye. Then suddenly, they began to scurry about, not comprehending why we were flying toward the docks. What if these were suicide boats? What if the boats began to blow up? Panic was imminent. The officers did everything to forestall it and ordered the soldiers to prepare weapons for action.

The lead cutter unexpectedly turned sharply and went along the spit to its end. The remaining cutters repeated the maneuver. And, again, slow speed, underwater exhaust, and complete silence. Of course, when a cutter at full speed sharply changes course, the wave created by that maneuver goes forward, sweeping away everything in its path. Thus it was here. The water struck at the low docks of the airfield, and the Japanese soldiers, together with their weapons, ended up in the water. They leaped up, shook their fists at us, and we quietly moved onward.

There were beaches here. There were no docks, of course, and we could not get the boats all the way up to the shore. But it was summer! Hot! We very calmly began to jump into the water, still on the move.

Thus we ended up at the airfield.

At first glance it seemed that we had gained nothing by this landing. But the spit was narrow where we'd landed, and on the other side of it, very near, were all the airfield logistic support facilities—weapons storage area, ammunition supply, spare parts, and three immense fuel storage containers. All that was now in our hands and under our sights. The landing field, which passed across the spit, and the aircraft that flew from it as if from an aircraft carrier were also under our control.

It goes without saying that having neighbors like us did not suit the Japanese, and we waited to see what they would do. It would have been dangerous to attack us: in front of us was a flat landing field, and at our backs the eight torpedo cutters were patrolling back and forth, with four large-caliber machine guns on each. And there we were, 140 men with automatic weapons! An attack would have been senseless.

Finally, two vehicles appeared: a light vehicle and a small truck. Officers arrived for negotiations, and soldiers carried stools for everyone. The Japanese could not talk standing up. Smiling ingratiatingly, officers approached us, extended their hands, and invited us to sit. I calmly said, "We came here not to talk with you, but to ask, when will you surrender?"

"To whom? What forces do you have at your disposal?" One of the officers smiled.

"Perhaps you do not see our strength?" I asked.

"It is small. We have a very powerful garrison here."

"If you do not surrender, we will begin to burn the fuel storage tanks, then blow up the supply dumps. There will be a sea of fire. Then we will climb aboard our cutters and move away, but what will you do? Think about it."

It was obvious that the Japanese had not expected this turn of events. They scurried about, and then the same officer said, "We do not have the right to decide such questions. We have an airfield commander. He invites you to the headquarters. Please use my vehicle."

It was clear that to go to the headquarters without documents that would guarantee us inviolability as negotiators was dangerous. But it was impossible not to go. While we had the police colonel and the admiral on our ship, no one could give the command to commence combat actions in the city. But one way or another, a clash or a battle was imminent. It would immediately spread into the city, and our assault force on the docks of the port would inevitably perish. We had to go to the headquarters.

We refused the vehicle. Ten of us went on foot. Perhaps this is what began the legend about "encirclement" of three-and-a-half thousand Japanese troops by ten scouts. The detachment under the command of Warrant Officer Nikandrov remained at the landing site.

The entire way, the Japanese officers extolled the might of the Imperial Army and the local garrison, clearly attempting to intimidate us, but we remained silent. I placed two scouts in front of the building, ordering them to give Nikandrov a signal to bring the detachment in the event of an aggravation in the situation in the headquarters. This would have been a last resort because it would have involved the amphibious force in the port.

We went into the office of the airfield commander, where a colonel sat behind a writing desk, and behind a long table, for guests, were twenty officers. At our appearance, all stood up. They greeted us with smiles and invited us to sit. Now not only we but also they began to ask questions. There were various issues. The first was the whereabouts of their commanders, the following ones were clearly provocational. To reply straight out that the admiral and the colonel were on our ship would significantly untie the hands of the airfield commander, who could then take command upon himself and move to evacuate his troops to the American zone.

We had to extricate ourselves from this situation somehow, and, when the colonel sharply raised his voice, saying, "Where are our commanders, you should know!" I threw up my hands.

I replied, "When they depart for somewhere, my command does not normally report to me, and yours even less. My command, perhaps, does not know about my presence here."

Then we were quiet for a while. A representative of fleet

headquarters, Captain Third Rank Kulebyakin, was with us, and he answered all of the remaining questions. I stepped in only when I saw that they were pressing him up against the wall. At one point, for example, the colonel jumped up, his face contorted by an evil grimace. "Why are your soldiers committing atrocities in our officer cantonment area?"

Kulebyakin began to speak about our enlightened discipline, about our absolute intolerance of any inhumane actions. This was all correct, but I had to help him because only the scouts knew the location of the officers' quarters, which were not nearby, but in the green zone. The naval infantry, crowded into the port, naturally had not been able to slip through the encirclement and cross the entire city just to find the officers' camp. So I very firmly stated, "I consider your question to be provocational. Not one of our soldiers has been to this place about which you speak and cannot have been. You yourself understand the absurdity of your assertions. If anything at all like this had happened, you always could have grabbed one or two soldiers at the scene of the crime. Show me the criminal, and I will immediately give the order to shoot him. But I implore you not to ask any more questions like this."

My decisive tone had a sobering effect on the colonel, and he did not ask any more questions. It was interesting to observe how their facial expressions changed. When we had entered, everyone was all smiles, and the first questions were asked in a syrupy tone. Then the smiles quickly faded, and they glared at us more frequently. Finally, it was obvious to everyone that they were stalling, so I got up and declared, "We didn't come here for an evening of questions and answers. We came here to clarify, finally, when you intend to surrender."

In reply, there was silence. And then I again promised to create a "sea of fire." This elicited a response: officers jumped up as though they had been stung. The colonel, pounding his fist on the table, began to yell hysterically, "This will not happen! A decision has been made. You will remain here, in the headquarters. They will escort you to another room, where there is comfortable furniture, and you will rest until the return of our commanders. Then they will release you. Order your troops to leave the airfield, or we will destroy them."

"That is not so simple, Honorable Colonel," I calmly replied.

"This is our concern. We will do our best," interrupted the colonel.

Now everything became clear. The lines had been drawn. There was no need to wonder how events would turn out. It was time to find a sure exit from this critical situation. Captain Third Rank Kulebyakin warned the colonel, "We know that the Japanese emperor has already signed the act of capitulation. We consider your actions to be unsanctioned."

"We do not know this. The army does not have an order, and we follow orders," the colonel answered.

We had to act quickly and energetically. The Japanese officers tensely followed our movements. It was felt that the scouts were prepared for anything. Operating on the principle of battle that says that in a fight between two enemies, one must surrender, it would have been possible to undertake a decisive action. We were convinced that these men were afraid and that we could take them, but what would that have gained? We couldn't take the entire garrison prisoner, and therefore our mission would not be accomplished. We needed the officers to remain alive, and we would have to use psychology to force them to lay down their weapons.

I permitted myself a small retreat.

More than once I'd come across lines in newspapers that were supposed to be from the letters of soldiers, something like: "My love, with joy I am prepared to give my life for you." They always bewildered me. I'd seen how soldiers really died, struggling with all of their will, gathering up their nerve. Sure, they'd give their lives for the Motherland, but only if there was no other way to accomplish the mission. Maybe these Japanese didn't want to die either. So it was necessary to make them believe that they would die before they could overcome us.

But how? To convince someone to believe your threat—to get him to raise his arms in surrender—it's necessary to rivet his glance to yours, hard and authoritative. Only then will he realize the futility of his situation and believe it. But it's not simple to make eye contact with twenty people. Nevertheless, there was a way! I wasn't alone in the office. My combat comrades were with me, and I knew they would immediately understand my plan. Therefore, turning for a moment toward my comrades, I said to the colonel, "Please explain to me the rights and obligations of hostages. We have never before been in such a role."

The colonel made a wry face but answered, "We simply will wait together for the return of our commanders. It is past time for them to be here."

"And if they do not come?"

The colonel was silent. I persisted. "We fought through the entire war in the West. We have adequate experience to evaluate the situation. No, we will not be hostages—better that we die. But we'll die together with you! The only difference is that you will die here, like rats, but we will try to break out."

Senior Sailor Mitya Sokolov, Hero of the Soviet Union, quickly stood up near the colonel's chair.[33] Forgetting about his handkerchief, the colonel wiped the sweat from his forehead with his sleeve. Petty Officer First Class Andrey Pshenichnykh, Hero of the Soviet Union, ignoring the fact that everyone was standing, was sitting near the door. Senior Sailor Volodya Olyashev—athlete, more than once champion of the Soviet Union in skiing, Meritorious Master of Sport—picked up Andrey and his chair and carried him over by the table and then took up the spot by the door himself. Petty Officer First Class Semyon Agafonov, Hero of the Soviet Union, began to juggle some grenades. Senior Lieutenant Ivan Ivanovich Guznenkov, having opened the window, looked below and lightheartedly said, "What's this about breaking out? It's only a short distance to the ground!"

The scouts were in their element. They did everything so quickly and precisely that the Japanese weren't able to come to their senses. Now they believed they were doomed, but, oh, they didn't want to die, especially since they knew that the war had been irrevocably lost.

Yes, they decided on capitulation, but they made one final attempt to deceive us. The colonel declared, "To avoid bloodshed, we agree to lay down our weapons. You wait in the other room or go for a stroll in the street, and we will summon the unit commanders and give them the order for their subsequent actions."

I answered him sharply. "No! We have paper and ink. Write the order. Do it now."

"But they will recognize this order only in the headquarters. It will have no effect."

"It will be valid," I persisted. "You have many telephones on the desk. Tell your unit commanders that the troops should form up without weapons on the landing field. When the formation is complete, we will go out to it."

Thus, everything was done at last. Forty minutes had passed. When we went out to the airstrip, we saw that three-and-a-half thousand soldiers stood in a column of four ranks. The scouts quietly watched over them. A group of sailors from the torpedo boats, armed with submachine guns, led by division commander Captain Lieutenant Malik, also had come up on the airfield.

This was a victory! But this was only half the mission, and perhaps not the most difficult. How were we to escort such an enormous mass along the narrow and winding streets to the collection point? I requested that the column re-form in eight ranks. Already they were carrying out our commands quickly, on the run. The colonel, perhaps understanding our difficulty with escorting, hastened to wash his hands. "We have accommodated your request. The troops are formed up. Now I absolve myself of any responsibility for anything that should happen."

"No, Honorable Colonel, not so fast, not so fast!" I interrupted. "Your troops will walk to the designated place under your command, but under our observation. You and the chief of staff sit in the light vehicle together with me, the remaining staff officers will go in the bus, and we will go behind the column. If even one soldier flees, then you alone are to blame."

He could do nothing. But he had to make a speech. The colonel spoke much and badly. He recalled the glory of Japanese arms and praised the samurai spirit to the sky. But he finished with the simple order, "Observing discipline and order, begin movement."

The column set off. Not three-and-a-half thousand but nearly five thousand Japanese soldiers and officers arrived at the designated site. Along the way other units had merged into the group. On one of the squares we met a (Japanese) machine-gun company, deploying in combat formation, preparing to open fire. But to fire at whom? They walked in march step, only without singing. And instead of machine-gun bursts, questions poured forth: "What happened?" From the column they answered: "An order for capitulation." "Whose?" "Airfield commander." Soldiers and officers encountered along the way threw away their weapons and joined the column. An hour later the entire garrison had surrendered. Thus ended this remarkable "encirclement."]

On our return to Russian Island, we received a congratulatory telegram from the command of the Pacific Fleet. All the detachment's scouts were awarded decorations for the Seisin operation. Warrant Officer Aleksandr Nikandrov and Chief Petty Officer Babikov were awarded the rank Hero of the Soviet Union. The government awarded me this rank a second time.[34]

* * *

Now the coast of Korea, which they called "land of the morning coolness" and "land of the morning calm," was behind us.

It was morning. Fresh, quiet, and calm. The sun was rising above the sea's horizon. From here it would take its usual path until it slipped away behind another ocean. The explosions of bombs and shells and the crack of shots would not be heard on the entire earth this day.

We stood on the deck and in thankful silence greeted the new day, a day of celebrating victory and peace.

In Place of
an Epilogue

NINE-AND-A-HALF YEARS after the close of the Second World War, a meeting took place in one of the rooms of the Oktyabrskaya [October, in honor of the October 1917 revolution] Hotel in Leningrad, and it is with this meeting that I wanted to finish my recollections about our detachment's naval scouts.

The hotel room belonged to a delegate who had come to attend a conference of agricultural workers of the northwestern regions of the country. The delegate was Makar Andreevich Babikov, Hero of the Soviet Union, secretary of the Komsomol oblast committee, and a deputy of the Supreme Soviet of the Komi Autonomous Republic.

Makar called at the Voroshilov Naval Academy [a midlevel military institution in Leningrad, roughly equivalent to the U.S. Naval War College but not as prestigious as the Voroshilov General Staff Academy in Moscow, a senior service college for all branches of the Soviet Armed Forces], where I was teaching, and after brief greetings we agreed upon a reunion. It would be nice, I said to Makar, to meet other wartime friends who lived in Leningrad: with the former detachment commissar, now Captain First Rank Dubrovskiy, with Captain Second Rank Sutyagin, with Senior Lieutenant Kolosov.

"Pashka Kolosov!" Babikov responded enthusiastically. "Pashka a senior lieutenant? How did you find him, Viktor Nikolaevich?"

"Very simple! I called the mechanical institute, the night

section, where Kolosov teaches. And we should call Kronshtadt, where Warrant Officer Baryshev works."

"Pashka Baryshev! Outstanding!" Again Makar cut me off.

"And did you know that Aleksey Radyshevtsev lives in Leningrad? He works in a sheet metal shop, but where exactly I don't know."

"We will find Alyosha! Through the address bureau! Who else can we meet with?"

I recalled people who lived near and far. Retired Colonel Leonid Vasilevich Dobrotin was in Moscow, and Guznenkov was teaching there. Aleksandr Nikandrov and Andrey Pshenichnykh were serving in the North, and Nikolay Arkadevich Inzartsev and Semyon Agafonov were on the Black Sea. [Agafonov died on New Year's Day 1977, at age fifty-nine.] It was possible now only to dream about a great gathering of wartime friends. In the meantime we decided to gather together a small group.

So here at a round table in a room in the Oktyabrskaya Hotel sat Dubrovskiy, Sutyagin, Babikov, Baryshev, Radyshevtsev, Kolosov, and I. There was no end to the questions and answers, the joyous exclamations.

Time had left its mark on the appearance of each of us. The former detachment commissar, senior *politruk*, was, I remembered, blond. But now in front of us sat Captain First Rank Vasiliy Mikhaylovich Dubrovskiy, remarkably heavy, with a graying head. Sutyagin was more lively and energetic, and it made him look younger. Kolosov was grasping for middle age, trying to appear older than his years. This was that same gray-eyed young boy Pasha Kolosov, whom I feared to send on reconnaissance. Radyshevtsev and Baryshev were true to themselves. The first said little, with measured tones, holding back his feelings, and did not take his eyes off the former clerk. Radyshevtsev rejoiced in the success of Makar Babikov, who after the war finished a higher party school and now occupied a responsible party post. Warrant Officer Baryshev poured forth in conversation. He was always a joker.

We recalled all our friends. Good memories of those who had died and those who survived. Someone began to list the professions of the former scouts. There were among us, it turned out, officers and party workers, teachers and engineers, candidates in technical sciences and metal craftsmen. There was a Master of Sport and even a national champion in skiing. These among those about whom we knew. With many others, ties had been broken. How we had wished that they had responded and let us know about themselves.

Countless times my wartime friends had expressed a desire that a book be written—a brief but accurate story about the detachment, its affairs and people. How many times each regretted that in the difficult days of the war, crammed with large events, he had not kept a diary that would now help recreate the combat chronicle of the detachment.

I told my friends that the Military Publishing House was planning to bring out such a book, and asked everyone to share his recollections with the author of a literary account. I use this occasion to express to them, as well as to L. V. Dobrotin and I. I. Guznenkov, my thanks. Many scouts, my former commanders, those equal to me in rank, and my subordinates, helped us write this book.

This also was a manifestation of that wartime friendship, that comradeship, which accompanied us in those bitter fights face-to-face with the enemy, that friendship which one needs in battle and in peacetime labor, and about which Edward Bagritskiy, the poet who fervently loved the sea, wrote:

> *Nevertheless, like a hunter, each is alert.*
> *The graying head is clear.*
> *And songs aplenty.*
> *And a dear wind.*
> *And friendship comes into its own.*

We said good-bye until we met once again.

We wished each other health and in all of our endeavors, as it goes among sailors, a following wind!

Appendix A

Reconnaissance Detachments in Other Fleets and Flotillas

BLACK SEA FLEET

The Black Sea Fleet formed a ground reconnaissance detachment in the late summer or early fall of 1941.[1] The approximately ninety men were recruited from naval and naval infantry units in the Sevastopol region and received parachute, land navigation, German and Romanian language and demolitions training in the fleet school. Their barracks was a former rest home located in a wooded valley several kilometers from Sevastopol.

In November 1941, after three or four months of training, this detachment conducted its first combat mission, ground reconnaissance of German positions twenty kilometers north of the fleet main base at Sevastopol. In early December, the detachment executed a successful raid on the German-occupied city of Evpatoriya, attacking the police station and airfield. In mid-December a small group of men landed on the south coast of the Crimea and for two weeks ambushed German military vehicles moving along the coastal highway.[2] The parent detachment operated out of its base at Sevastopol until May 1942, when some of its men were sent to the Azov Flotilla base at Novorossiisk. Others remained at Sevastopol to aid in the defense of the city, while a third group went to Tuapse, on the east shore of the Black Sea.[3]

After another period of training for newly assigned personnel, the Azov Flotilla component moved to its new base at Taman, east of Kerch Straits. From there the detachment operated for two months along the German-occupied coast of Kerch Peninsula, reporting on German coastal shipping and land traffic. In August 1942, the group stood down for a brief rest, then moved to the Caucasus. Deployed in several small detachments, it conducted ground reconnaissance and raids in support of and subordinated to units of the Red Army against German mountain troops for about six weeks.

In October 1942, the detachment was resubordinated to the Black Sea Fleet, and in early 1943 it resumed ground reconnaissance along the coastline north of Novorossiisk. In one action in early May, an entire Soviet platoon was surrounded and destroyed by German troops.[4] The detachment commander, D. S. Kalinin, received the Hero of the Soviet Union award posthumously for his fight to the death. Another platoon avoided capture and walked out by an overland route. Its commander, N. Zemtsov, was also named a Hero of the Soviet Union.

In June 1943 several members of the detachment parachuted into the southern coast of the Crimea to conduct operations with the partisans.[5] The naval scouts conducted reconnaissance against German airfields, garrisons, and supply centers and radioed the information they obtained back to fleet headquarters. Other patrols from the detachment, which included female radio operators, parachuted into the hills overlooking the south coast near Yalta. Over a period of several months these groups directed air strikes against German coastal shipping.[6]

In December 1943, the naval scouts established contact with the underground organization in Sevastopol and began to supply it with leaflets, explosives, and a radio for sabotage operations within the city.[7] These activities continued until the liberation of the peninsula and the city in April–May 1944. Subsequently the reconnaissance detachment personnel were transferred to the Danube Flotilla.

AZOV FLOTILLA

The history of the Azov Flotilla reconnaissance detachment dates to 1941, when the flotilla, commanded by the young admiral Sergey Georgievich Gorshkov, was based at Primorsko-Akhtarsk, on the east coast of the Sea of Azov.[8] Memoir accounts indicate that this flotilla had an active ground reconnaissance force in October 1941 that, until mid-1942, operated against German garrisons and positions along the north coast of the Sea of Azov, from Berdyansk to Taganrog, penetrating inland as far as fifty kilometers.[9] When the German ground offensive threatened the flotilla base in the summer of 1942, that base was displaced to the west and south, eventually winding up at Novorossiisk. There in June 1942 scouts from the Black Sea Fleet merged with the Azov unit for operations in the mountains along the southeast coast of the Black Sea.

The Azov Flotilla did not return to its home ports until after the spring of 1943, when the Germans slowly began to withdraw after their defeat at Stalingrad. Ground reconnaissance operations resumed against the German-occupied north shore of the Sea of Azov. Naval scouts conducted many raids along the coast either in support of landing operations or to gather intelligence. By October 1943, the front was once again on the east shore of the Crimea at Kerch Peninsula, and Azov Flotilla reconnaissance detachment elements, among them a female intelligence agent, were on the peninsula itself, sending reports back by radio.[10] In November 1943, in support of the Kerch-El'tigen operation, the naval scouts went ashore ahead of amphibious landing units to determine the precise location and strength of German defenses. After the complete liberation of Kerch Peninsula in April 1944, the Azov Flotilla was disbanded. Its boats, commander, staff, and personnel, including the reconnaissance detachment, were transferred to the Danube Flotilla, then preparing for the offensive into Romania.

DANUBE FLOTILLA

In August 1944 the first boats of the Danube Flotilla moved from Soviet ports into the Danube River. The reconnaissance detachment of this flotilla consisted of veterans of the Azov Flotilla and Black Sea Fleet detachments, commanded by Senior Lieutenant Viktor Kalganov, formerly of the Black Sea Fleet detachment.[11] From late 1944 until the end of the war in Europe in May 1945, this detachment reconnoitered the Danube River in advance of the flotilla, performing several missions: selecting the safest route up the river for the flotilla; locating any mines or mine fields the Germans had placed in the water, often through interrogation of local nationals; determining the precise position of German shore batteries that could interfere with movement of the flotilla; and capturing enemy soldiers (in Russian *yazyki*, "tongues") ashore for interrogation. Because the flotilla was subordinated to a *front* of the Red Army, reconnaissance reports were quickly passed from the flotilla to the *front* commander.

A good example of the unique style of this detachment is shown in its contribution to the battle for Budapest in January 1945.[12] Naval scouts went into the German-occupied city and, with help from a local national, found the office of the river control authority. They blew open a safe and took from it a document containing the complete obstacle plan for the river through and above Budapest. On another occasion the scouts made their way to the island between the two halves of the city and determined the precise location of a particularly active German artillery battery. Still another time a small group of scouts crawled through the city sewer system for three hours, came out near the German garrison headquarters in the palace in

...a, abducted two German officers, and took them back through the sewer to Soviet lines.

The reconnaissance detachment of the Danube Flotilla fought along the river as far as Vienna, where several of its members were killed in the capture of the city's bridges. At the conclusion of hostilities in May 1945, the remaining men of the detachment sailed back downstream and helped clear the Danube of debris and mines.

DNEPR RIVER FLOTILLA

The history of the reconnaissance detachment of the Dnepr River Flotilla is brief and somewhat obscure.[13] The flotilla was formed for the third time in September 1943, based on the personnel and vessels of the Volga River Flotilla.[14] In the early summer of 1944 the flotilla was subordinated to Marshal K. K. Rokossovskiy's First Belorussian *Front* to support the left flank of the *front* along the Pripyat River. In late June, in preparation for offensive actions toward the city of Pinsk, the flotilla commander formed a reconnaissance detachment from sailors of the flotilla's smoke-laying and decontamination unit.[15] The detachment commander was a junior lieutenant, a veteran of the defensive battles at Odessa and Sevastopol, with ground reconnaissance experience. Several of his scouts had fought as naval infantrymen in ground combat before being assigned to the flotilla.

In late June and into July, the platoon-size detachment conducted several landing operations behind German lines, during which ten of its thirty-two members earned the award Hero of the Soviet Union.[16] The Dnepr River Flotilla went on to fight in Poland and Germany, taking part in the capture of Berlin. The reconnaissance detachment does not appear in Soviet sources under that name but appears to have been reorganized or subsumed into another organization named the 1st Separate Fast Boat Detachment (in Russian, *1-yy otdel'nyy otryad poluglisserov*), attached to the Dnepr River Flotilla's 1st Brigade.[17] This unit was created in the fall of 1944, after the completion of the Soviet campaign into Belorussia, but did not go into action until April 1945 after the spring thaw. In the battle for Berlin, this unit conducted amphibious assaults across the river Spree. Its commanding officer and eight men earned the award Hero of the Soviet Union for their actions in these final days of the war.

BALTIC FLEET

Baltic Fleet headquarters formed a reconnaissance detachment in mid- to late 1941, subordinated it to the intelligence staff,[18] and based it on Kronshtadt Island. Its members infiltrated into Finnish territory north of Leningrad by boat and later across the ice to locate Finnish army positions and airfields.[19] Teams of sailor-scouts later parachuted into German-occupied territory west of Leningrad to locate German positions and units. There are also references in Soviet sources to small diversionary groups landed by submarine and torpedo cutter west of Leningrad to attack German rear area objectives.[20]

A second type of operation conducted by this detachment was the parachute insertion of several female agents into German-occupied Estonia in mid-1942. Equipped with communications gear, they were assigned to reconnoiter Estonian ports to establish the frequency, routes, and cargo of German naval and commercial ship traffic. These agents were part of a larger effort of the Baltic Fleet to interdict the shipment of iron ore from Sweden to Germany.[21]

In 1943–44, the Baltic Fleet reconnaissance detachment also supported partisan operations, with the insertion by parachute of men and supplies to organize, lead, and support partisan units operating along the Baltic littoral west of Leningrad.[22]

Finally, among the personnel assigned to the intelligence section of the fleet staff was a group of trained divers from the Red Navy's underwater salvage and rescue service, EPRON.[23] Stranded in Leningrad by the rapid German advance, this group of approximately twenty-five men, at the suggestion of Admiral I. S. Isakov, was assigned to the intelligence section of Baltic Fleet staff.[24] They were employed for prelanding reconnaissance of the German-occupied shorelines of Lake Ladoga, Narva Bay, and the Neva River. They also executed attacks against isolated and unguarded bridges and other targets.

Because this group was based on Decembrist Island, between Leningrad and Kronshtadt, and not with the fleet's ground reconnaissance detachment on Kronshtadt, its subordination is uncertain.[25] Men of physically small stature in the unit were trained to swim out of the torpedo tubes of submarines, indicating a possible connection to the submarine reconnaissance element of fleet intelligence. But these EPRON divers clearly executed missions similar to those of the larger reconnaissance detachment and could well have performed them jointly.

AMUR RIVER FLOTILLA

The Amur River Flotilla was based in the city of Khabarovsk in the Far East.[26] When the Soviets attacked the Japanese forces in Manchuria in August, the Amur River Flotilla was subordinated to the Second Far Eastern *Front* supporting that *front*'s offensive along the course of the Sungari River toward Harbin. The 71st Special Purpose Detachment of the Amur River Flotilla distinguished itself in combat during several amphibious landings in August 1945 against Japanese forces.[27] The detachment commander, Captain S. M. Kuznetsov, earned the award Hero of the Soviet Union for his actions in one of these battles.

PACIFIC FLEET

The 140th Reconnaissance Detachment of Headquarters, Pacific Fleet, was formed some weeks before the Soviets declared war on Japan, from a mixture of inexperienced Pacific Fleet personnel and combat veterans of Viktor Leonov's Northern Fleet detachment. Because Leonov wrote about this brief period in the concluding chapter of his memoir, a discussion will be found in that chapter and supporting notes.

Appendix B

Supreme Commander of the 20th (Mountain) Army
22.2.1943
  Section Ic Az A 8 Nr. 810/43 secret

Secret!

Enemy situation from 21.1 to 20.2.1943

[base document begins at frame 001305]

[Annex 3 to base document, beginning at frame 001328]

*Partisan activity and Organization in the sector of 20th
(Mountain) Army*

b) *Changes in the partisan organization and in the structure, strength, and armament of the partisan organization
and deployed troops.*

[frame 001329]

4) The *Reconnaissance (and Diversionary) Detachment of*

Source: Germany, Heer, AOK 20 [Germany, Army, 20th Army],
Kriegstagebuch nr. 1 [War diary no. 1], microfilm series T-312, roll 1649,

the Northern Fleet is controlled from Murmansk or Polyarnoye. This detachment belongs to the Red Navy, Russian partisans, and Norwegian volunteers together. There are also many criminals in their complement, who through the reconnaissance detachment have the opportunity to exculpate their guilt. The personnel of the reconnaissance detachment receive general military training, especially topography, compass, and map reading, but no special training.

The insertion occurs frequently in the form of ski patrols, sometimes in civilian clothes made of reindeer fur or also in Russian ski uniforms with camouflage outer garments.

The so-called "Diversionaries" are inserted into the Norwegian and Finnish coastal areas. It is believed that these partisan groups are among those which were landed by submarine or from rubber boats in quiet fjords. Most of these people have mastered the Norwegian language. The groups are up to sixty men in strength and primarily under Norwegian leadership. For the accomplishment of their missions the diversionaries go singly into the Norwegian northern coast.

The leadership of the diversionary groups lies in the hands of Captain Second Rank Visgin, whose deputy is Lieutenant Colonel Dubrotin. Landings of the diversionaries are carried out only in civilian clothes.

The headquarters of the Reconnaissance Detachment of the Northern Fleet is in Polyarnoye. Two groups are subordinated to this headquarters [end of frame 001329], of which Visgin is the chief. The first group operates for reconnaissance in the rear area, the second group (diversionaries) operates only in Norway. The Reconnaissance Detachment is subordinated to the commander of the Northern Fleet and to the Central Intelligence Directorate in Moscow.

frames 001305–30, National Archives and Records Administration, Washington, D.C. Translated by James F. Gebhardt.

Appendix C

Supreme Commander of the 20th (Mountain-) Army
19 November 1943
Ic/AO Journal Nr. 96/43 Top Secret
Soviet Espionage Activity in the Varanger Region
1 Sketch

5 Copies
1st of 5 copies

To
Oberkommando des Herres
Army actions section (Abwehr) with the General [staff] for
special duty at OKH

   Below is a report about a case of Soviet-Norwegian
agent activity in the Varanger Region, of which this disclo-

Source: Germany, Heer, AOK 20 [Germany, Army, 20th Army],
Kriegstagebuch nr. 1 [War diary no. 1], microfilm series T-312, roll 1651,
frames 000682–89, National Archives and Records Administration, Washington, D.C. Translated by Harold S. Orenstein and James F. Gebhardt. This
document names thirteen Norwegian and Soviet personnel as members of
Northern Fleet's intelligence department deployed on Varanger Peninsula.
Of this group, Richard Johansen, Franz Mathisen, Harald Utne, Leif Utne,
Trygve Eriksen, Aage Halvari, (Henri) Petersen, and Oscar Johnsen are also
named in Babikov, *Otryad*, or in *Voyna*. This book contains several references to the Norwegian-Soviet platoon's actions in late 1942 and early 1943.
Babikov's account of the German success in luring in a Soviet submarine
(M-105) in October 1943, noted in the above document, is contained in chap-
ter 14.

sure covers the months of July, August, September, and October 1943.

A. *Persons*:

a. *Vertyanskiy*, Georgiy, Russian prisoner of war, 20 years old, member of the intelligence department of the Northern Fleet, Polyarnoye, taken prisoner on 17 September 1942 at Titovka. He supplied the first accounts concerning agent activity in northern Norway.

b. *Members of the intelligence department of the Northern Fleet deployed on Varanger were:*

1. *Yessipov*, Vasiliy, Russian soldier, 20 years old, taken prisoner on 15 July 1943 at Seglodden (Varanger).

2. *Vlasov*, Boris, Russian soldier, was separated from Yessipov on 1 April 1943. Not captured.

3. Harald *Utne*, fled from Kiberg at the beginning of the war, Norwegian, 32 years old, taken prisoner on 27 August 1943 at Komagvaer (Varanger).

4. Leif *Utne*, fled from Kiberg at the beginning of the war, Norwegian, 20 years old, taken prisoner on 27 August 1943 at Komagvaer (Varanger).

5. Haakon *Halvari*, fled from Kiberg at the beginning of the war, Norwegian, 38 years old, shot in a skirmish at Persfjord on 28 July 1943.

6. Oscar *Johnsen*, from Kiberg, Norwegian, 42 years old, shot in a skirmish at Persfjord on 28 July 1943.

7. Trygve *Eriksen*, fled from Kiberg at the beginning of the war, Norwegian, 42 years old, departed in spring 1943 and returned to Murmansk.

8. Franz *Mathisen*, fled from Kiberg at the beginning of the war, Norwegian. Shot himself during capture at Persfjord on 27 August 1943.

9. Ricard *Johansen*, fled from Kiberg at the beginning of the war, Norwegian, 24 years old, not captured.

10. Bjorne *Jorstad*, Norwegian, emigrated to Russia before age 24, 26 years old, not captured.

11. *Kore*, fled from Kiberg at the beginning of

the war, Norwegian, shot in the skirmish at Persfjord on 28 July 1943.

      12. Aage *Halvari*, fled from Kiberg at the beginning of the war, Norwegian, taken prisoner on 20 October 1943 at Seglodden.

      13. *Petersen*, fled from Kiberg at the beginning of the war, Norwegian, taken prisoner on 24 October 1943 at Havningsberg.

  c. *Informers from among the population of the Varanger Peninsula: 41 Norwegian men and women.*

B. *Background:*

    a. Since the summer of 1942, an increasing number of German convoys to Kirkenes and other supply ports of the 20th (Mountain) Army have been attacked by Russian submarines and aircraft near the North Varanger coast. At the same time, many freighters with valuable cargo and military vehicles have been lost. These attacks, according to observation, have been by enemy submarines which lie in wait in fjords. Radio communication from land was not detectable.

    b. In November 1942 a Russian prisoner of war named Vertyanskiy, who was taken prisoner in a combined attack operation against Mogilnyy and was treated as a prisoner of war, voluntarily came forward and declared that he was a member of the Northern Fleet intelligence section, Polyarnoye, and could give information about the activity of Soviet espionage troops.

  His interrogation by AOK 20 (Mtn) Ic/AO [Abwehr liaison officer to the operations staff of the Twentieth Mountain Army] established that the intelligence section of the Northern Fleet has formed a combined "diversionary unit" made up of Norwegian fugitives and Russians and is sending this espionage troop unit in groups of about four men to the Kirkenes area. *Their mission:* discovery of positions, determining the arrivals and departures of ships, and sending radio messages to Murmansk and to the submarines.

Mode of operation: in civilian clothes, observation of ship traffic out from the coast. Formation of a network of informers within the Norwegian population. *Landing of troops at mission location:* by submarine and rubber boat in isolated fjords.

In March 1943 Vertyanskiy was put at the disposal of the Kirkenes Abwehr Office for the Conduct of Undercover Investigations for use as an informant. Commander Kuhl, Abwehr Office Kirkenes, put the Kirkenes radio direction-finding squad and undercover agents into action with Vertyanskiy's participation. The Kirkenes radio direction-finding squad reported a radio message with the call signal VKO on 27 April 1943. Via Radar Station Oslo Nr. 11 on 3 May 1943, journal Nr. 266/43 (classified), on the basis of a determination of the Radar Net Control Station Berlin, the radio message was declared to be from the Finnish service, and cessation of monitoring was ordered. In fact, a later discovery from radio data and the arrest of a Soviet radio operator established that it had concerned a radio message from a Soviet agent's radio station in Kola. On 10 July 1943 Commander Kuhl's successor, Captain Terlinden, had use elsewhere for Vertyanskiy on the grounds that he had shown himself unsuitable for intelligence work. Subsequently Vertyanskiy was turned over to the prisoner-of-war section, Commandant of the Lapland District, by the AOK 10, Ic/AO, and was assigned to the liberation army [this is a reference to ROA, Rossiyskaya osvoboditelnaya armiya (Russian liberation army), commanded by General Vlasov].

C. *Search Operation. Locating the Radio Station:*

Through statements by Vertyanskiy and through reports from other sources, the suspicion grew stronger that the enemy was getting intelligence out of the country and had established more radio stations in the Varanger region. The Varanger Peninsula was combed by reconnaissance patrols jointly by the 210th Infantry Division, Kirkenes Secret Service, Abwehr Office Kirkenes, and the commander of the Kirkenes sea defense (operation "Midnight Sun"), the population investigated and identified by name. In addition, there followed a request, with reward money, for information on enemy agents and suspicious observations. On 14 July 1943, during an ensuing search for submarine bases in Kongsfjord, the remnants of a Russian radio station (see sketch, radio station 4) were found near Lokvik.

At the same time there followed a report from the people of Syltefjord about observation of a parachute drop. An extension of the search operation to Syltefjord and Persfjord resulted in finding a radio station (2) with a transmitter at Syltevik on 14 July 1943, finding a radio station (1) with two transmitters in Persfjord on 15 July 1943, and the capture of the Russian radio operator Yessipov, who was staying there.

On 23 July 1943, a subsequent search operation involving the cooperation of army and navy and conducted on the entire northern coast of the Varanger Peninsula led to the discovery of another radio station (3) in Kongsfjord. This only came about because of our evaluation of captured documents and statements by prisoners.

Finally, one more radio station (5) was found in the area of Buevandet, which had evidently avoided detection.

On 28 July 1943, a surprise search operation by naval reconnaissance in Persfjord resulted in a clash with three agents, who were killed while resisting. Two radio transmitters and important radio documents were found. The dead agents turned out to be Ricard Johansen, Kore, and Haakon Halvari.

In the course of these operations, the population of the entire area was screened by the 210th Infantry Division and Kirkenes secret service. [end of frame 000684]

The evaluation of captured documents and the confrontation with prisoner Yessipov led to the arrest of a total of forty-one Norwegians, some of whom were guilty of being informers and others of offering lodging and support. Of these, nineteen were convicted, eleven sentenced to death by a court-martial of the 210th Infantry Division, and eight sentenced to extensive imprisonment. The verdicts were carried out, and the executions were publicly announced. The remaining prisoners were sent to a labor camp because of unprovable suspicions.

On the basis of reports from the population, on 27 August 1943 two agents, the Norwegians Harald and Leif Utne, were taken prisoner at Komagvaer, and two radio transmitters were secured. A third agent, Franz Mathisen, shot himself.

With the help of the agent Leif Utne, a radio game began with Murmansk. Purpose: to lure more agents. Extraction by submarine. Destruction of submarines.

As a result of the call for help, there followed many drops of provisions by airplanes; on 5 October 1943 two agents were parachuted into the interior of the Varanger Peninsula. On 20 October 1943 a submarine approached the designated pickup site at Seglodden, and an agent, Aage Halvari from Kiberg, was put ashore; he was taken prisoner. An alert antitank gun hit the submarine; a depth charge launched by the navy was unsuccessful so that the submarine presumably escaped.

An agent named Petersen, who, according to Halvari, was landed by a submarine at Seglodden on 19 October 1943, was arrested at Havningsberg on 24 October 1943.

D. *From Events and Interrogations: A Picture of the Process of Agent Activity in the Varanger Region:*

From the interrogation of Vertyanskiy, the office directing the mission is known as the Intelligence Section (RO [*razvedyvatel'nyy otdel*]) of the Northern Fleet in Polyarnoye, the head of which is *Captain Visgin*. Apart from commandos carrying out measures against German strongpoints, this section has as its main mission the reconnaissance of northern Norwegian coastal areas, the German ship supply lines to and from Kirkenes and other supply ports of the 20th (Mountain) Army naturally being the most important target, and with that the maintenance of bases for operations.

The section drew its agents, as knowledgeable of the area

as possible, from a group of sixty Norwegian communists, who had fled in a cutter from the area of Vardo and Kiberg to Murmansk at the beginning of the war. Training and assembly of the espionage troops took place in a special "Saboteur Department."

Makeup of Troops: Three to six men (excluding the radio operator, who in most cases is Russian) composed of the above-mentioned Norwegians.

Dress: Civilian clothing with uniforms (with no indication of rank) underneath; good winter clothing.

Equipment: Radio transmitters, firearms, egg-shaped hand grenades, essential utensils, leaflets, writing materials, medical supplies, small cameras, field glasses, *money.*

Transport to the deployment area was by submarine; landing was by rubber boat.

Supply by means of parachute drop and submarine; otherwise from the local area.

Mission: With help from the communists among the population, observation of ship traffic and collection of all obtainable information about shipping and other military objectives, mine fields, forbidden waterways, coastal fortifications, batteries, etc. Transmission by radio.

The method of operation is best described in the mission of the agent mentioned above in A:

On 25 October 1942, the squad consisting of Leif Utne, Harald Utne, and Trygve Eriksen received from Captain *Visgin* the mission to go to Lokvik; they had been brought to Polyarnoye on 26 August 1942 on a submarine and on 28 October 1942 were put ashore at Lokvik with many months' worth of rations. The leader was Eriksen, who after a few days undertook to get in touch with the communists of the population. Following this, a whole series of Norwegian communists, who had arranged to bring information to the patrol on the shore, came voluntarily to the radio station (4). They were paid off with only a little money because, as communists, they were gladly ready to volunteer. On Eriksen's instructions, some ten of these Norwegians undertook a reconnaissance mission to Vardø, Vadsø, Tanafjord, and Hammerfest.

According to instructions, there followed a radio report to Murmansk about transports and warships, troop movements, guardposts and military construction, transfers from guardposts, areas of mine fields and prohibited waterways, impact of Russian aircraft and warships, German objectives, and patrols. In the course of time, an enormous quantity of such intelligence was obtained.

On 6 April 1943, *Eriksen* was extracted and provisions for the summer months were brought in by submarine. Franz *Mathisen* replaced Eriksen. Eriksen took all the written records.

On 22 June 1943, the patrol moved to radio station (3) in Kongsfjord, which provided better observation and protection.

With the approach of German soldiers on 13 July 1943, the patrol fled inland, received more provisions on request, and was captured at Komagvaer on 27 August 1943.

Likewise, the two Kores and Oskar Johnsen operated from Kiberg near Syltevik at radio station (2) with the help of four of the local people. Their work resulted in a voluminous handbook with notes about dispatched radio messages (which was captured).

One of the Kores and Johnsen were shot on 28 July 1943 in Persfjord during a visit to the radio station.

Radio station (1) at Seglodden had been in existence since January 1943 and was occupied by the agents H. Halvari, R. Johannsen, Bjorne Jorstad, and Yessipov. The circle of informers of this radio station consisted of four Norwegians from the surrounding area.

H. Halvari was shot at radio station (1) on 28 July 1943.

Each of the patrols was assigned a specific sector, thereby watching over the north Varanger coast without any gaps. The coastal area of Vardø, Vadsø, Hammerfest, and Kirkenes was included in the reconnaissance by the group of informers, who were enthusiastically and extensively busy with their communist activities. The successes of the agents were undoubtedly significant.

E. *Countermeasures:*

The principal search operations for discovering agent networks are described under C.

The families of the arrested Norwegians were evacuated from the coastal area by the Kirkenes secret service.

They refrained from further evacuation for the following reasons:

a) The occupation by German troops of the northern coast of the Varanger Peninsula without any gaps is not possible.

b) With a complete evacuation the enemy would be offered an even larger area for landing operations and for hiding than before, when he had to reckon with part of the population which betrayed him.

c) Reports from the people were decisive for discovering radio station 2 in Syltevik and radio station 5 in Kongsfjord.

The registration of civilian personnel, begun by the 210th Division, will be continued.

Cooperating with the Kirkenes secret service, Abwehr Office Kirkenes, and the navy, the 210th Infantry Division is maintaining continuous surveillance of the civilian population.

Patrols and posts on the coast increase the risk for Soviet agents.

The "radio game" that was begun with the help of agents who had been taken prisoner, and which had as its purpose to lure and destroy submarines and agents, has already been successful and will be continued.

The population will function as a net of agents. Reindeer herders in the interior of the peninsula will be won over to conduct observation.

The well-meaning portion of the Norwegian population, which now is aware of severe punishment, will be enlisted by means of rewards, partly in kind, to cooperate in reconnaissance and reports concerning agents.

For the Army Supreme Commander

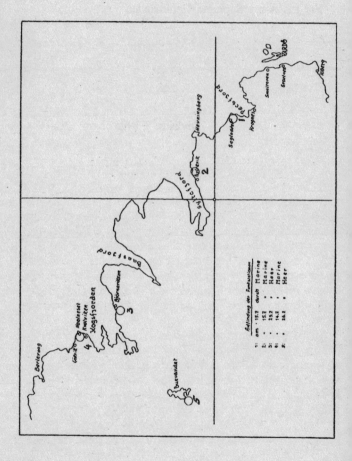

Notes   267

look at Soviet naval torpedo boats in all the fleets, see Meister, *Soviet Warships of the Second World War*, 213–39.

Appendix D

2d Mountain Division   Division Headquarters 12.9.1944
Commander

Soldiers of the 2d Mountain Division!

Although the enemy has not launched any major attacks against us this year, he has forced Finland to lay down its arms and now threatens to extend his grasp to Petsamo.

In front of our strongpoint front, the 31st Ski Rifle Brigade for days has been preparing an attack. Additional forces are probably arrayed behind it. We will permit the enemy to hurl himself against our diligently and solidly built strongpoints and then destroy him through a counterattack.

All advantages are on our side.

The strongpoint garrisons should know that behind them all available battalions and batteries of the 2d Mountain Division are ready for action. The counterattack reserves know what to do when the enemy bloodies himself on the withering defensive fire of our strongpoints.

Above all, I know that the fighting spirit of the 2d Mountain Division is more mature, that every infantryman,

Source: Germany, Heer, 2. Gebirgs-division [Germany, Army, 2d Mountain Division], Kriegstagebuch nr. 1 [War diary no. 1], microfilm seies T-315, roll 109, frame 00823, National Archives and Records Administration, Washington, D.C. Translated by Samuel Lewis and James F. Gebhardt.

every gunner, every engineer soldier will do his best, that none of you will let down the honor of our proud division.

It is ordered that we, in spite of the political changes in Finland, must hold our front. All of you know why this must be so: because we need the nickel and copper from the Kolosjoki works, whose ovens will soon be smoking again, because we must here show the Russians that there is still one front on which their hunger for territory will not be satisfied.

Soldiers of the 2d Mountain Division! The homeland is looking to you! I put my trust in you! We will master every situation, no matter how and when it may develop.

> Hail the Führer!
> /s/Degen
> Commander, 2d Mountain Division

This order is to be issued by 14 September [1944] to all soldiers at roll call or in bunkers by the unit commander or strongpoint commander.

> Chief of the General Staff
> Jodl
> Authorized to sign:
>
> /signature/
>
> Lieutenant colonel

Appendix E

World War II Rank Equivalents

U.S. Navy	U.S. Army	Red Navy
Seaman recruit	Private	Sailor
Seaman apprentice	Private First Class	
Seaman	Corporal	Senior Sailor
Petty Officer Third Class	Sergeant	
Petty Officer Second Class	Staff Sergeant	Petty Officer Second Class
Petty Officer First Class	First Sergeant	Petty Officer First Class
Chief Petty Officer	Master Sergeant	Chief Petty Officer
Warrant Officer	Warrant Officer	Warrant Officer
		Junior Lieutenant
Ensign	Second Lieutenant	Lieutenant
Lieutenant Junior Grade	First Lieutenant	Senior Lieutenant
Lieutenant	Captain	Captain Lieutenant
Lieutenant Commander	Major	Captain Third Rank
Commander	Lieutenant Colonel	Captain Second Rank
Captain	Colonel	Captain First Rank
Commodore	Brigadier General	Rear Admiral
Rear Admiral	Major General	Vice Admiral
Vice Admiral	Lieutenant General	Admiral
Admiral	General	Fleet Admiral
Fleet Admiral	General of the Army	

Notes

INTRODUCTION

1. Hero of the Soviet Union is the highest Soviet award that can be earned for valor or service. Its rough equivalents in the award system of the United States armed forces are Congressional Medal of Honor; Distinguished Service, Air Force, and Navy Crosses; and Distinguished Service Medal(s). This award was given to 11,635 Soviet servicemen and women during World War II. A complete listing of all recipients of this award since its inception in 1934 is contained in the two-volume *Geroi Sovetskogo Soyuza*.

2. Biographical information on Viktor Leonov is from Velichko, *Dvazhdy*.

3. Komsomol is short for Kommunisticheskiy soyuz molodyozhi, the organization that prepared young people for subsequent Communist Party membership.

4. Nikitin, "Podvig."

5. A defensive region (in Russian *oboronitel'nyy rayon*) in this context should be thought of not as a place but as a military unit. The Northern Defensive Region, for example, was a joint service command in the Northern Fleet, responsible for the defense of Rybachiy and Sredniy peninsulas. Led by a coastal defense major general, the command consisted of at least two brigades of naval infantry (Soviet marines), bolstered by several separate battalions of artillery, engineers, machine-gun units, and support troops. For a detailed discussion of the origin and purpose of these commands, see Achkasov, "Iz opyta oborony voyennomorskikh baz (1941–1942gg.)." See also Dvoryanov and Oppokov, "Organizatsiya vzaimodeystviya."

6. See "razvedyvatel'nyy otryad" [reconnaissance detachment], *SVE*, 7:39.

7. Isakov, *Izbrannyye trudy*, 178–83.

8. Ibid., 179.

9. This conclusion is drawn from an indirect reference in the collection

Pobeda, 18: "In the detachment were Kronshtadt sailors, who had the experience of combat on land. . . . A year and a half ago they went into the Finns' rear area on skis."

10. This unique organization has not previously been discussed in Western general or special histories of World War II; a close examination of the Northern Fleet appears below, that of the other fleet and flotilla detachments in Appendix A.

11. The best account in English of the activities of the German army in this theater is U.S. Department of the Army Pamphlet 20-271. There are three excellent accounts of this early fighting in Russian: Babikov, *Letom*, Khudalov, *U kromki kontinenta*, and Veshchezerskiy, *U khladnykh skal*. Khudalov was a regimental commander in the 52d Rifle Division, commanded by Veshchezerskiy, that withstood the brunt of the German attack in the summer and early autumn of 1941.

12. Golovko's meeting with his intelligence chief is described in Babikov, *Letom*, 67–68.

13. Ibid., 69. Vizgin is mentioned in Kvyatkovskiy, "Bespokoynaya," as one of the "leaders and chiefs of intelligence organs" in the Soviet navy during World War II.

14. Babikov, *Letom*, 110.

15. Ibid., 111.

16. The commissar was an officer, normally equal to or one rank lower than the commander, who was responsible for ensuring the political training and reliability of every person in the unit, including the commander himself. He was the unit's deputy commander and at the same time ranking Communist Party member.

17. Babikov, *Letom*, 199. According to Babikov, the Intendant rank was frequently given to accomplished athletes. Historically, however, holders of this rank generally served in rear support elements. Leonov talks about Inzartsev in his 1957 memoir.

18. An account of this operation is given in Babikov, *Otryad*, chaps. 5–8. There is another account of this first submarine insertion in the memoir of the former commander of the Northern Fleet's submarine brigade, Admiral N. I. Vinogradov, *Podvodnyy front*, 58–61.

19. Babikov, *Otryad*, 102.

20. Ibid., 104. According to Babikov, Krymova was a language and area specialist who had lived in Sweden and Norway before the war. She was fluent in all the Scandinavian languages, plus English, French, and German. Biographical data on Krymova is in Babikov, *Voyna*, 116–19. According to Leonov's memoir, Sutyagin spoke Norwegian.

21. Babikov, *Voyna*, 115.

22. This analysis is supported by both Soviet and German documents. A 1950 Soviet Navy report on Northern Fleet intelligence activities during the war describes submarine insertion and extraction of small scout teams in a section of the report distinctly separate from the accounts of the activities of Leonov's detachment. See *Sbornik materialov*, No. 38, 14–20.

The German support for this analysis is an intelligence assessment from February 1943. See Germany, Heer, Kriegstagebuch nr. 1, *Oberkommando der 20. (Geb.) Armee Abt. Ic Az. A 8 Nr. 810/4*, 22.2. 1943, Annex 3, "Bandentätigkeit und Organisation vor (Geb.) A. O. K. 20" [Band activities and organization in front of 20th Mountain Army], microfilm series T-312, roll 1649, frames 001328–29, NARA. See Appendix B for a translation of this document.

23. Babikov, *Otryad*, 103–5.

24. Ibid., chap. 15. Another source indicates that the submarine S-102, commanded by Captain Lieutenant L. I. Gorodnichiy, inserted a reconnaissance group [*razvedgruppa*] in this area on 5 January 1942. After he landed the reconnaissance team, he moved his vessel offshore and over the next several days attacked and sank three German transports. The submarine returned to the pickup site on 18 January and retrieved the team, then returned to base. See Alekseyev, "Primeneniye," 63.

On another occasion, a submarine with a minelaying mission was used to insert a reconnaissance team. See Kolpakov and Shubochkin, "Minnozagraditel'nyye deystviya." *Sbornik materialov*, No. 38, 15, clearly states that the submarines participated in these insertions and extractions in the course of routine patrols along German sea lanes. Only in exceptional cases did a submarine insert and extract reconnaissance teams simultaneously or even on the same patrol.

25. Because of the latitude of this region (between 69 and 70 degrees north latitude, approximately two hundred miles north of the Arctic Circle), light conditions vary dramatically between winter and summer. The terrain and vegetation afforded little natural concealment so darkness was a great ally to the scouts. For a detailed description of the terrain in the Petsamo area, see Kuehnelt-Leddihn, "Petsamo Region."

26. Babikov, *Otryad*, chap. 18.

27. See Ruge, *The Soviets as Naval Opponents*, 154–55. S. I. Kovalenko, the captain of the submarine, was pulled out of the water by the crew of the German minesweeper that had rammed his boat. His foot or leg had apparently become caught in the hatch. For a more complete Soviet perspective of this incident, see Vinogradov, *Podvodnyy*, 92–100. According to Vinogradov, Kovalenko's leg was amputated in a German hospital. The Soviet submarine commander was later imprisoned in France and subsequently was executed by the Germans. Before his death, he told his story to a British submarine captain, himself a prisoner, who passed it along to Soviet naval officials in London after the war.

28. The account of this incident continues in Babikov, *Otryad*, chap. 21, and in chapters 2, 4, and 6 of Babikov, *Voyna*. Vinogradov, *Podvodnyy*, 100, indicates that two of the Norwegians died of injuries sustained during the landing, and the third was probably captured by the Germans. The two sailors from the submarine were also captured but later escaped and rejoined Red Army units. Babikov, in *Voyna*, chap. 6, contends that one Nor-

wegian died of injuries, the Soviet radio operator died of illness ten days later, and the remaining Norwegian agent eluded capture.

29. Babikov, *Otryad*, chaps. 18–21.

30. Ibid., chap. 21. The M class (*malyutka*—small) submarines were extremely small (206 tons surfaced, 258 tons submerged), with a serious shortcoming in buoyancy. They occasionally surfaced involuntarily after firing a torpedo. They were generally employed for a very short-range missions because their fuel supply was limited. It is noteworthy that even these platforms, with their severe space and weight limitations, were used for inserting teams.

31. Ibid., 171.

32. *Sbornik materialov*, No. 38, 14–20, contains brief descriptions of six insertions between September 1941 and October 1943. A German document dated 27 September 1942 notes that two Russian agents with a transmitter were inserted by submarine north of Tromsø and subsequently captured. See *Wehrmachtbefehlshaber Norwegen Ia/O. Qu/Qu 2/Ic/Ao Nr. 951/42*, "Befehl für den Schutz von Wehrwirtschaftsbetrieben" [Order for the defense of military-industrial facilities], Annex 1, microfilm series T-312, roll 1648, frame 000903, NARA.

33. An extraordinary German document describes in detail the mixed Soviet-Norwegian platoon and its activities. See Germany, Heer, Kriegstagebuch nr. 1, *Oberkommando der 20. (Gebirgs-) Armee Ic/AO Tgb. Nr. 96/43*, 19 November 1943, "Sowjetrussische Spionagetätigkeit im Varanger-Raum" [Soviet-Russian espionage activity in the Varanger area], microfilm series T-312, roll 1651, frames 000682–89, NARA. See Appendix C for a translation of this document.

Another document summarizes the November 1943 report and adds a brief account of December 1943 incidents. See Germany, Heer, Kriegstagebuch nr. 1, *Oberkommando der 20. (Gebirgs-) Armee Ic/AO Tgb. Nr. 136/44*, 22 August 1944, "Tätigkeitsbericht der Abt. Ic/AO (Abwehroffizier III) beim Oberkommando der 20. (Gebirgs-) Armee, Zeit: 1.7.–31.12.1943" [Activity report of section Ic.AO (Abwehr officer III) of high command of Twentieth Mountain Army for the period 1 July–31 December 1943], paragraph V.1.C. "Tätigkeit des sowjetrussischen militärischen und zivilen Nachrichtendienstes in der Berichtszeit" [Activities of Soviet-Russian military and civilian intelligence services in the reporting period], microfilm series T-312, roll 1651, relevant passages in frames 000562–64, NARA.

34. See Germany, Heer, Kreigstagebuch nr. 1, *Oberkommando der 20. (Gebirgs-) Armee Ic/AO Tgb. Nr. 1055/43 geh.*, "Tätigkeitsbericht der Abt. Ic/AO (Abwehroffizier) beim Oberkommando der 20. (Geb.) Armee, Zeit 1.1.1943 bis 30.6.1943" [Activity report of section Ic.AO (Abwehr officer) of 20th Mountain Army command for the period 1 January to 30 June 1943], paragraph V. "Abwehr des feindl. (Sowjetr.) Nachrichtendienstes und der sowjetr. Banden." [Intelligence on enemy (Soviet) security services and Soviet partisan/guerrilla groups], microfilm series T-312, roll

1650, beginning at frame 000061 with relevant material at frames 000082–83, NARA. There is no mention of the use of German personnel for these missions in any Soviet source that I have seen.

35. Babikov, *Voyna*, 156–57.

36. Ibid., 175. The four were Semyon Agafonov, Aleksey Antonov, Andrey Pshenichnykh, and Sergey Grigorashchenko. Agafonov and Pshenichnykh are frequently mentioned in Leonov's memoir, and both became Heroes of the Soviet Union in 1944 for their actions at Cape Krestovyy.

37. Babikov discusses this mission at length in *Voyna*, chap. 20. Also see Leonov, *Gotov'sya*, 17–19.

38. The March, April, and June insertions are discussed in Babikov, *Voyna*, chap. 23, and the two October missions are discussed in chap. 28.

39. Ibid., chap. 29. Naturally, one might ask if there were Northern Fleet or other Soviet intelligence teams inserted into Norway who did not return to Soviet control at war's end. It is clear from Babikov's writings that another Soviet intelligence activity, based in Murmansk, was inserting teams into Norway. See *Otryad*, 32, and *Voyna*, 143, 148, and 149. There were postwar consequences to all of this Norwegian involvement in Soviet intelligence collection, one of which pertained to American U-2 flights. Selmer Nilsen, whose family had aided a Soviet reconnaissance team during the war, was recruited and trained in 1949 and later assisted the Soviets in tracking U-2 reconnaissance aircraft flights into the airfield at Bodo. See Vatne, *Jeg Var Russisk Spion*.

40. *Sbornik materialov*, No. 38, 17.

41. These detachments were named as follows: in the Northern Fleet, 181st Special Reconnaissance Detachment *(osobogo razvedyvatel'nogo otryada)*; in the Amur Flotilla, 71st Special Purpose Detachment *(otryada osobogo naznacheniya)*; and in the Pacific Fleet, 140th Special Purpose Reconnaissance Detachment *(razvedyvatel'nogo otryada osobogo naznacheniya)*.

42. See Chernomys, "Podvig desanta v rayone mysa Pikshuev."

43. Redanskiy, "V ryadakh," 71.

44. Leonov, *Gotov'sya*, 24 (Northern Fleet), and 73 (Pacific Fleet).

45. See Mosalev, "Razvedyvatel'no-diversionnye podrazdeleniya."

46. Alekseev, "Primeneniye," 63.

47. Yashin, "Sily spetsial'nykh operatsiy."

48. See Kondrat'ev, "Sily spetsial'nykh operatsiy."

49. According to *Sbornik materialov*, No. 38, 6, Northern Fleet intelligence staff were subject to tasking by Main Naval Staff in Moscow, and also Headquarters, Karelian *Front*.

50. According to Babikov, *Voyna*, 78, Admiral Golovko ordered that information gained by Soviet air reconnaissance on German combatant ship movements in northern Norway be passed to Admiral Fisher. It is probable that the strategic intelligence information from other sources, such as the

scout teams, was also passed through this channel. No acknowledgment of this connection has been found, however, in published British sources.

51. Master of Sport and Meritorious Master of Sport are rankings approaching Olympic level, earned by victories in major competitions. One of Leonov's men in the Northern Fleet, Vladimir Olyashev, was a champion of the Soviet Union and Meritorious Master of Sport in skiing. Six other men, Tikhonov, Saratovskiy, Agafonov, Zubkov, Baryshev, and Ken'ev, were Masters of Sport in skiing. Inzasrtsev was the fleet weightlifting champion in his weight class. Ivan Lysenko was a wrestling champion. Ivan Guznenkov was a competitive rock climber and martial arts fighter. All these examples are from the Northern Fleet, but there were many athletes in the other fleet detachments as well.

52. See Chkheidze, *Zapiski Dunayskogo razvedchika*, 64.

53. Babikov, *Na vostochnom*, 232.

54. Until recently, it was difficult to pin down a precise date from unclassified sources, leaving one in the unfortunate predicament of having to turn to Viktor Suvorov, who cites no documents in support of his claims. In *Spetsnaz*, 31, he indicates that *spetsnaz* formations appeared in experimental form during Marshal Zhukov's tenure, that is, as early as 1957, the year of Zhukov's dismissal by Krushchev. This conclusion may be bolstered by Penkovskiy, *Penkoviskiy Papers*, 237. Penkovskiy indicates that during Zhukov's tenure, the GRU had organized a school near Moscow for training about two hundred "inveterate cutthroats as saboteur agents and terrorists." The contradiction between these two sources is that Suvorov is discussing an engineer-based *spetsnaz*, while Penkovskiy is referring to an intelligence-based *spetsnaz*. In either case, the time period is the late 1950s so the supposition that regular *spetsnaz* formations were in existence by the early 1960s could not be dismissed out of hand. A recently published Soviet journal article stated unequivocally that 1962 was the year that *spetsnaz* formations were formed in the post–World War II era. See Ptichkin and Kliment'yev, "Komandirovka v spetsnaz."

55. Kvyatkovskiy, "Bespokoynaya."

56. Leonov would not acknowledge this direct involvement with any military organization in our September 1990 interview. In separate discussions, both he and his daughter indicated that after he left active duty, he worked for DOSAAF as a motivational lecturer. In this position he traveled throughout the Soviet Union, giving talks to both military and nonmilitary audiences. He expressed great pride in his public speaking ability, saying that flag-rank officers were very reluctant to speak on the same dais with him.

CHAPTER 1

1. According to a September 1990 interview with Leonov in Moscow, the base was Polyarnyy, at the time the main base of the Northern Fleet.

Polyarnyy is located on the west side of Kola Bay, about thirty-five kilometers northeast of Murmansk.

2. Vinogradov, *Podvodnyy*, 19, also makes reference to the three Nikolays but places them in a different order: Losev, Ryabov, and Damanov. He indicates that the other submariners called them Kolya number one, Kolya number two, and Kolya number three.

3. According to Babikov, *Otryad*, 16, Radyshevtsev was recruited to the detachment in August 1941. He had served four to five years in the navy, most recently as a torpedoman in a submarine. He neither drank nor smoked.

4. Petr Frantsevich Lesgaft (1837–1909) was a Russian doctor, a specialist in anatomy and physiology. He was also a teacher and created a uniquely Russian system of training instructors in physical education. See *BSE*, 14:354.

5. *Jäger* is German for hunter and also for a type of infantryman in the eighteenth, nineteenth, and early twentieth centuries. It is the term used in much of the Soviet literature of this northern theater to describe troops of the German mountain divisions.

6. The Military Council of the fleet consisted of the commander in chief (Admiral A. G. Golovko), the deputy commander for political affairs (Division Commissar A. A. Nikolaev), and the chief of staff (Rear Admiral S. G. Kucherov). Since both the fleet commander and chief of staff were always referred to by their titles, the reference is clearly to the deputy commander for political affairs. The Military Council served as an institution of collective leadership in both the Red Army and Navy during World War II. *Front* and fleet orders, for example, were signed by all three members of the council, not just the commander alone. For a lengthy and detailed description of the military council, see *SVE*, s.v. "voyennyy sovyet," 2:272.

7. Pioneer is the Communist Party's organization for youth aged ten to fifteen. Pioneers can graduate to Komsomol membership at age fourteen with a recommendation from their adult leaders. Until the dissolution of the Soviet Union, Pioneer members could be seen wearing red scarves visiting museums and walking guard at war memorials throughout the USSR.

8. Despite this humble beginning, Leonov continued to write poetry in his later years. When I visited with him in Moscow in November 1990, he recited some of his poetry to me.

9. In Russian, *Studenoye morye*, literally "frozen sea," a reference to the White Sea.

10. Konstantin Mikhaylovich Stanyukovich (1843–1903), noted Russian author, came from a seafaring family and was the son of an admiral in the Russian fleet. After studying in the Naval Cadet Corps in Petrograd in 1857–60, he went on a long cruise. In 1864 he left the service and took up a career as writer and schoolteacher. He is most famous for a collection of stories that he wrote between 1886 and his death about his life at sea

that earned him the Pushkin Prize in 1901. These stories were translated into many foreign languages. See *BSE*, 24:422–23.

11. *Osoaviakhim* is the Russian acronym for *Obshchestvo Sodeystviya Oborone i Aviatsionnomu i Khimicheskomu stroitel'stvu SSSR* [Society for Support of Defense in the Aviation and Chemical Construction of the USSR]. Despite the long name, it was in essence an organization to conduct preinduction military training among Soviet youth. Its current role in Soviet society is fulfilled by *DOSAAF—Dobrovol'noye Obshchestvo Sodeystviya Armii, Aviatsii i Flota* [Voluntary Society for Support of the Army, Air Force, and Navy].

12. In Russian, *Gotov k trudu i oborone*. This was one of many awards Komsomol members could earn for demonstrated expertise in various individual military skills such as marksmanship, parachuting, and military-related sports. In a September 1990 interview in Moscow, Leonov indicated that he made one parachute jump while a member of the Komsomol organization at the factory.

13. This mission is described in Babikov, *Letom*, 186–94, and Velichko, *Dvazhdy*, 14. A German document dated 24 July 1941 briefly mentions this raid, fixing the date of the actual attack at 22 July. See Germany, Heer, Kriegstagebuch nr. 1, AOK 20 [Headquarters, 20th German Army], "Aktennotiz" [Memorandum], microfilm series T-312, roll 1647, frame 001173, NARA.

14. The Russian here is *yazyk*, and it means literally "tongue," like the tongue in a person's mouth. In both the Red Army and Navy, this term was used to refer to a live prisoner, one who could speak, as opposed to a dead prisoner, who could not.

15. In 1941 the Soviets had a number of small arms in their inventory. Photographs from the early war period show Leonov and others armed with the *PPSh—pistolet-pulemyot Shpagin* [submachine gun of the Shpagin design], a 7.62mm submachine gun with a 71-round drum magazine; the 7.62mm Tokarev semi-automatic rifle; and the sniper version of the 1891/30 Mosin bolt-action rifle. Although members of the detachment carried light machine guns, there are no photographs of them or specific references that would permit identification. According to *Sbornik materialov*, No. 38, 66, depending on the size of the detachment for a given mission, it carried one or two light machine guns. Approximately 75 percent of the men carried submachine guns, the remainder rifles. Each scout was issued four hand grenades and three hundred rifle/submachine-gun cartridges. Distributed within the detachment were five to ten antitank grenades and twenty-five to fifty antipersonnel mines.

16. The grenade Leonov was using required a plunger to be inserted into a fuse body, which activated a time-delay fuse. The hissing noise emanating from the grenade indicated that the fuse was ignited.

17. The necessity to leave behind the body of a comrade apparently made a lasting impression on Leonov, for by the time he became

commander of the detachment in late 1943, the detachment had an unwritten law: "Northern Fleet scouts never left their wounded behind, and never left the body of a hero for the enemy to gloat over." See Velichko, *Dvazhdy*, 23–24.

18. Major Dobrotin was Captain Third Rank Vizgin's deputy and was in charge of ground reconnaissance and intelligence. He was responsible for both the reconnaissance detachment and the mixed Soviet-Norwegian platoon (see Figure 1).

19. Budenny's cavalry is a reference to the 1st Cavalry Army of Marshal Semyon Budenny, perhaps the most famous fighting unit of the civil war. Other renowned veterans of this unit include marshals Timoshenko and Zhukov, who are recognized in the West as among the great Soviet generals of World War II. Budenny, who died in 1970, began his military career in the tsar's army in 1903. Although he commanded major troop formations in World War II, he is not remembered for his strategic or operational-level leadership.

20. Just as in English we say "Bill" for "William," "Beth" or "Betty" or "Liz" for "Elizabeth," so also do the Russians abbreviate names. They call it a diminutive, and say "Sasha" for "Aleksandr," "Vitya" and "Vitek" for "Viktor," and "Misha" for "Mikhail."

21. The original Russian here is *tribunal*, an English cognate, which in the Soviet military justice system equates to a court-martial in the American military justice system. During World War II, a tribunal was empowered to render extremely harsh sentences, including death by firing squad.

22. Major General Eduard Dietl came to northern Norway as commander, 3d Mountain Division, in the German invasion at Narvik in April 1940. Just a few days later he was promoted to lieutenant general. By the time of the invasion of the Soviet Union in June 1941, Dietl was commanding Mountain Corps Norway, a formation that was later to become the XIXth Mountain Corps. In November 1941 Dietl was elevated to command of all German army forces in Finland, later named the 20th Mountain Army. Dietl was promoted to colonel general in June 1942, the rank he held until his death in a plane crash in Austria in June 1944, while returning to his command from a visit with Hitler.

The 2d Mountain Division was formed in 1938 after the annexation of Austria. It fought in Poland in 1939 and in the 1940 invasion of Norway. In June 1941, the division participated in the invasion of the Soviet Union on the Murmansk axis, where it suffered heavy losses. Following a brief respite in northern Norway after the front stabilized in late 1941, the division returned to the Petsamo area in 1942 and remained there until October 1944. In January 1945 the division was transferred to the Colmar area of southeastern France, where it fought against American troops in the final months of the war.

The 3d Mountain Division was also formed in Austria in 1938, and it too fought in Poland in 1939 and in Norway in 1940. After the front stabilized in the Petsamo region, the division was transferred to the Baltic area in mid-1942 and then to the southeastern region of the Soviet Union in early 1943.

The 6th Mountain Division was activated in the winter of 1939–40 and fought in the campaign in the West in 1940. In April 1941 it was in Greece and in May fought against British forces on Crete. The division was transferred from Greece to the Petsamo area in the summer of 1941.

CHAPTER 2

1. The Musta-Tunturi Range is the group of low mountains that lies across the isthmus of Sredniy Peninsula. The Soviet troops defending this narrow neck of land belonged to the Northern Defensive Region, a joint service command subordinated to the Northern Fleet. The commander of this force from mid-July 1942 to late September 1944, Major General S. I. Kabanov, has written an excellent memoir, *Polye boya*.

2. Leonov also discusses Paraeva in *Gotov'sya*, 27. In the September 1990 interview, Leonov stated that Paraeva stayed with the detachment for about a year. He showed me a photograph of her after the war placing flowers at a memorial on Cape Krestovyy. Babikov mentions her in *Letom*, 204 and 213.

3. Karelia is a vast area of Soviet and Finnish territory that lies north and northeast of Leningrad. It is principally forests, lakes, and swamps.

4. *Ruslan and Lyudmila* is an epic poem by Alexander Pushkin, perhaps the most famous Russian poet, who lived during the Napoleonic era.

5. In Pushkin's poem, Chernomor was an evil sorcerer who debauched Lyudmila on her wedding night. Belomor was a good sorcerer. The names are also a pun on the Russian words for black and white, i.e., "hairy" and "bald."

6. This raid is described in great detail in Babikov, *Letom*, chap. 22.

7. *Oberleutnant* is equivalent to a first lieutenant in the U.S. Army.

8. The scouts generally carried a certain quantity of demolitions on these missions, which they used to destroy German positions or supplies. One of the scouts, Vyacheslav Mikhailovich Dogadkin, was nicknamed Dynamite-man in recognition of his special skill in these matters. See Nikitin, "Podvig," 63.

9. According to Babikov, *Letom*, 223, eight men were killed and over thirty wounded by this strafing.

10. Leonov and the others had been evacuated to a hospital in Arkhangelsk. See Velichko, *Dvazhdy*, 18.

11. General N. N. Yudenich, a former tsarist officer, led the Northwestern Army in an offensive against Petrograd in October 1919. His forces advanced to within twenty miles of the heart of the city before they were halted. For additional information, see Mawdsley, *Russian Civil War*, 196–201.

12. *Ovod* means gadfly in Russian. The author of the novel by this title referred to in the text is unknown.

13. Babikov, *Letom*, 254–74.

14. This action is recorded in German records as follows: "Yesterday evening a deserter appeared south of Luostari Airfield, who declared himself to be a member of a reconnaissance and partisan detachment that was advancing south of Luostari airfield and had the mission to attack the airfield and destroy everything." See Germany, Heer, Kriegstagebuch nr. 1, AOK 20, "Fernspruch Gebirgs Korps Norwegen [Telephone message Mountain Corps Norway] Ic 1.9.1941 1745 hours," microfilm series T-312, roll 1013, frame 9209088. Based on this incident and the interrogation of the deserter, a reconnaissance detachment was added to the Soviet order of battle by German intelligence analysts: "Aufklärungs Abteilung: (Partisanen-Abt.) Gesamtstärke etwa 300 Mann, davon etwa 200 Matrosen." [Reconnaissance detachment: (Partisan det.) total strength about 300 men, of whom approximately 200 are sailors]. See ibid., "Vermutliche Feindkräfte vor Gesamtraum des A.O.K. Norwegen Stand 5.9.1941" [Probable enemy strength in the operating area of AOK Norway as of 5.9.1941], microfilm series T-312, roll 1012, frame 9207906, NARA.

15. Leonov was hospitalized for approximately two months. See Velichko, *Dvazhdy*, 18.

16. Ibid., 19, indicates that Leonov, an accomplished competitive cross-country skier, was named the detachment's chief of ski training. Babikov, in *Letom*, 252–53, names several ski instructors who came in from Leningrad. According to Babikov, Leonov was put in charge of the important task of procuring the detachment's winter clothing and ski equipment. Leonov selected a military ski that met the needs of the detachment. For advice on clothing and boots, he turned to the community of reindeer herders. Photographs of members of the detachment show a white fur garment that reached below the knees, with a fur hood.

17. According to Babikov, *Otryad*, 22, Kashutin had served first in the army, then four to five years in the navy. He liked to wear army fatigues and enjoyed a reputation as a ladies' man.

18. I asked Leonov about Agafonov in our September 1990 interview. He said that Agafonov had missed a deployment of his submarine from base and was sentenced to seven years' confinement by a court-martial. From his previous duty as athletic director of the submarine brigade, Inzartsev knew Agafonov well and convinced the fleet commander to allow him personally to vouch for the convicted sailor. Leonov spoke with sincerity about the unjustness of Agafonov's sentence and with respect for Inzartsev's mitigating actions. In 1944 Agafonov became a Hero of the Soviet Union (see Chapter 8).

19. Babikov, *Otryad*, chap. 9. Leonov, in *Gotov'sya*, 84–88, suggests that this mission was conducted on the night of 6–7 November with a naval infantry reconnaissance company.

20. Several German documents describe this raid and establish the time

of the attack as 0200 hours 25 October. See Germany, Heer, Kriegstagebuch nr. 1, AOK 20, morning reports, evening reports, and teletype messages, series T-312, microfilm roll 1013, frames 9208536–38, 9208836, 9208852, 54, 57, 59 and 61, NARA.

21. Babikov, *Otryad*, chap. 11.

22. Ibid., chap. 12.

23. Ibid., chap. 13.

24. According to a German report, "Russian reconnaissance troops have been repeatedly identified in German uniforms and with German weapons.... In one action on the Litsa Front [the sector around the Litsa River], the enemy took the uniforms off of German prisoners and casualties for the purpose of equipping partisans [*Banden*]." See Germany, Heer, Kreigstagebuch nr. 1, *Armeeoberkommando Norwegen Ic Nr. 1080/42*, 14 November 1942, "Feindnachrichtenblatt Nr. 24, Stand: 14. November 1942 [Enemy information report No. 24, as of 14 November 1942]," microfilm series T-312, roll 1649, frame 000201, NARA.

25. Babikov, *Otryad*, chap. 16.

26. Viktor Leonov was among those wounded. He briefly mentioned this action in *Gotov'sya*, 81–83.

27. Babikov, *Otryad*, chap. 19.

28. Every German soldier carried a small booklet in his pocket that fully identified him and his unit. Soviet reconnaissance troops always attempted to recover these booklets from German casualties. They were a vital source of information upon which to base the German order of battle.

29. Babikov, *Otryad*, chap. 20.

CHAPTER 3

1. The Russian term here is *desantnik*, literally "member of a landing force." This word is used in the context of amphibious landings, airborne or airmobile landings, and also for troops that ride into battle hanging onto the sides of tanks.

2. Although the detachment normally worked the immediate coastline, on more than one occasion it reconnoitered as deep inland as the German airfield at Luostari, a straight-line distance of approximately fifty kilometers from the coast.

3. This passage infers that on occasion the detachment had to leave bodies behind, although reluctant to do so.

4. The headquarters element consisted, in addition to the detachment commander and deputy commander (political officer), of radio operators, medics, runners, armorer, cook, supply clerk, bootmaker, light vehicle driver, and others. According to Babikov, in *Na vostochnom*, 24, these personnel were frequently men of the line platoons who because of their wounds were no longer able to participate fully in combat operations.

Rather than lose their experience entirely, they were allowed to remain in the detachment and serve in a less physically demanding position.

5. Trophy weapons were captured German or Finnish small arms. Although their ammunition requirements differed from those of Soviet-manufactured weapons, they were available, reliable, and useful for practical as well as deceptive purposes. When they were fired near a German position, the Germans might not become alarmed at hearing *German* weapons, not realizing it was Soviet troops firing them. All weapons have distinctive identifying sound signatures.

6. According to Babikov, in *Otryad*, 172, for this particular mission the reconnaissance detachment was subordinated to 12th Naval Infantry Brigade. A detailed description of the larger amphibious operation from the Soviet perspective can be found in Rumyantsev, *Razgrom*, chap. 3. A recently declassified Soviet document describes in detail the medical support of this operation. See *Sbornik materialov*, No. 17. The German perspective is in U.S. Department of the Army, Pamphlet 20-271, 223–28.

7. Landing at a point some distance from the main landing site to deceive the Germans as to the main axis was a frequent mission for the Black Sea Fleet's reconnaissance detachment. See Volunchuk, *Po tylam*, 123.

8. Boris Abramov was one of the detachment's premier cross-country skiers and a frequent winner in fleet competitions at ten and twenty kilometers. See Velichko, *Dvazhdy*, 29, and Babikov, *Otryad*, 171.

9. It is frequently mentioned in the literature of other fleet detachments that naval scouts did not allow themselves to be captured alive. As the German document in Appendix B clearly states, however, *razvedchiki* did not always succeed in avoiding capture.

10. U.S. Department of the Army, Pamphlet 20-271, map 19, shows the axis of the 12th Naval Infantry Brigade but not the reconnaissance detachment. A better map can be found in Rumyantsev, *Razgrom*, 69.

11. The medical support for the detachment was provided by an officer, who in this and other sources is referred to as "doctor" (in Russian, *doktor*), not "medic" (in Russian, *sanitar* or *saninstruktor*). Babikov, in *Voyna*, 159, uses the Russian *feld'sher*, which is frequently translated as "physician's assistant." The Black Sea Fleet detachment also had a doctor (in Russian *vrach*); see Volunchuk, *Po tylam*, 85.

12. According to Babikov, in *Otryad*, 177, Sheremet was given a pistol and he shot himself.

13. Vologda is a city that in 1982 had a population of 254,000, located 400 kilometers (250 miles) north and slightly to the east of Moscow. Just as Americans from Maine and Texas speak English somewhat differently, so too do Russians from different parts of the Russian Republic speak their language with unique accents. In addition, sailors and soldiers from non-Russian nationalities speak Russian as a second language, adding to the difficulties of oral communication within units of the Soviet Armed Forces.

14. This is a reference to the German decoration for valor, the Iron Cross.

15. *Shashlik* is pieces of mutton roasted on a spit, similar to our shish kebab.

16. The reconnaissance detachment, dressed in reindeer fur outer garments, was far better prepared for this sudden late spring storm than were the conventional naval infantry forces. This freezing weather significantly reduced the effectiveness of the Soviet forces and contributed greatly to the failure of the overall operation.

17. This description is supported by photographs. See Khaldey, *Ot Murmanska*. There is a photograph of Viktor Leonov near the front of this photograph collection and a photograph of Stepan Motovilin near the back, both dressed in fur outer garments and wearing skis.

18. This was a reference to the time Baryshev carried the skier Kolikov on his back.

19. Semyon Agafonov, the former cook from the submarine *Shch*-401, was the detachment's sharpshooter. He is shown holding a Mosin-Nagan sniper rifle with a much larger than normal scope in "Pechenga snova nasha!", 65. I asked Leonov in our September 1990 interview if Agafonov was the detachment sniper, and he immediately corrected me. When I showed Leonov the photograph cited above, he chuckled and said he knew all about the photo, but Agafonov was not a sniper.

20. Of the seventy men who landed ashore on 27 April, ten were healthy, two had died, two were wounded, and the remainder were suffering from frostbite or snow blindness when extracted. See Babikov, *Otryad*, 184. These numbers coincide exactly with those given in *Sbornik materialov*, no. 17, 24.

21. Babikov discusses this mission in *Otryad*, chap. 23.

CHAPTER 4

1. Each of the Soviet navy's four fleet (Northern, Baltic, Black Sea, and Pacific) maintained a school for basic and advanced individual training of enlisted sailors. The Northern Fleet's school was in the Solovetskiy Islands, in the White Sea southwest of Arkhangelsk.

2. "Old Believers" were those followers of the Russian Orthodox faith who adhered to certain religious traditions and rituals that were modified by decree in 1666. A massive upheaval resulted from the decree, when lmillions of Old Believers refused to accept new forms of worship that were closer to the Greek Orthodox faith. For more information see Pipes, *Russia under the Old Regime*, 234–39.

The Pechora River originates on the west slopes of the middle Ural Mountains, and flows some eighteen hundred kilometers northward to drain into the Barents Sea.

3. Ust-Tsylma lies along the Pechora River at the great bend where the

river turns from a westward flow to a northward flow. It is about 125 kilometers (75 miles) south of the Arctic Circle.

4. This could have been a five-ruble coin or his grade from school. In the Soviet school system, grades are given in the form of numbers, one being the lowest grade and five the highest.

5. A military commission in this context is roughly equivalent to a local draft board in the United States. Among the members of the military commission are representatives of the branches of service, who have some say in determining the fate of young conscripts.

6. Soviet sailors wear a blue-black hat with the fleet's name in white letters around the hatband and two short pieces of ribbon at the back. In Russian it is called a *beskozyrka*.

7. Kronshtadt is a Baltic Fleet base with a history dating back to the time of Peter the Great (early eighteenth century).

8. Khasan is a lake near the Soviet-Chinese-North Korean border, about 130 kilometers (80 miles) southwest of Vladivostok. In late July 1938 the Soviets and Japanese, who were occupying Manchuria, fought a sharp battle that led to several days of small-scale war. For more information, see Coox, *Anatomy of a Small War*.

Khalkhin-Gol is the name of a river that separates eastern Mongolia from western Manchuria. Soviet and Japanese forces fought a several-week war here in July and August 1939. It was at Khalkhin-Gol that Georgiy Zhukov established his reputation as a brilliant combat leader. For more information, see Coox, *Nomonhan*.

9. This is the only mention of Vladimir Lyande in this book. Babikov tells us much more about Lyande in *Morskiye*, 12–14, and *Voyna*, chap. 20. Leonov also wrote about him in *Gotov'sya*, 17–19. Lyande came to the reconnaissance detachment from the Black Sea Fleet after recuperating in a hospital from wounds received during the defense of Sevastopol. He was reputedly one of the best boxers in the Northern Fleet. There is no question that Lyande belonged to Leonov's detachment, for during our September 1990 interview, without any prompting from me, Leonov talked about Lyande. He said that Lyande was the best man in his detachment for snatching German prisoners alive. Lyande, according to Leonov, knew several different forms of unarmed combat and could disarm any German regardless of what method or technique the German fought with.

10. In Russian, as in German, there is a polite form of "you," *vy*, and a familiar form, *ty*. The polite form connotes respect.

11. *TASS* is the Russian acronym for *Telegrafnoye Agenstvo Sovetskogo Soyuza* [Telegraph Agency of the Soviet Union], the government-owned and operated press service.

CHAPTER 5

1. Babikov, in his account of this action in *Otryad*, chap. 24, indicates that the detachment moved to the small port of Ozerko on Rybachiy Peninsula on 16 September 1942. This new base was only temporary, to support the detachment's participation in the upcoming operation. Both Babikov and Leonov refer to the detachment's permanent base at Polyarnyy after this time period in other accounts.

2. *Mogila* in Russian means grave or tomb, and *mogilnyy* is the adjectival form. Thus Cape Mogilnyy becomes literally Cape Sepulchre, or more loosely translated, Cape of Death in English.

3. Captain Inzartsev renewed his association with the reconnaissance detachment as a lieutenant colonel in June 1945, as an officer in the Pacific Fleet intelligence staff.

4. Leonov is somewhat circumspect here concerning his attitude and feelings toward Frolov, although in *Gotov'sya*, 81, Leonov held Frolov responsible for the failure of the aborted January raid toward Nikel. Babikov, however, minces no words in *Otryad*, 193–94. Using the pseudonym Frol Nikolaev for Frolov (whose first initial coincidentally was "N."), Babikov wrote the following in 1986, describing Frolov's assumption of command: "The most experienced scouts, who had been going into the enemy's rear for a year already, did not accept Frol Nikolaev in the role of new commander of the detachment. And not only because he differed greatly from Inzartsev. Frol very much loved to talk and sometimes to invent stories and exaggerate. His stories didn't set well with veterans in the detachment. They were more experienced than Nikolaev in service, in reconnaissance, and in daily life. Nikolaev had to do too much to win authority in the detachment. In the meantime he received only the position, but he still lacked the prestige and respect of the position." Babikov further indicates in *Voyna*, chap. 19, that by November 1943 Frolov had lost the confidence of several of the scouts, some of whom requested release back to their former units rather than serve under him.

5. The larger operation is described in some detail in *Sbornik materialov*, No. 1, 34–53. A complement of fifty men under Frolov's command was subordinated to the commander, 12th Naval Infantry Brigade (Colonel V. V. Rassokhin). Lieutenant General S. I. Kabanov, who in 1942 was Rassokhin's immediate commander, recalls this incident in his memoir, *Polye boya*, 88–99. In our September 1990 interview, I asked Leonov about working with the naval infantry. He talked at length, in essence saying that the naval infantry had its own methods, which were not conducive to the establishment of close working relations with his reconnaissance detachment.

6. The remark is a reference to a Russian fairy tale, the point of which is that the magpie could neither fly nor walk. In this context the lieutenant was bemoaning his inability to move his unit.

7. The reconnaissance detachment was operating under the direct command of a naval infantry captain, V. S. Buyanov, who, according to Kabanov (*Polya boya*, 93), returned to the embarkation site about eight hours after the landing without his troops. Kabanov met him at the dock and ordered the captain to return to the battlefield and find his men. Although Kabanov does not mention the captain's eventual fate, a recently published excerpt from Admiral Golovko's personal diary, dated 20 September 1942, supports Leonov's account: "Captain B. ran to the cutters . . . and raced to Eyna. B. will have to be charged." See Golovko, "Otets bez flota sebya ne myslil," 84.

8. U.S. soldiers and marines called their hand grenades "pineapples," and the Soviets called theirs "lemons."

9. Zhdanov did blow himself up with this grenade. Babikov, *Otryad*, 203, writes that Zhdanov was from a submarine and on his first mission. Leonov also mentions this incident in *Gotov'sya*, 20–21.

10. According to Velichko, *Dvazhdy*, 25, Mikheev was the fleet champion in grenade throwing.

11. Boris Lyakh was one of the boat commanders with whom the detachment formed a habitual and lasting relationship. Lyakh received his Hero of the Soviet Union award after the Petsamo-Kirkenes battle in early November 1944. Both Leonov and Babikov have maintained contact with Lyakh in recent years. On the occasion of the fortieth anniversary of the Petsamo-Kirkenes operation, Lyakh and Leonov were interviewed in the same article. See "Podvig Zapolyar'ya." In 1985 Lyakh was photographed sitting next to Babikov at a veterans' conference. See Nikanorov, "Sluzhat rodine veterany," 14.

12. Order of the Red Banner is a decoration dating from 1924, awarded to individuals or units of the Soviet Armed Forces for the display of courage and bravery in combat with the enemy. When a unit such as a rifle division receives this award, it becomes part of the name of the organization in perpetuity. It is a very prestigious award.

13. Dates given in both Babikov's and Kabanov's accounts show that Leonov was appointed an officer on or about 20 September 1942.

CHAPTER 6

1. Leonov was appointed *zampolit* (deputy commander for political affairs) in December 1942. See *SVE*, 4:622. It is an interesting contrast to the recent practice in the Soviet Armed Forces, wherein political officers were specially trained for that role from the beginning of their military careers. In Leonov's case, they took a "warrior" and made him a *zampolit*, thus ensuring a political officer with a strong leadership image.

2. Leonov spent the fall of 1941 at the ski base while he recovered from his wound. In *Gotov'sya*, 25, Leonov tells an anecdote about Pshenychnykh's fear of parachute jumping. Through sheer force of will,

Pshenychnykh overcame this fear and participated in both day and night training jumps. He also was involved in the combat jump into the Varanger Peninsula in late October 1944 (see Chapter 8).

3. Voronezh is a city on the Don River, about 150 kilometers due east of Kursk. It was overrun by the Germans in June 1942.

4. Velichko, *Dvazhdy*, 26–27, places much emphasis on this subject. As the following quotations clearly demonstrate, arduous physical training and athletic competition were hallmarks of the detachment. "In the breaks between operations, the detachment was transformed into a sports group. People were involved in running with rucksacks, ski jumping for both height and distance, throwing grenades, fencing, competition in swimming and rowing, and organizing wrestling matches.... To an uninitiated person, it could seem that the men were preparing for a competition. Leonov was tireless in this matter. He dreamed about the ideal scout—an ardent patriot, mindful of the war, physically developed in all aspects, strong and clever. Normally they only took people into the detachment who were fully engaged in sports. But just the same, it was impossible to select the ideal fighting men. One turned out to be an accomplished swimmer but a weak fencer; another was an outstanding boxer but could not swim. The majority of those who came to the detachment suffered from 'sports disease'—expertise in only one area. 'Healing' was begun. Leonov required everyone who joined the detachment to take up all types of sport.... Sport, sport, sport! In all types and applications. No allowances were given to anyone. The entire combat curriculum was focused on a single theme: the training of the soldier for single combat in the most difficult and unexpected situations.... In the detachment there emerged a cult of admiration of physical strength and endurance, and a love for sport was born." This theme was also picked up by the author of a 1987 tribute to Leonov: "Those who arrived in Leonov's detachment could not at first comprehend where they were: in a troop unit or a sports school. Several men were practicing methods of hand-to-hand combat right out in the snow. Nearby a group of men were working out on pieces of exercise equipment. Skiers feverishly glided by on waxed skis with enormous rucksacks on their backs." See Nikitin, "Podvig," 62.

5. *Sambo* is derived from the Russian words *samooborona bez oruzhiya*, or self-defense. It is a Soviet-originated system of hand-to-hand combat, derived from Greco-Roman wrestling, but also influenced by Asian martial arts, that combines both offensive and defensive moves.

6. *Tekhnikum* is Russian for technical school, what in the United States would be called a vocational or trade school.

7. Onega is a city at the mouth of the river Onega, which flows northward into the White Sea.

8. Velichko, *Dvazhdy*, 26, also described the heaving gangplank, indicating that it was nicknamed Leonov's ladder.

9. According to Velichko, *Dvazhdy*, 27–28, Leonov imposed five rules on every member of the detachment: (1) He had to be able to cross-

country ski on heavily broken terrain. (2) He had to maintain the qualities of a sailor—steer a small boat, run along a narrow heaving gangplank, swim with weapon and rucksack. (3) He had to be highly proficient in the methods of hand-to-hand combat—all types of fighting unarmed against an enemy who had a weapon, to master the use of cold weapons (knives and swords), including, when it was required, the "Finnish dagger." (4) He had to be able to use weapons effectively: to shoot aimed fire and to throw a grenade far and accurately in any conditions, especially after a long and intense march. (5) He had to harden his body so that it could withstand cold and hunger, long marches, and lying in a freezing position.

10. Compasses were of limited use in this area because of the proximity of the North Pole and the high mineral content of the ground, and maps were poorly surveyed and in short supply, so the scouts probably did a lot of celestial navigation.

11. The text reads "bay N." The Soviets use the letter "N" whenever they do not wish to disclose the name of a place or unit. Makar Babikov, however, conveniently mentions the site of this training in *Na vostochnom*, 7. It was the Solovetskiy Islands in the White Sea, the same place where Babikov received his initial training in 1940.

12. Sutyagin was the platoon commander of the mixed Soviet-Norwegian platoon that had been conducting coast-watching operations on the Varanger Peninsula since early 1942. Leonov's mention of him is further corroboration, if any is needed, of the linkage between the two organizations.

13. Tsar Saltan is the subject of a Russian fairy tale.

14. Aleksandr Vasil'evich Suvorov (1730–1800) was perhaps the most famous battle captain in Russian military history. His quotation, "Difficult in training, easy in battle," is frequently found in contemporary Soviet tactical references. Fyodor Fyodorovich Ushakov (1744–1817) was to the tsar's navy what Suvorov was to the army. In an attempt to exploit feelings of Russian patriotism and nationalism among his army and fleet, Stalin had decorations created in the names of both these heroes from the Russian past, the Order of Suvorov (three gradations) on 29 July 1942 and the Order of Ushakov (two gradations) on 3 March 1944.

15. Normally the plan for a specific insertion in the enemy's rear area was developed by the intelligence section of fleet staff and then approved by the fleet chief of staff. The basic elements of the plan included mission, composition and weapons of the scout force, composition of the delivery force, instructions for uploading and passage by sea to the landing site, landing plan, actions ashore, extraction plan, organization of communications, and measures to prepare the men for the specific mission. See *Sbornik materialov*, No. 38, 68.

16. Shabalin, like Boris Lyakh, frequently delivered or extracted the men of the reconnaissance detachment to or from a hostile shore beginning in October 1941. He was awarded his first Hero of the Soviet Union medal in February 1944 and his second in November of the same year. In

September 1990, Leonov proudly showed me a photograph of him and Shabalin together taken shortly after the war. Shabalin attained the rank of rear admiral in 1969, when he commanded the Frunze Naval Academy. He died in October 1982 at age sixty-seven. See *SVE*, 8:488.

17. A German document describes the raid: "On 15.12 [15 December 1943] the Norwegian lighthouse operator was abducted from Lille Ekkeroy Island. The attackers came from an enemy submarine. On 21.12 an enemy commando group (15 men) destroyed 4 light Luftwaffe trucks southeast of Langbunes [moving] southward from Kiberg, Varanger Peninsula." See "Fernschreiben" [Teleprinter] 1.1.1944, microfilm series T-312, roll 1650, frame 000462, NARA.

18. Leonov, *Gotov'sya*, 53–55; *Sbornik materialov*, No. 38, 69–72.

19. *Sbornik materialov*, No. 38, 68–70.

20. Babikov, *Morskiye*, 17–18.

CHAPTER 7

1. Petty Officer Polyakov used the familiar, and in this circumstance rude, form of "you" [*tebye*] when he should have used the polite and respectful, as to a superior officer, form [*vam*].

2. Polyakov appears in a photograph with Leonov in an October 1988 article in *Morskoy sbornik*, 14. He is standing to Leonov's immediate left, with his hat tilted far toward his right ear. In *Gotov'sya*, 11, Leonov indicates that Polyakov was eventually kicked out of the detachment, apparently for malingering.

3. A *telnyashka* is the striped T-shirt that all naval infantrymen and sailors wear. This clothing item was added to the uniform of Soviet airborne troops in the 1970s, apparently at the insistence of the late general of the army V. F. Margelov, himself a naval infantryman during the early days of World War II. The two T-shirts are easily distinguishable by their colors: the naval version has dark blue stripes and the airborne version a lighter shade of blue.

4. *Salazhonka* means young sailor, and a rough equivalent in English might be "boot," one who has just completed boot camp, or basic training.

5. In the Soviet Armed Forces, it is normal for personnel to wear decorations on their fatigue uniforms when performing certain types of duty.

6. The Order of the Red Star dates from 1930 and is awarded to personnel of the Soviet Armed Forces for a broad range of activities, from personal bravery or skillful leadership in combat to participation in the development of an important item of military equipment.

7. *Partorg* is the Russian acronym for "party organizer," the Communist Party activist in a unit.

8. *Komsorg* is the Russian acronym for Komosomol organizer, the Komosomol activist in a unit.

9. The member of fleet Military Council was the senior Communist Party leader in the fleet, and he countersigned the orders of the fleet commander. Since Leonov's detachment was directly subordinated to fleet headquarters, the detachment *zampolit* in effect worked for the fleet *zampolit*.

10. Any item captured from the enemy, whether a weapon or piece of personal gear, was called "trophy property" *(trofeynoye imushchestvo)*. It was considered the detachment's property and therefore was not available for personal use except when properly authorized. Many of these items were probably worn or used by detachment members when they conducted missions wearing German uniforms.

11. *Troika* in Russian means a group of three—three men, three horses, and so on. The word *troika* comes from the Russian word for three, *tri*.

12. Hanko is a peninsula in southwestern Finland that Soviet naval forces occupied in March 1940 after defeating Finland in the Soviet-Finnish War. From this position, Soviet forces could exert some control over passage in and out of the Bay of Finland. Finnish and German ground, air, and naval forces defeated the Soviet defenders by December 1941.

13. Musta-Tunturi was a hill mass on the southern approach to Sredniy Peninsula and the scene of many sharp tactical engagements between Soviet and German troops.

14. *Politruk* is the Russian acronym for political instructor *(politicheskiy rukovoditel')*, a term that in the World War II context is equivalent to *zampolit*.

15. Leonov's men had more than a hobby interest in photography. According to Babikov, *Morskiye*, 8–9, Warrant Officer Viktor Maksimov led an entire squad of photographers. Whenever a mission required special photographic support, Maksimov either provided the necessary personnel or took his squad. Babikov briefly describes an unsuccessful photographic mission in March 1944 in *Voyna*, 239–42.

16. These are references to the 6th Mountain Division (Crete), and the 2d Mountain Division (Narvik), the two principal German units in the XIXth Mountain Corps.

17. This one-page order, translated in Appendix D, was captured on the first or second day of the Soviet offensive by troops of the 10th Guards Rifle Division, 99th Rifle Corps, attacking on the main axis against the 2d Mountain Division. See Khudalov, *U kromki*, 151.

18. This movement to a temporary base on Rybachiy Peninsula occurred around 11 September 1944. The effort to rehearse on terrain that resembled the objective area was a standing operating procedure from very early in the detachment's history.

19. Every unit in the Soviet Armed Forces had a Lenin Room. It was both a shrine to V. I. Lenin and a classroom where political instruction and indoctrination were carried out.

20. Novosibirsk was a major industrial city east of the Ural Mountains

in southwestern Siberia. It was not unusual for delegations from military production facilities to visit units at the front.

21. Spassk is a small town in Ryazan oblast about 150 kilometers (75 miles) southeast of Moscow.

22. Major General E. T. Dubovtsev commanded the Northern Defensive Region, the joint service command responsible for the defense of Rybachiy Peninsula. He succeeded Major General S. I. Kabanov in mid-September 1944. Kabanov later went to the Far East, where he commanded the Southern Defensive Region during the August 1945 battle with Japanese forces.

23. For the most comprehensive account of this operation in English, see Gebhardt, *Petsamo-Kirkenes Operation*.

24. Captain I. P. Barchenko-Emelyanov [Leonov used only the first half of his hyphenated surname] was an experienced naval infantryman, who had served in reconnaissance units of the 12th Naval Infantry Brigade in the Murmansk area since November 1941. In June 1943, he took command of the Northern Defensive Region reconnaissance detachment, a collection of naval infantrymen who were veteran scouts of many reconnaissance and raid operations against German units and positions along the coast of occupied Finnish and Soviet territory.

Barchenko-Emelyanov finished a brief memoir shortly before his death in January 1984, *Frontovye budnyy Rybach'ego*. Barchenko-Emelyanov and Leonov do not write much about each other in their respective memoirs. Although there are no clear indications of personal animosity between the two leaders, there probably existed a strong spirit of competitiveness. Leonov's detachment was based at the fleet main base in Polyarnyy and worked directly for the fleet commander. Barchenko-Emelyanov's detachment was based on Rybachiy Peninsula and was one level below Leonov's in the reconnaissance "pecking order."

During our September 1990 interview, Leonov offered the information that after the Petsamo-Kirkenes operation, Admiral Golovko did not recommend Barchenko-Emelyanov for Hero of the Soviet Union. Rather, army general Meretskov, commander of the Karelian Front, submitted the recommendation. The existence of these two separate reconnaissance detachments, one naval and the other naval infantry, is a force structure issue with significant current implications. Soviet naval *spetsnaz* formations may appear in diverse guises, subordinated to various levels of the chain of command.

CHAPTER 8

1. Konstantin Simonov (1915–79) was a famous Soviet writer and poet, whose first association with the Soviet Armed Forces was as a war correspondent during the battle at Khalkhin Gol in 1939. Simonov spent the entire period of the Great Patriotic War moving from one sector of the

Soviet-German front to the other, writing both poetry and prose for the troops as well as the civilian population, in support of the war effort. He spent several weeks in the Murmansk area in October and November 1941. Simonov left at least one account of a patrol with the reconnaissance detachment. See Ehrenburg and Simonov, *In One Newspaper*. According to Babikov, *Otryad*, 72–82, Simonov wrote "Wait for Me" while visiting the reconnaissance detachment. In the postwar period he served as a correspondent for *Pravda* in various Soviet capitals and abroad. He also served as the chief editor for *Novyy mir* [New world] for eight years, and for *Literaturnaya gazeta* [Literary gazette] for three. In 1974 Simonov received the award Hero of Socialist Labor and the Lenin Prize.

2. Konstantin Simonov, *Stikhotvoreniya poemy* [Poems] (Moscow: "Sovetskaya Rossiya," 1985), 135–36. Translated by James F. Gebhardt.

3. The expression "take the devil by the horns" [in Russian *'k chertu na roga popadesh'*] has the connotation of "face death head-on."

4. In the text these two words have the accent marks shown on the second syllable, indicating the English names Victor and Victoria, from the Latin root *vincere*, past participle of the verb meaning "to conquer."

5. The implication of the text here is that Leonov's and Barchenko-Emelyanov's detachments moved by different routes from the landing site to the objective area. Babikov, *Voyna*, 280, confirms this, saying that two routes were used to present less of a target for German detection. The two detachments were close enough to each other to provide mutual support.

6. Liinakhamari was a small village on the west side of Petsamo Bay. In 1944 it was the terminus of the Great Arctic Highway, the road from Rovaniemi on the Arctic Circle to the Barents Sea, named Eismeerstrasse by the Germans and Arctic Ocean Highway by the Soviets. Liinakhamari had a large tourist hotel, a fish-processing factory, a post office, and a deep harbor.

7. Early in the morning the 12th Naval Infantry Brigade had attacked across the narrow Sredniy Isthmus behind a forty-seven-thousand-round artillery preparation. The 63d Naval Infantry Brigade, which landed at the same time as Leonov's detachment a few kilometers to the east, was fighting its way south and eastward to link up with the 12th Naval Infantry Brigade.

8. An agitator in this context was a Communist Party propagandist or activist, whose duty it was to inspire and motivate the men.

9. Leonov's and Barchenko-Emelyanov's detachments had to climb down a steep slope, which, according to one source, took six hours. This brought them to the base of the hill that formed the center of the cape. On the western portion of the cape was a four-gun 88mm antiaircraft battery, at the top of the hill in the center of the cape was a German strongpoint, and on the northern shore of the cape at the bottom of the hill was a four-gun 150mm shore battery.

10. Throughout the text, the first battery is the antiaircraft battery,

Leonov's objective. The strongpoint and the second battery—the shore battery—were Barchenko-Emelyanov's objectives.

11. Two different Russian words for "doctor" were used in these two sentences, *vrach* and *doktor*.

12. The crews from the second battery, the shore battery, were housed near their guns several hundred meters away and were at this very moment fighting off the attacks of Barchenko-Emelyanov's detachment. The men referred to by Leonov were probably antiaircraft gun crews or support personnel.

13. Attachments to the composite detachment included an unspecified number of artillerymen. Leonov may have had a few with him who were familiar with the workings of these German guns.

14. In Russian, *litsom k litsu*. It is from this passage that Leonov titled the chapter and the book.

15. Despite their elite status, these men wore steel helmets when appropriate.

16. A *shturmovik* is a low-flying attack aircraft or helicopter. Although it is a generic word, one aircraft in particular carried this name in the Red Air Force, the Ilyushin Il-2. This was a single-engined heavily armed and armored attack aircraft, commonly referred to as a flying tank. Thirty-five thousand such aircraft were built during the war. According to an official Soviet postwar report, Lend-Lease P-40 Kittyhawks accompanied the Ilyushins, and the supplies were dropped from an A-20 Boston. See *Sbornik materialov*, No. 27, 49.

17. Leonov withdrew his men to the center of the cape, toward the strong-point that was by this time controlled by Barchenko-Emelyanov's men.

18. The time of the amphibious landing was 2250 hours, 12 October 1944.

19. Leonov, Pshenichnykh, and Agafonov were awarded Hero of the Soviet Union for their actions at Cape Krestovyy. In our September 1990 interview, Leonov called Agafonov "the most fearless sailor" he had ever known. Leonov credited Agafonov with having personally killed sixty Germans at Cape Krestovyy, with submachine gun, hand grenades, and in hand-to-hand combat.

20. The total casualties for the composite detachment were 53 killed and wounded a total force of 195. The number of German soldiers killed is unknown, and the number of those captured ranges from a low of 75 to a high of 114 in available written accounts. Leonov put the number of prisoners of war at 127 in our September 1990 interview.

21. Pechenga is the Russian name for this area, some four thousand square miles of territory that was ceded to Finland in 1920 under the terms of the Treaty of Dorpat. Petsamo and Pechenga are used interchangeably in Russian-language sources.

22. This is not Soviet propaganda but a matter of historical record. The Germans demolished much of the infrastructure of northern Norway as

they retreated. The destructive conduct of German forces in this part of Norway has left its mark on regional politics to this day.

23. See V. Leonov, "Vperedsmotryashchiye" [The lookouts], in Korshunov, *Cherez fiordy*, 174–76. Leonov also mentions this incident in *Gotov'sya*, 59–60. In our September 1990 interview, Leonov indicated that he was to have made the parachute jump but had injured several ribs at Cape Krestovyy two weeks earlier. Makar Babikov wrote at length about this final voyage to Varanger Peninsula in *Morskiye*, 20–40, and *Voyna*, chap. 28. See also *Sbornik materialov*, No. 38, 85.

24. In this sentence Leonov used the Russian verb *rukovodit'*, which means to lead or direct. Colonel Orlov clearly flew in the plane to the drop zone and returned to base with the aircraft. Orlov's position in Russian is *nachal'nik parashyutnodesantnoy sluzhby flota*. It was an analogous organization in the Black Sea Fleet, subordinated to that fleet's aviation arm, that conducted an airborne raid on the German airfield at Maikop, in the Kuban, in October 1942. See Furtatov, *Ognennyye desanty*.

25. Kiberg was apparently a center of communist political activity before the war. It is probably not coincidental that ten of the eleven Norwegians listed in the German document in Appendix B were from the Kiberg area.

26. Sutyagin commanded the mixed Soviet-Norwegian agent platoon and also had participated in the training of Leonov's detachment in the Solovetskiy Islands in early 1943, then later accompanied Leonov in the raid on Lille Ekkeroy island in December 1943.

27. The final objective was the port of Vardø on the northeast shore of Varanger Peninsula.

28. It is interesting that the Soviets turned weapons over to Norwegian civilians. They were probably local communists, perhaps even relatives of some of the communists who had fled to Murmansk after the German occupation.

29. The detachment's main base throughout the war was Polyarnyy, Northern Fleet headquarters.

30. The Soviets have always celebrated the victory over the Germans on 9 May, rather than 8 May as in the United States.

31. In our September 1990 interview, Leonov stated that the total number of sailors transferred from Murmansk to Vladivostok was fifty. A photograph in Babikov, *Na vostochnom*, following page 112, shows forty-four men.

CHAPTER 9

1. Data added from Babikov, *Na vostochnom*, 6, according to which the detachment left Murmansk around 20 May, departed from Moscow on 31 May (p. 8), and arrived in Vladivostok on 12 June (p. 17). Vladivostok is the largest city and port in the Soviet far east, with a population of

584,000 in 1983. The railroad line mentioned is the trans-Siberian line, the vital rail link between the European Soviet Union and its resource and industrial centers in Siberia.

2. Russian Island is an island thirteen kilometers long and eighteen kilometers wide in Peter the Great Bay off Vladivostok.

3. According to Babikov, *Na vostochnom*, 18, the northerners made up one-third of the Pacific Fleet detachment. If there were 44 northerners, then the new detachment numbered approximately 130. Babikov goes on to write (p. 20) that in consultation with Lieutenant Colonel Inzartsev, former commander of the Northern Fleet detachment and now in the intelligence section of the Pacific Fleet staff, Leonov formed two line platoons and a support section, the latter about half platoon strength. This structure duplicated that developed and tested in combat with the Germans in the Northern Fleet. A recently declassified Soviet naval report establishes the strength of the Pacific Fleet detachment at 139 or 140 men. See *Sbornik materialov*, No. 30, 28.

4. Leonov had about seven weeks, from 19 June, when the detachment occupied its barracks on Russian Island to 9 August, when the Soviets declared war on Japan, to train his new inexperienced men. He built his program around physical conditioning, movement techniques in both urban and nonurban settings, the use of various types of vessels for amphibious landings, map reading, and recognition of enemy weapons, signatures, and uniforms. See Babikov, *Na vostochnom*, 26–28. Velichko, *Dvazhdy*, 35, indicates that Leonov also set up his heaving gangplank here. In *Gotov'sya*, 74, Leonov gives the following description of this training: "First of all, we had to improve the physical endurance of all the scouts, and this we did to the degree possible. It went something like this. A group received a mission—at one site to simulate the defeat of a headquarters, in another, fifteen kilometers distant, the demolition of a bridge, and after midday, when it seemed their strength was exhausted, to attack a hill."

5. For a detailed examination of the Soviet campaign in Manchruia, see Glantz, *August Storm: The Soviet 1945 Strategic Offensive in Manchuria*, and *August Storm: Soviet Tactical and Operational Combat in Manchuria*.

6. Leonov and Guznenkov, his *zampolit*, went to Vladivostok to receive the order on 10 August (copies of the orders, issued at the fleet main command post, are in *Sbornik materialov*, No. 30, Appendixes 1 and 2). On 11 August, when the detachment was about halfway to its objective, Leonov called his platoon leaders below deck to give them a more detailed order. Babikov described this process: "Leonov called me and my squad leaders into the bow cabin, where the noise of the motors was quieter and would not disturb our conversation so much. Here he told us more details about the assigned mission.

"During the entire war years in the north there was developed and observed in the detachment a strict process of receiving the order. An indispensable condition of intelligence/reconnaissance [*razvedka*] is secrecy. If the enemy manages to learn about the information that has been gained, the information will be much less valuable and could even lead to harm. This is why the enemy should not know about the dispatch [of a unit] on reconnaissance or the essence of their mission. The details of the mission were given to the detachment commander just before embarkation. They briefed us, platoon commanders and squad leaders, during the movement by sea, when it was obvious that everything was taking shape favorably, that return to base on account of weather or other reasons was not likely. The squad leaders, in general terms, using a sketch, passed the mission down to the men. Before the landing, and sometimes even afterward, right up to return to base, none of us knew the precise geographic location and place name of the objective. Such strict secrecy protected us from many accidents and failures." See Babikov, *Na vostochnom*, 36–37.

7. The four Korean ports where Leonov's detachment fought have both Japanese and Korean names, respectively, as follows: Yuki—Unggi; Rasin—Najin; Seisin—Ch'ongjin; and Genzan—Wonsan.

8. Not all of this smoke resulted from Japanese actions. Earlier in the day, Soviet naval aviation flew 150 sorties against the port and Japanese shipping in the harbor, setting many of the fires. See Vnotchenko, *Pobeda*, 270.

9. Leonov does not mention it in either of his books, but Babikov notes that in this first landing operation there was a "strap-hanger," a representative of the fleet staff intelligence section, Captain Third Rank Kolyubakin. He was responsible for ensuring that the landing was carried out in accordance with the fleet commander's orders. See *Na vostochnom*, 34. This same officer accompanied Leonov's detachment in the subsequent landing at Wonsan. According to *Sbornik materialov*, No. 38, 66, a Northern Fleet intelligence staff representative went out on every mission to facilitate command and control. Thus the practice was carried to the Pacific Fleet.

Babikov, in *Na vostochnom*, 41–62, discusses the detachment's actions in Yuki in far greater detail than Leonov does. The most interesting portion of this description (p. 52) reads as follows: "Leonov, Guznenkov, and one of the interpreters left the detachment position and went away, as we later found out, for a meeting with our Soviet agent [*razvedchik*], who had been inserted in Yuki long before the outbreak of hostilities. The conversation, which lasted more than an hour. helped our officers to know better the situation in the city on the eve and in the first days of the war and to receive a more detailed characterization of the Japanese garrison and its command." This suggests the existence in the Pacific Fleet intelligence staff of an agent organization, perhaps patterned on the analogous organization in the Northern Fleet. This topic will resurface in the discussion of a subsequent landing.

10. This column belonged to the 393d Rifle Division, 25th Army, 1st Far Eastern *Front*. This linkup is mentioned in the memoir of the 25th Army commander, Colonel General I. M. Chistyakov. See *Sluzhim*

otchizne, 275–76. The *front* commander was Marshal K. A. Meretskov, who was promoted to that rank immediately after his Karelian *Front* completed the Petsamo-Kirkenes operation. His *front* staff then was sent to the Far East to begin preparation for this campaign. Meretskov followed in the spring of 1945. See Meretskov, *Na sluzhbe narodu*.

11. Babikov, *Na vostochnom*, 62–78. *Sbornik materialov*, No. 30, 29–35, also describes the landing at Rasin. According to this source, only sixty-eight men from Leonov's detachment participated in this landing.

12. Vnotchenko, *Pobeda*, 270.

13. The Soviet Union abrogated the April 1941 nonaggression treaty between the two governments when it launched its ground and naval offensive on 8 August. Japanese forces in northern Korea and Manchuria did not attack Soviet forces.

14. Senior Lieutenant I. M. Yarotskiy commanded a company of submachine gunners from the 390th Naval Infantry Battalion. *Sbornik materialov*, No. 30, contains a lengthy account of the Seisin landing on pages 37–52 and copies of some fleet orders and planning documents in Appendixes 3–8. Interestingly, according to a footnote on page 40, this official account is based largely on the post-battle report of Twice Hero of the Soviet Union Captain Lieutenant Leonov.

15. Barabolko commanded the 355th Separate Naval Infantry Battalion.

16. En route back to the base, the detachment ran into some mines, allegedly placed by U.S. naval air forces. Four scouts were killed, two of them veterans of the Northern Fleet, and many of the detachment's weapons were drenched in salt water. Babikov writes that after only five hours of sleep, the detachment was awakened early on 13 August and ordered to prepare for the landing in Seisin. Part of this preparation was the exchange of these weapons for new, which, Babikov says, still had protective storage grease on them. The men cleaned and test-fired them on the way to Seisin. See Babikov, *Na vostochnom*, 80–81, 92–97. According to *Sbornik materialov*, No. 30, 42, 140 men participated in this operation.

17. Babikov does not mention this incident in any of his writings.

18. Babikov, *Na vostochnom*, 97.

19. Babikov has written a lengthy description of the Seisin battle in *Na vostochnom*, 98–162. See also chapter 16 in Kabanov's *Polye boya*. Kabanov had earlier commanded the Northern Defensive Region (on Rybachiy Peninsula) in the Northern Fleet and had been transferred to the Pacific Fleet in the autumn of 1944. In August 1945, he commanded first the Vladivostok Defensive Region and later the Southern Defensive Region, joint service commands subordinated to the Pacific Fleet.

20. Apparently Leonov did not have good intelligence concerning the physical layout of the harbor and city. The Pacific Fleet's air arm had attacked the harbor in the days immediately preceding this landing so at the least the detachment should have had aerial photographs or pilot debriefing notes.

21. Babikov, *Na vostochnom*, 121–22.

22. The original Russian here [*sukhoputnyy ofitser*] suggests that Denisin came from the Red Army into the naval infantry. The need for his intelligence specialty apparently was sufficient to warrant interservice transfer, something not unusual in the Soviet Armed Forces today.

23. Tyarosov was the detachment medic, in Russian *saninstruktor*. See Babikov, *Na vostochnom*, 105. On the next page, 106, Babikov mentions the detachment *doktor*, Goncharuk. From this passage, it is clear that the detachment had both a medical doctor and medics or corpsmen to assist in medical treatment of casualties.

24. Barabolko's battalion landed early on the morning of 14 August. See Vnotchenko, *Pobeda*, 273.

25. Yarotskiy was wounded three times before the Seisin battle was over and on 14 September 1945 received the title Hero of the Soviet Union. He retired from active service as a lieutenant colonel in 1971 and died in 1980 at age sixty-four.

26. This main force was the 13th Naval Infantry Brigade. See Vnotchenko, *Pobeda*, 274.

27. Leonov, *Gotov'sya*, 38–48. Babikov wrote a lengthy description of the Wonsan operation in *Na vostochnom*, 173–233. See also Kabanov, *Polye boya*, chap. 17, and *Sbornik materialov*, No. 30, 59–63. According to the latter source, eighty-two men from Leonov's detachment landed at Wonsan. It does not specifically discuss the role or actions of Leonov's detachment.

28. The main force was again the 13th Naval Infantry Brigade, now commanded by Captain First Rank A. F. Studenichnikov.

29. Again note the presence of Japanese linguists in Leonov's group. It is not clear in any source if they are assigned or attached personnel.

30. After he returned to the port, Leonov was ordered to go back into the city and confront Admiral Khori, the Japanese naval commander, in his headquarters. Leonov took two squads from each of his two platoons and moved back into the city. After some discussions, Leonov convinced the admiral to come to the assault force's flagship to continue negotiations with the landing operation's senior commander, Captain First Rank Studenichnikov. For a detailed description of these actions, see Babikov, *Na vostochnom*, 208–14.

31. Captain Lieutenant M. G. Malik was awarded Hero of the Soviet Union on 14 September 1945 for his actions in landing assault forces in three Korean ports and participation in clearing mines from another. He retired as a captain first rank in 1960 and died in October 1980 at age sixty-nine.

32. If these were American-manufactured Higgins or Vosper patrol torpedo boats, given to the USSR in the Lend-Lease program, each was powered by three Packard V-12 engines. The common Soviet G-5 class patrol torpedo boats were powered by a Soviet version of an Italian Isotta Fraschini engine, two each, or two Packard V-12 engines. For a complete

look at Soviet patrol torpedo boats in all the fleets, see Meister, *Soviet Warships of the Second World War*, 213–39.

33. D. I. Sokolov joined a partisan group in the Leningrad area at age eighteen in 1942. He fought as a machine gunner, demolitions specialist, and scout, reaching the rank of sergeant and the position of commander, regimental reconnaissance of the Third Regiment, Fifth Leningrad Partisan Brigade. He was awarded the title Hero of the Soviet Union in April 1944. In our September 1990 interview I asked Leonov how Sokolov came to the detachment. Leonov said that Sokolov was drafted in 1944 into the regular forces and sent to the Pacific Fleet. Someone informed Leonov of this experienced scout's presence in the fleet, Leonov asked for him by name, and Sokolov came to the detachment.

34. Even the detachment's return to its base at Russian Island was not an ordinary voyage. According to Babikov's account, Leonov's men commandeered a Japanese naval schooner, prepared it for sea, and sailed it back to base. En route, the detachment received a radio message that they had been designated "guards" status. See Babikov, *Na vostochnom*, 232–33. (Guards status is roughly equivalent to a Presidential Unit Citation in the U.S. armed forces. Soviet units so designated have the word "guards" added to their unit title, and frequently their numerical designation also changes.) Leonov's Pacific Fleet detachment is thus referred to in Soviet sources as the 140th Guards Reconnaissance Detachment (with "Special Purpose" [*osobogo naznacheniya*] often added), of Headquarters, Pacific Fleet. According to a recent Soviet article, Leonov's Pacific Fleet detachment was demobilized immediately after the war. See Baryshev, "Traditsii v otstavku?"

APPENDIX A

1. Like the Baltic Fleet detachment, the Black Sea Fleet detachment was unnumbered. In all the literature it is referred to as *razvedyvatel'nyy otryad shtaba flota* (reconnaissance detachment of headquarters fleet). A good memoir account of the early days of this detachment is Volonchuk, *Po tylam*.

2. Whether the reconnaissance detachment participated in the Kerch-Feodosia operation (26 December 1941–2 January 1942) cannot be discerned from available sources.

3. The group that went to Tuapse is described in Strekhnin, *Otryad "borody."* The "beard" *(borody)* was the leader of this group, Viktor Kalganov. Most of the book deals with their exploits in the Danube Flotilla.

4. Lengthy descriptions of this action can be found in Slavich, *Posleslovie*, 7–93, and Volunchuk, *Po tylam*, 111–33.

5. Volonchuk, *Po tylam*, 134–42. See also Redanskiy, "*V ryadakh.*"

6. Strekhnin, *Otryad "borody,"* 31–80.

7. Volunchuk, *Po tylam*, 138, gives the December 1943 date; Basov, *Krym v velikoy otechestvennoy*, 225, indicates that this association began in February 1944.

8. Admiral Sergey Georgievich Gorshkov commanded the Azov Flotilla from October 1941 through its redesignation as the Danube River Flotilla in April 1944 until December 1944. In a sudden personnel change that has never been fully explained in Soviet sources, he was replaced by Admiral G. N. Kholostyakov. Gorshkov went on to serve in increasingly responsible positions, becoming the commander in chief of the Soviet Navy in 1955.

9. In the Soviet Navy, a flotilla was in essence a riverine force. It contained units both afloat and ashore, frequently including naval infantry. Depending on the strategic and operational situation, a flotilla could be subordinated to a ground commander to support the Red Army units fighting in areas proximate to the river or sea in which the flotilla operated. The memoir of the former chief of staff of the flotilla, A. V. Sverdlov, *Voploshcheniye*, contains many references to an unnumbered ground reconnaissance detachment subordinated to the flotilla staff intelligence chief, A. S. Barkhotkin. The recently declassified *Sbornik materialov*, No. 26, does not specifically mention the reconnaissance detachment.

10. Sverdlov, *Voploshcheiniye*, 75. The female agent was Sofia Osetrova, and when later she was presented to the flotilla chief of staff, she wore the standard naval blue-and-white striped T-shirt under her uniform blouse.

11. Several Soviet memoirs and secondary works discuss the combat actions of the unnumbered Danube Flotilla reconnaissance detachment: Sverdlov, *Voploshcheniye*, beginning on 90; Strekhnin, *Otryad "borody,"* beginning on 91; Chkheidze, *Zapiski razvedchika*; and Chkheidze, *Zapiski Dunayskogo razvedchika*.

12. Sverdlov, *Voploshcheniye*, beginning on 136; Strekhnin, *Otryad "borody,"* 163–226; Chkheidze, *Zapiski razvedchika*, chap. 5; and Chkheidze, *Zapiski Dunayskogo razvedchika*, 88–118.

13. Although the Dnepr Flotilla itself has a long history, there is no available evidence to indicate the existence of a reconnaissance detachment until late June 1944, when this organization emerged. Its characterization as a reconnaissance detachment comes from Kislyi, *Na pritokakh dnepra*, 68.

14. During the Soviet period, the Dnepr Flotilla was in being from April 1919 to late 1920, then was formed again in June 1931. In June 1940 it was disbanded and its assets split between the Danube and Pinsk flotillas. See *SVE*, 3:206, s.v. "Dneprovskaya voyennaya flotiliya" [Dnepr River Flotilla]. For a detailed history of the flotilla during World War II, see Loktionov, *Pinskaya i Dneprovskaya flotilii*. See also *Sbornik materialov*, No. 22.

15. Despite its reconnaissance function in combat and its

characterization as a reconnaissance detachment in narrative passages, in official sources this unit has retained its title of 66-go otdel'nogo otryada dymomaskirovki i degazatsii (Dneprovaya voyennaya flotiliya) [66th Separate Smoke-Laying and Decontamination Detachment (Dnepr River Flotilla)].

16. All ten names are listed in Kislyi, *Na pritokakh dnepra*, 116. Biographical sketches of these men may be found in *Geroi Sovetskogo Soyuza*.

17. See Grigor'yev, *Desant v Berlin*. In this book the former commander of the Dnepr Flotilla focuses on the combat actions of this unique group of men. Included among the photographs are pictures of all the Heroes of the Soviet Union from the 66th Separate Smoke-Laying and Decontamination Detachment, establishing some connection between that organization and the 1st Separate Fast Boat Detachment.

18. The Baltic Fleet was a leader in matters of naval intelligence. It was the first fleet in the Soviet navy to form a radio intercept unit (1927). See Kvyatkovskiy, "Bespokonynaya."

19. See Fedorov, *Surovyye tropy*.

20. Submarine M-96, for example, commanded by Captain Lieutenant A. I. Marinesko, landed a six-man reconnaissance group in Narva Bay, behind German lines, on 9 November 1942. See "Aleksandr Ivanovich Marinesko," 36. Also in 1942, perhaps a few months earlier, a torpedo cutter landed two diversionary groups in the Narva area. One of these groups destroyed a German ammunition dump containing aviation bombs. See Gumanenko and Mushtaev, *Po ottsovskomu sledu*, 62–63.

21. This group is described in Karpenko and Noskov, *Doch' respubliki*. The former chief of the intelligence section of the Baltic Fleet staff, N. S. Frumkin, describes their mission on pages 270–72.

22. Redanskiy, "V ryadakh," 65–71.

23. In Russian, Ekspeditsiya podvodnykh rabot osobogo naznacheniya [Special Purpose Expedition for Underwater Work]. For a history of EPRON, see Chiker, *Sluzhba*.

24. See Kapitsa, "Podvodnaya pekhota."

25. There are, for example, accounts of Baltic Fleet divers who raised the German submarine U-250 from the bottom of Bjorkesund, in the vicinity of Tallin harbor, in July–August of 1944, I believe, on the basis of textual analysis. The U-boat, which had been depth-charged, was towed in great secrecy to Kronshtadt, where Soviet engineers removed the latest German T-5 acoustical torpedoes for study. The five crew members and captain of the U-boat who came to the surface after the sinking were taken to the intelligence section of Baltic Fleet headquarters for interrogation. The nature of the mission suggests that these were divers assigned or, more likely, attached to the intelligence section. It is another interesting and important connection between Soviet underwater salvage and rescue personnel and the intelligence section of a fleet headquarters. For more details, see Vol'skiy, "Deyatel'nost' minno-tral'nykh i protivolodochnykh

sil KBF," photograph on 131 and text on 146; and Mosgov, "Tayna zatonuvshey submariny," which names Senior Lieutenant A. Razuvayev as the officer in charge of the divers. The name of the experienced diver A. D. Razuvayev appears in Chiker, *Sluzhba*, 195, thus clearly indicating that the submarine retrieval was an EPRON operation.

26. For a history of the flotilla, see Bagrov and Sungorkin, *Krasnoznamennaya amurskaya flotiliya.* See also *Sbornik materialov*, No. 33.

27. The most detailed description of the specific actions of the reconnaissance detachment is in Korolev, *Geroi velikogo okeana*, 299–303.

Bibliography

Achkasov, V. "Iz opyta oborony voyenno-morskikh baz (1941–1942gg.)" [From the experience of defending naval bases (1941–1942)]. *Voyenno-istoricheskiy zhurnal* [Military history journal], No. 2 (February 1979): 24–30.

Akulov, P., and Tolodol'nikov, G., comps. *V boyakh za Belorussiyu* [In battles for Belorussia]. Minsk: Belarus', 1974.

"Aleksandr Ivanovich Marinesko (Shtrikhi K biografii)" [Aleksandr Ivanovich Marinesko (biographical notes)]. *Morskoy sbornik*, No. 4 (April 1990): 33–47.

Alekseev, V. P. "Primeneniye podvodnykh lodok v interesakh vedeniya razvedki" [Utilization of submarines for the conduct of reconnaissance]. *Voyenno-istoricheskiy zhurnal* [Military history journal], No. 1 (January 1987): 59–65.

Babikov, M. A. *Letom sorok pervogo* [The summer of forty-one]. Moscow: "Sovetskaya rossiya," 1980.

———. *Morskiye razvedchiki* [Naval scouts]. Syktyvkar: Komi knizhnoye izda-tel'stvo, 1966.

———. *Na vostochnom beregu* [On the eastern shore]. Moscow: "Sovetskaya rossiya," 1969.

———. *Otryad osobogo naznacheniya* [Special purpose detachment]. Moscow: "Sovetskaya rossiya," 1986.

———. *Voyna v arktike* [War in the Arctic]. Moscow: "Sovetskaya rossiya," 1991.

Bagrov, V. N., and Sungorkin, N. F. *Krasno-znamennaya Amurskaya flotiliya* [Red Banner Amur Flotilla]. Moscow: Voyenizdat, 1976.

Barchenko-Emel'yanov, I. P. *Frontovyye budni Rybach'yego* [Days on the front on Rybachiy Peninsula]. Murmansk: Murmansk knizhnoye izdatel'stvo, 1984.

Baryshev, V. "Traditsii v otstavku?" [Are traditions retired?]. *Sovetskiy voin* [Soviet soldier], No. 21 (1990): 51.

Basov, A. V. *Krym v Velikoy Otechestvennoy voyne 1941–1945* [The Crimea in the Great Patriotic War, 1941–1945]. Moscow: Nauka, 1987.

271

BSE. See Prokhonov, A. M.

Burgess, William H. III, ed. *Inside Spetsnaz: Soviet Special Operations, A Critical Analysis.* Novato, Calif.: Presidio Press, 1989.

Chernomys, A. "Podvig desanta v rayone mysa Pikshuev" [The feat of the assault landing in the Cape Pikshuev area]. *Morskoy sbornik* [Naval digest], No. 4 (April 1972): 73–75.

Chiker, N. P. *Sluzhba osobogo naznacheniya* [Special purpose service]. Moscow: DOSAAF, 1975.

Chistyakov, I. M. *Sluzhim otchizne* [We serve the fatherland]. Moscow: Voyenizdat, 1985.

Chkheidze, A. A. *Zapiski Dunayskogo razvedchika* [Notes of a Danube scout]. Moscow: "Molodaya guardiya," 1982.

———. *Zapiski razvedchika* [Notes of a scout]. Moscow: Voyenizdat, 1981.

Coox, Alvin D. *The Anatomy of a Small War: The Soviet-Japanese Struggle for Chang-kufeng/Khasan, 1938.* Westport, Conn.: Greenwood Press, 1977.

———. *Nomonhan: Japan Against Russia, 1939.* 2 vols. Stanford: Stanford University Press, 1985.

Danilin, A. "Ne stareyut dushoy veterany" [Veterans are not aging in spirit]. *Morskoy sbornik* [Naval digest], No. 5 (May 1988): 16–18.

Dvoryanov, Ye. Ya., and V. G. Oppokov. "Organizatsiya vzaimodeystviya sil flota s sukhoputnymi voyskami pri oborone voyenno-morskikh baz, portov i gorodov" [The organization of coordination of the forces of the fleet with ground forces in the defense of naval bases, ports, and cities]. *Voyenno-istoricheskiy zhurnal* [Military history journal], No. 11 (November 1986): 19–27.

Ehrenburg, Ilya, and Konstantin Simonov. *In One Newspaper: A Chronicle of Unforgettable Years.* New York: Sphinx Press, 1985.

Fedorov, V. D. *Devyat'sot dney razvedchika* [Nine hundred days of a scout]. Moscow: Voyenizdat, 1967.

———. *Surovyye tropy: zapiski razvedchika* [Difficult paths: Notes of a scout]. Moscow: Voyenizdat, 1961.

Fedorov, V. S. "Stranitsy pamyati" [Pages of memory]. In I. V. Vasilevich, *Daleko za liniey fronta* [Far behind the front line]. Moscow: Voyenizdat, 1988, 202–44.

Furtatov, V. M. *Ognennyye desanty* [Fiery assaults]. Moscow: Voyenizdat, 1989.

Gebhardt, James F. *The Petsamo-Kirkenes Operation: Soviet Breakthrough and Pursuit in the Arctic, October 1944.* In Leavenworth Papers Series No. 17, Fort Leavenworth, Kan.: U.S. Army Command and General Staff College, 1990.

Germany. Heer. 2 Gebirgs-division, Kriegstagebuch nr. 1 [War diary no. 1]. Microfilm series T-315, roll 109, National Archives and Records Administration, Washington, D.C.

———. 20. Heer. Kriegstagebuch nr. 1 [War diary no. 1]. Microfilm series

T-312, rolls 1013, 1647, 1648, 1649, 1650, and 1651, National Archives and Records Administration, Washington, D.C.

Geroi Sovetskogo Soyuza: Kratkiy biograficheskiy slovar' [Heroes of the Soviet Union: Brief biographical dictionary]. 2 vols. Moscow: Voyenizdat, 1987–88.

Glantz, David M. *August Storm: The Soviet 1945 Strategic Offensive in Manchuria.* In Leavenworth Papers Series No. 7, Ft. Leavenworth, Kan.: Combat Studies Institute, U.S. Army Command and General Staff College, 1983.

———. *August Storm: Soviet Tactical and Operational Combat in Manchuria.* In Leavenworth Paper Series No. 8, Ft. Leavenworth, Kan.: Combat Studies Institute, U.S. Army Command and General Staff College, 1983.

Golovko, A. G. *Vmeste flotom* [Together with the fleet]. 3d ed. Moscow: Voyenizdat, 1984. An English translation was published by Progress Publishers in 1988 under the title *With the Fleet.*

Golovko, Mikhail. "Otets bez flota sebya ne myslil . . ." [My father could not think of himself apart from the navy]. *Morskoy sbornik* [Naval digest], No. 5 (May 1990): 82–86.

Grigor'ev, G. "Desant na Pripyati" [Assault on the Pripet]. *Morskoy sbornik* [Naval digest], No. 7 (July 1984): 65–68.

Grigor'yev, V. V. *Desant v Berlin* [Assault on Berlin]. Moscow: DOSAAF, 1989.

Gumanenko, L., and V. Mushtaev. *Po ottsovskomu sledu* [Along my father's tracks.] Moscow: "Molodaya gvardiya," 1989.

Isakov, I. S. *Izbrannyye trudy: Okeanologiya, geografiya, i voyennaya istoriya* [Collected works: Oceanology, geography, and military history]. Edited by N. D. Sergeev. Moscow: Izdatel'stvo "Nauka," 1984.

Kabanov, S. I. *Polye boya—bereg* [The battlefield is the shore]. Moscow: Voyenizdat, 1977.

Kamalov, Kh. Kh. *Morskaya pekhota v boyakh za rodinu* [Naval infantry in battles for the Motherland]. Moscow: Voyenizdat, 1983.

Kapitsa, Petr. "Podvodnaya pekhota" [Underwater infantry]. In *Legendami oveyannaya* [Covered by legends], comp. A. P. Vorontsov and Kh. Kh. Kamalov, 277–89. Leningrad: Lenizdat, 1975.

Karpenko, P., and Yu. Noskov. *Doch' respubliki* [Daughter of the republic]. Tallin: "Eesti Raamat," 1968.

Khaldey, Evgeniy. *Ot Murmanska do Berlina* [From Murmansk to Berlin]. Murmansk: Murmansk knizhnoye izdatel'stvo, 1984.

Khudalov, Kh. A. *U kromki kontinenta* [At the edge of the continent]. Moscow: Voyenizdat, 1974.

Kislyy, G. *Na pritokakh Dnepra* [On the tributaries of the Dnepr.] Moscow: Voyenizdat, 1959.

Kolpakov, A., and E. Shubochkin. "Minno-zagraditel'nyye deystviya sovetskikh podvodnykh lodok v Velikoy otechestvennoy voyne" [Mine

barrier activities of Soviet submarines in the Great Patriotic War].
Morskoy sbornik [Naval digest], No. 5 (May 1989): 33–37.

Kondrat'ev, V. "Sily spetsial'nykh operatsiy VVS SShA" [Special operations forces of the U.S. Air Force]. *Zarubezhnoye voyennoye obozreniye* [Foreign military review], No. 10 (October 1989): 31–37.

Korolev, V. T. *Geroi velikogo okeana* [Heroes of the great ocean]. Vladivostok: Dal'nevostochnoye knizhnoye izdatel'stvo, 1972.

Korshunov, V. G. *Cherez fiordy* [Through the fjords]. Moscow: Voyenizdat, 1969.

Kozlov, I. A., and V. S. Shlomin. *Krasnoznamennyy severnyy flot* [Red Banner Northern Fleet]. Moscow: Voyenizdat, 1983.

Kuehnelt-Leddihn, Erik R. von. "The Petsamo Region." *Geographical Review* 34 (July 1944): 405–17.

Kvyatkovskiy, Yu. "Bespokoynaya vakhta razvedki VMF" [Troubled watch of naval intelligence]. *Morskoy sbornik* [Naval digest], No. 10 (October 1988): 13–14.

Leonov, V. N. *Gotov'sya k podvigu* [Prepare for a great feat]. Moscow: Izdatel'stvo DOSAAF, 1985.

———. *Litsom k litsu: Vospominaniya morskogo razvedchika v literaturnoy zapisi S. Glukhovskogo* [Face to Face: Recollections of a Naval Scout in the Literary Notes of S. Glukhovskiy]. Moscow: Voyenizdat, 1957.

———. *Uroki muzhestva* [Lessons of courage]. Moscow: "Molodaya gvardiya," 1977.

Loktionov, I. I. *Pinskaya i Dneprovskaya flotilii v Velikoy Otechestvennoy voyne* [Pinsk and Dnepr river flotillas in the Great Patriotic War]. Moscow: Voyenizdat, 1958.

Mawdsley, Evan. *The Russian Civil War.* Boston: Allen & Unwin, 1987.

Meister, Jurg. *Soviet Warships of the Second World War.* New York: Arco, 1977.

Meretskov, K. A. *Na sluzhbe narodu* [In service to the people]. Moscow: Voyenizdat, 1983.

Mosalev, V. "Razvedyvatel'no-diversionnye podrazdeleniya VMS SShA" [Reconnaissance-diversionary subunits of the U.S. Navy]. *Zarubezhnoye voyennoye obozreniye* [Foreign military review], No. 2 (February 1984): 76–80.

Mozgov, N. "Tayna zatonuvshey submariny" [Secret of the sunken submarine]. *Krasnaya zvezda* [Red Star], 14 June 1990.

Naval General Staff, Fleet Academic Directorate. *Sbornik materialov po opytu boyevoy deyatel'nosti voyenno-morskikh sil soyuza ssr* [Collection of materials on the experience of the combat activities of the Soviet fleet]. No. 1. "Diverionno-desantnyye operatsii Severnogo flota po unichtozheniyu opornykh punktov protivnika na yuzhnom poberezh'ye Motovskogo zaliva v 1942" [Northern Fleet diversionary-amphibious operations for the destruction of enemy strongpoints on the southern coastline of Motovskiy bay in 1942.] Moscow and Leningrad: Directorate of the Naval Press of the People's Commissariat of the Navy of the USSR, 1943.

———. No. 17. "Mediko-sanitarnoye obespecheniye desantnoy operatsii Severnogo flota v Motovskom zalive (27 aprelya–13 maya 1942 g.)" [Medical support of the Northern Fleet's amphibious assault in Motovskiy Bay (27 April–13 May 1942)]. Moscow and Leningrad: Directorate of the Naval Press of the People's Commissariat of the Navy of the USSR, 1944.

———. No. 22. "Boyevaya deyatel'nost' krasnoznamennoy dneprovskoy flotilii v kampaniyu 1944 g." [Combat activity of Red Banner Dnepr Flotilla in the 1944 campaign]. Moscow and Leningrad: Voyenno-morskoye izdatel'stvo, 1948.

———. No. 26. "Boyevaya deyatel'nost' krasnoznamennoy ordenov nakhimova i kutuzova dynayskoy flotilii v 1944–1945 gg." [Combat activity of Red Banner Orders of Nakhimov and Kutuzov Danube Flotilla in 1944–1945]. Moscow: Voyenno-morskoye izdatel'stvo, 1945.

———. No. 27. "Severnyy flot v operatsii po osvobozhdeniyu sovetskogo zapolyar'ya (7–31 oktyabrya 1944 g.)" [The Northern Fleet in the operation for the liberation of the Soviet Far North (7–31 October 1944)]. Moscow and Leningrad: Directorate of the Naval Press of the People's Commissariat of the Navy of the USSR, 1945.

———. No. 30. "Boyevaya deyatel'nost' tikhookeanskogo flota v voyne s yaponiyey" [Combat activity of the Pacific Fleet in the war with Japan]. Moscow: Publishing House of the Ministry of the Soviet Fleet, 1946.

———. No. 33. "Boyevaya deyatel'nost' krasnoznamennoy armurskoy flotilii v voyne s yaponiyey" [Combat activity of Red Banner Amur Flotilla in the war with Japan]. Moscow: Voyenizdat, 1947.

———. No. 38. "Razvedyvatel'noye obespecheniye severnogo flota v velikuyu otechestvennuyu voynu (1941–1945gg.)" [Intelligence support of the Northern Fleet in the Great Patriotic War (1941–1945)]. Moscow: Publishing House of the Ministry of the Soviet Fleet, 1950.

Nikanorov, A. "Sluzhat rodine veterany" [Veterans serve the Motherland]. *Morskoy sbornik* [Naval digest], No. 7 (July 1985): 14–15.

Nikitin, Ye. "Podvig, voshedshiy v serdtsa istoriyu" [The feat that has gone into our hearts and our history]. *Morskoy sbornik* [Naval digest], No. 5 (May 1987): 60–63.

"140-y gvardeyskiy razvedyvatel'nyy otryad shtaba Tikhookeanskogo flota" [140th guards reconnaissance detachment of headquarters Pacific Fleet], *Morskoy sbornik* [Naval digest], No. 1 (January 1985): 54–55.

"Pechenga snova nasha!" [Pechenga is ours once again!]. *Morskoy sbornik*, No. 10 (1979): 64–65.

Penkovskiy, Oleg. *The Penkovskiy Papers.* New York: Doubleday, 1965.

Pipes, Richard. *Russia under the Old Regime.* New York: Scribner's, 1974.

Pobeda [Victory]. Moscow: DOSAAF, 1975.

"Podvig Zapolyar'ya" [Victory in the Transpolar]. *Morskoy sbornik* [Naval digest], No. 10 (October 1984): 52–55.

Prokhonov, A. M., ed., *Bol'shaya Sovetskaya Entsiklopediya* [Great Soviet encyclopedia]. 30 vols. Moscow: Izdatel'stvo "Sovetskaya entsiklopedia," 1970–78.

Ptichkin, S., and M. Kliment'yev, "Komandirovka v spetsnaz" [Temporary duty with *spetsnaz*]. *Sovetsky voin* [Soviet soldier], No. 22 (1990): 9–14.

Redanskiy, V. "V ryadakh narodnykh mstiteley" [In the ranks of the people's avengers]. *Morskoy sbornik* [Naval digest], No. 2 (February 1985): 65–71.

Ruge, Friedrich. *The Soviets as Naval Opponents, 1941–1945.* Annapolis: Naval Institute Press, 1979.

Rumyanstev, A. M. "V shtabe severnogo flota" [In the headquarters of the Northern Fleet]. In *Na zemle, v nebesakh i na more* [On the ground, in the skies, and on the sea], 54–118. Moscow: Voyenizdat, 1988.

Rumyanstev, N. M. *Razgrom vraga v Zapolyarye (1941–1944gg): Voyenno-istoricheskiy ocherk* [The defeat of the enemy in the polar region (1941–1944): A military historical outline]. Moscow: Voyenizdat, 1963.

Sadovskiy, V. "Komandir 'Chernykh d'yavolov' " [Commander of the 'black devils']. *Sovetskiy voin* [Soviet soldier], No. 3 (March 1985): 36–37.

Sbornik materialov. See Naval General Staff.

Slavich, S. *Posleslovie k podvigu: Povesti o razvedchikakh* [Postscript to a feat: Stories about scouts]. Simferopol': "Tavriya," 1975.

Sovetskaya voyennaya entsiklopediya [Soviet military encyclopedia]. 8 vols. Moscow: Voyenizdat, 1976–80.

Strekhnin, Yu. *Otryad "borody"* [Detachment of the "beard"]. Moscow: DOSAAF, 1962.

Suvorov, Viktor. *Spetsnaz: The Inside Story of the Soviet Special Forces.* New York: Norton, 1988.

SVE. See *Sovetskaya voyennaya entsiklopediya.*

Sverdlov, A. V. *Na more Azovskom* [On the sea of Azov]. Moscow: Voyenizdat, 1966.

———. *Voploshcheniye zamysla* [The embodiment of intent]. Moscow: Voyenizdat, 1987.

U. S. Department of the Army, Pamphlet 20-271. *The German Northern Theater of Operations, 1940–1945,* by Earl F. Ziemke. Washington, D.C.: U.S. Government Printing Office, 1959.

"V boy shli vmeste" [They went into battle together]. *Krasnaya zvezda* [Red star], 31 July 1991.

Vatne, P. E. *Jeg Var Russisk Spion—Historien om Selmer Nilsen* [I was a Russian Spy—The Story of Selmer Nilsen]. Oslo: H. Aschehoug & Co., 1981.

Velichko, M. *Dvazhdy Geroy Sovetskogo Soyuza V. N. Leonov* [Twice Hero of the Soviet Union V. N. Leonov]. Moscow: Voyenizdat, 1948.

Verbovoy, O. "Iz opyta desantnykh deystviy Sovetskogo VMF na rekakh v strategicheskikh nastupatel'nykh operatsiyakh 1944–1945" [From the experience of amphibious actions of the Soviet navy on rivers in the strategic offensive operations of 1944–1945. *Morskoy sbornik* [Naval digest], No. 11 (November 1984): 18–23.

Veshchezerskiy, G. A. *U khladnykh skal* [By the cold cliffs]. Moscow: Voyenizdat, 1965.

Vinogradov, N. I. *Podvodnyy front* [Underwater front]. Moscow: Voyenizdat, 1989.

Vishnyakov, N. "Pechenga snova nasha!" [Pechenga is ours once again]. *Morskoy sbornik* [Naval digest], No. 10 (October 1979): 64–65.

Vnotchenko, L. N. *Pobeda na dal'nem vostoke* [Victory in the Far East]. Moscow: Voyenizdat, 1971.

Vol'skiy, L. Ya. "Deyatel'nost' minno-tral'nykh i protivolodochnykh sil KBF" [Activities of minesweeping and antisubmarine forces of the Baltic Fleet]. In A. M. Samsonov, *Moryaki-Baltitsy na zashchite Rodiny 1941–1945* [Baltic Fleet sailors in defense of the Motherland, 1941–1945]. Moscow: Nauka, 1986.

Volunchuk, F. F. *Po tylam braga* [In the enemy rear areas]. Moscow: Voyenizdat, 1961.

Yashin, S. "Sily spetsial'nykh operatsiy VMS SShA" [Special operations forces of the U.S. Navy]. *Zarubezhnoye voyennoye obozreniye* [Foreign military review], No. 9 (September 1989): 67–70.

Zakharov, S. E., et al. *Krasnoznamennyy tikhookeanskiy flot* [Red Banner Pacific Fleet]. Moscow: Voyenizdat, 1973.

Zyryanov, B. "Razvedchik" [Scout]. *Sovetskoye voyennoye obozreniye* [Soviet military review], No. 6 (June 1989): 22–23.

Index